# THE GLOBAL SCHOLAR

## IMPLICATIONS FOR POSTGRADUATE STUDIES AND SUPERVISION

EDITORS
PETER RULE
ELI BITZER
LIEZEL FRICK

*The Global Scholar: Impications for Postgraduate Studies and Supervision*

Published by African Sun Media under the SUN PReSS imprint

All rights reserved

Copyright © 2021 African Sun Media and the authors

This publication was subjected to an independent double-blind peer evaluation by the publisher.

The authors and the publisher have made every effort to obtain permission for and acknowledge the use of copyrighted material. Refer all enquiries to the publisher.

No part of this book may be reproduced or transmitted in any form or by any electronic, photographic or mechanical means, including photocopying and recording on record, tape or laser disk, on microfilm, via the Internet, by e-mail, or by any other information storage and retrieval system, without prior written permission by the publisher.

Views reflected in this publication are not necessarily those of the publisher.

First edition 2021

ISBN 978-1-991201-22-5
ISBN 978-1-991201-23-2 (e-book)
https://doi.org/10.52779/9781991201232

Set in Futura Lt BT 10.25/14.5

Cover design, typesetting and production by African Sun Media

SUN PReSS is an imprint of African Sun Media. Scholarly, professional and reference works are published under this imprint in print and electronic formats.

This publication can be ordered from:
orders@africansunmedia.co.za
Takealot: bit.ly/2monsfl
Google Books: bit.ly/2k1Uilm
africansunmedia.store.it.si *(e-books)*
Amazon Kindle: amzn.to/2ktL.pkL

Visit africansunmedia.co.za for more information.

# ACKNOWLEDGEMENT

Thank you to the authors of the chapters in this book. We greatly appreciate your patience, encouragement and support during the long process of the development of the book, which was complicated by Covid-19 and its ramifications.

Thanks also to our language editor, Ella Belcher, for her meticulous work. You certainly added to the quality of this publication!

We would also like to thank Wikus van Zyl and Anina Joubert of African Sun Media for accompanying us through the process with expert advice and support. We value your collaborative spirit.

To the three external reviewers (Professor LOK Lategan, Associate Professor Michelle Picard and Associate Professor Susan Carter), your carefully considered feedback and recommendations on the manuscript helped us to improve the book and prompted us to add the final chapter on Covid-19 and the global scholar, bringing the book right up to date. We are most appreciative of the time, effort and expertise that you contributed in service of scholarship.

## THE EDITORS
June 2021

# CONTENTS

List of Tables .................................................................................................. ix
List of Figures ................................................................................................. ix

**Introduction**
    The global scholar: Three conceptual lenses - horizon, currency, trajectory ............ 1
    *Peter Rule, Eli Bitzer & Liezel Frick*

## PART ONE • Horizons

1. Opportunities and challenges of international research experiences during doctoral studies in a globalised doctoral education world ................................. 17
   *Maresi Nerad*

2. Doctoral education as a field of global scholarship: An analysis of Anglophone published research (2005-2018) ................................................. 43
   *Liezel Frick & Johann Mouton*

3. The Vitae Researcher Development Framework in South African postgraduate education ........................................................................... 63
   *Pia Lamberti & Moyra Keane*

4. Is international benchmarking appropriate for improving the quality of thesis examination? ................................................................................ 83
   *Margaret Kiley*

## PART TWO • Currents and currencies

5. The politics of postgraduate education: Supervising in a troubled world ................ 97
   *Sioux Mckenna*

6. Academic mobility in the digital academy: Questions for supervision .................... 113
   *Anna Morozov & Cally Guerin*

7. The implications of doctoral mobility for doctoral programme design and supervision ..................................................................................... 131
   *Rebekah Smith McGloin*

8. Quality doctoral education in Africa: A question of setting the right standards? ...... 149
   *Jan Botha, Marc Wilde, Mike Kuria & Murat Özgören*

**PART THREE • Trajectories**

9 The interdisciplinary PhD: Processes, outcomes and challenges .......................... 175
  *Karri A. Holley*

10 Finding academic jobs in stratified countries: The effects of social class of
   origin in the development of academic networks for Chilean PhDs ...................... 189
   *Roxana Chiappa*

11 Towards a theoretical framework for exploring emotion in doctoral education:
   Critically exploring familiar narratives in student experiences ............................... 215
   *Sherran Clarence*

12 Working together beyond the PhD ................................................................... 231
   *Gina Wisker, Gillian Robinson & Shosh Leshem*

**PART FOUR • Reflections and directions**

13 Reflections on Covid-19 and the global scholar ................................................ 253
   *Peter Rule*

Index .................................................................................................................. 267

Contributing Authors ........................................................................................... 271

# LIST OF TABLES

| | | |
|---|---|---|
| TABLE 2.1 | Comparison of cited journals across four sources (Evans 2011; Hopwood 2018; Jones 2013; Tight 2012) | 46 |
| TABLE 8.1 | Areas requiring effective QA arrangements: A comparison across regions | 167 |
| TABLE 10.1 | Characterisation of participants in the sample | 196 |
| TABLE 10.2 | The process of securing an academic job | 200 |

# LIST OF FIGURES

| | | |
|---|---|---|
| FIGURE A.1 | Postgraduate supervision and local, international and global contexts | 5 |
| FIGURE A.2 | Currency and the global scholar | 9 |
| FIGURE 1.1 | Conceptual assessment framework of Before-During-After | 33 |
| FIGURE 1.2 | An outcomes-oriented logic model for international programmes and initiatives | 33 |
| FIGURE 2.1 | Contributions to the scholarship on doctoral education per journal (N=907) | 52 |
| FIGURE 2.2 | Number of articles per year overall (2005-2018) | 53 |
| FIGURE 2.3 | Contributions per country in overall sample (N=907) | 54 |
| FIGURE 2.4 | Article contributions per region | 55 |
| FIGURE 2.5 | Themes related to doctoral education scholarship (1) | 57 |
| FIGURE 2.6 | Themes related to doctoral education scholarship (2) | 58 |
| FIGURE 2.7 | Themes related to doctoral education scholarship (3) | 59 |
| FIGURE 3.1 | The RDF domains and sub-domains | 73 |

| | | |
|---|---|---|
| **FIGURE 7.1** | Percentage of doctoral candidates classified as international | 135 |
| **FIGURE 8.1** | Rules and guidelines on supervision (Source: Hasgall *et al.* 2019:23) | 159 |
| **FIGURE 12.1** | The continuum of supervisors and graduated students working together: From the 'lightside' to the 'darkside' | 239 |

# THE GLOBAL SCHOLAR

## THREE CONCEPTUAL LENSES - HORIZON, CURRENCY, TRAJECTORY

Peter Rule, Eli Bitzer and Liezel Frick

## INTRODUCTION

The theme of 'the global scholar', as it relates to postgraduate studies and supervision, is complex and multi-layered. Postgraduate supervisors and their students are often also 'global scholars' as members of international disciplinary and interdisciplinary networks, digital platforms and research teams, contributors to global scholarship, global travellers, participants on the international conference circuit (currently severely curtailed by Covid-19), and in many other ways. They are also global citizens in an increasingly complex, connected and compressed world. An academic's profile as a global scholar emerges and evolves as their career develops, for example, as they publish in international journals, collaborate across national boundaries and participate in international conferences. It also evolves as scholarship evolves: new interdisciplinary and transdisciplinary areas emerge, creating new opportunities for collaboration; as the world changes, new problems of global interest arise and new international alignments open or close funding channels (Brexit, BRICS, joint research on pandemics); and as technology changes in the form, for example, of new digital platforms and sources of 'big data'.

However, the 'global scholar' is usually also, and simultaneously, a 'local scholar' with an institution that serves as a 'home base', a local group of scholars and students that form an immediate academic community and a local context that informs teaching, research and community engagement activities. In our globalised world, the local and the global are not necessarily opposite poles but often inform and even constitute each other – captured by the awkward hybrid term 'glocal'. Thus, the local 'indigenous knowledge' of Western Europe had evolved since the 17th century to become 'universal' science. Reactions in the global South to epistemological and cultural impositions from the West might begin as local movements of 'decolonisation' but take on global dimensions as they resonate across national and continental boundaries (Pimblott 2020). The horizons of the local and the global are continuously reconfiguring one another. Of course, this is not a 'natural' process but is informed by global power dynamics such as 'market forces', global and regional geopolitics, and international media platforms and priorities. As an extremely complex and multi-faceted process, it is perhaps not surprising that globalisation is seen in both utopian and dystopian terms: celebrated by some for its opportunities and affordances, and repudiated by others for its destructive social, cultural and ecological impacts.

This book explores the theme of 'the global scholar' in relation to postgraduate studies and supervision. 'The global scholar' is an abstraction that collates 'scholar' and 'globe', a kind of composite of 'global scholars', which in turn is short-hand for scholars that straddle different localities in a variety of ways. Is 'the global scholar' one whose research focuses on issues at a global scale and import, such as global warming and climate change, the Earth's magnetic field, the epidemiology of pandemics, or the evolution of the internet? These 'scholars of the global' are perhaps also 'global scholars'. Does it refer to a scholar who has an international profile, whose work is known in diverse places across the globe? Perhaps 'international scholar' is a better moniker: how many are truly 'global' in this sense? Or perhaps to one who travels in real time or virtually across and between the hemispheres, a 'scholarly international traveller' who thrives on the international conference circuit? Academia is known to count among the most internationally mobile of professions, but does this mobility make academics 'global scholars'? Digitalisation contracts the globe to a screen and global networking to a social networking site, and so makes 'the global scholar' ubiquitous, as mobile as a fingertip. This book does not provide a definitive answer to this question but a variety of perspectives, that together perhaps contribute to developing a useful horizon.

This chapter elaborates three conceptual lenses for understanding the 'global scholar' theme: horizon, currency, and trajectory. Modell (2009:6) describes metaphor as a "currency of the mind": a form of cognition, a way of coming to know the world. All three terms can be used metaphorically to illuminate the idea of the global scholar and its implications for postgraduate education. Horizon refers to the broad frameworks – whether conceptual or contextual – that we employ to understand postgraduate studies and supervision. Currency is a suggestive conceptual tool that we expand here in four senses: means of exchange, mobility, immediacy and intellectual charge. Trajectory refers to the particular courses that the careers of academics, early career researchers, postgraduate students or other groups take, and the forces that shape these courses. We link each of these conceptual lenses to relevant chapters in the book and use them as our organising logic in arranging and sequencing the chapters.

## HORIZON

Hans-Georg Gadamer's concept of 'horizon' (Gadamer 1975) offers a compelling spatiotemporal lens for understanding the notion of the global scholar and its implications for postgraduate studies and supervision. Gadamer developed it in the context of a hermeneutical theory of interpretation with reference to the process of interpreting texts and situations, especially those foreign to the interpreter. For Gadamer, horizon is "the range of vision that includes everything that can be seen from a particular standpoint" (Gadamer 1975:269). An interpreter has to achieve "the right horizon of enquiry for the questions evoked by the encounter with tradition" (*ibid.*). In other words, interpreters have to uncover the horizon assumed by the text or situation which they encounter, and engage this horizon with their own, thus achieving a 'fusion of horizons' – the movement towards a common understanding. This fusion changes their own horizon as they incorporate elements of the horizons of others, a continuing process that reflects their moving standpoint in time, space and socio-cultural context.

As a spatiotemporal construct, horizon is useful for understanding what supervisor and student bring to the supervision relationship. A supervisor's horizon might be informed by aspects such as disciplinary and interdisciplinary knowledge, methodological expertise, experiences of supervision and institutional location, as well as their positionality regarding aspects such as gender, race, age, class and profession. All these aspects might be shaped by both local and global dimensions. The students, on the other hand, have their own horizons, also shaped by local and global factors. These might include, besides their academic backgrounds, home and work situations, motivation and career trajectory, as well as their socio-cultural positionality. Supervision as a dialogic space (Rule 2015) brings together these horizons and can facilitate their generative engagement, but can also effect a 'confusion' of horizons (where participants misunderstand or overlook key aspects of one another's horizons), or a 'transfusion' of horizons (where one party imposes a horizon of assumptions and expectations on the other).

In this volume, Maresi Nerad provides a useful global horizon by focusing on doctoral education through the prism of doctoral students' study-abroad experiences. This focus also resonates with the theme of currency as mobility discussed below. Nerad explores the pervasive influence of globalisation on doctoral education by discussing both macro- and micro-level impacts, as well as tensions related, for example, to quality and quantity, equity, and the funding priority afforded science, technology, engineering and mathematics (STEM) disciplines at the expense of humanities and social sciences. The chapter concludes by identifying important challenges and lessons that need to be shared. Her postscript provides a telling reminder of how a global phenomenon such as the Covid-19 pandemic impacts doctoral education.

Liezel Frick and Johann Mouton offer a horizon by presenting a 'big picture' of the global scholarship. This takes the form of a scoping review of "doctoral education as a field of global scholarship". Their analysis of published Anglophone research (2005-2018) synthesises published work on doctoral education and supervision, It provides readers with a framework within which to locate not only the various chapters in this book but also their own understandings and practices of postgraduate education and supervision. Notably, the chapter also indicates the gaps in the scholarship; for example, the absence of a substantial Africa-wide scholarship on doctoral supervision brings into question the 'global' nature of the scholarship.

Margaret Kiley explores the horizon of doctoral assessment by interrogating thesis examination as an international benchmark for quality. The notion of benchmarking reflects the movement towards globalisation and common standards in doctoral education, a problematic process if it ignores the local and institutional factors at play. Her chapter questions how doctoral standards apply in the procedures and practices of doctoral examination. This movement often manifests in the examination of a thesis by national and international examiners, and the differing horizons reflected in their reports. These differences are sometimes attributed merely to personal preferences and preoccupations ("Oh, she has a bee in her bonnet about methods!") but may reflect collective forces and contexts, often implicit and unexamined. The process of examining theses can generate new horizons and fusions of horizons, but how we harness these to improve the quality of doctoral education is, as Kiley shows, an open and significant question.

Pia Lambert and Moyra Keane bring into dialogue the horizon of the Vitae Researcher Development Framework (RDF), which originated in the United Kingdom but has had wider international uptake, and the South African context of postgraduate education in its decolonising 'Rhodes Must Fall' moment. Their engagement of horizons raises fascinating questions about the complex relation between the local and the global: to what extent a local (UK) framework, which has attained some international traction, is applicable to another local (SA) context with its own peculiar history and higher education landscape. The processes of contextualisation (local UK), de-contextualisation (global) and re-contextualisation (other local SA) raise possibilities regarding "imported theory" (Jansen 2019) ranging from wholesale adoption of the framework to critical modification or even outright rejection. Lamberti and Keane lean towards critical modification of the Vitae RDF, suggesting a fusion of horizons which might involve the adaptation of the framework, as well as a re-viewing of the South African context of application. Figure A.1 is a schematic representation of postgraduate supervision and local, international and global contexts.

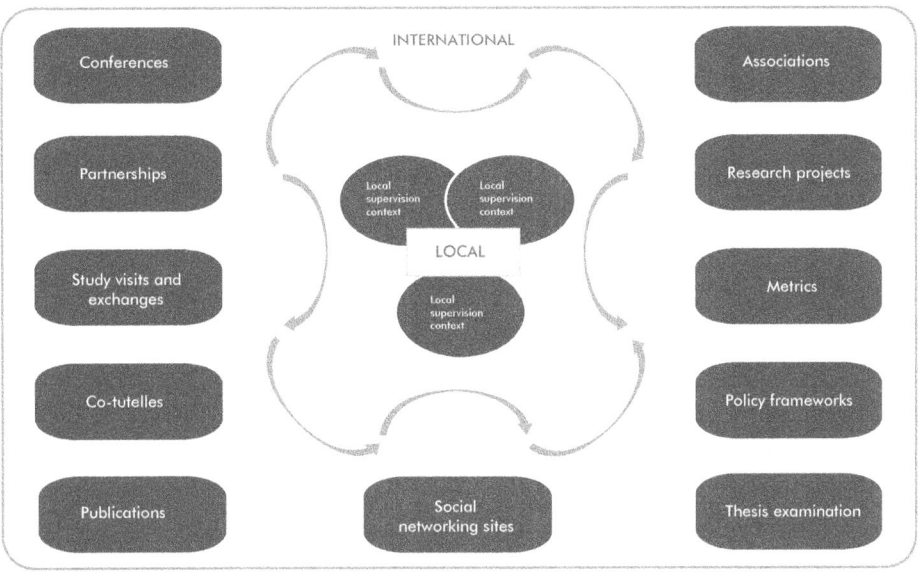

**FIGURE A.1**   Postgraduate supervision and local, international and global contexts

In Figure A.1 we suggest a fluid wave-like connection between local supervision contexts and international events and developments. A supervisor might present material at an international conference which reflects his or her local reality and in turn bring back ideas that influence the local supervision context. It also suggests that the relation between the local and international is not uniform: different kinds of international influences might affect the local supervision context at different times; for example, if a university department is involved in an international research project with partners in several countries, this might strongly influence students who are involved in the project. If the project generates cutting-edge research with international import, it might in turn influence international discourse through publications and presentations in the international arena. The figure also points to the danger of collapsing the international into the global. Whereas the global encompasses the globe as a whole, including both the local and the international in their various forms, and goes beyond nations to include ecological and other systems, the international refers to the engagement of two or more nations. This might be limited to a bilateral partnership, a regional association, or a continental body, none of which necessarily has a truly global reach. Using 'global' as a synonym for 'international' entails the danger of elevating certain international activities to a status that may not be justified and that disguises uneven reach and representation. We recognise, however, that it is difficult to sustain this distinction between 'global' and 'international' when they are so often used interchangeably, but perhaps worth the effort.

## CURRENCY

The suggestive compound notion of 'currency' can also serve as a useful conceptual lens for understanding the theme and contents of this volume. This notion has related meanings that can be developed and extrapolated in relevant ways to illuminate the central theme. Here we present four senses of currency:

First, *currency as academic exchange value*: Here we draw on the economic sense of currency as a means of exchange and apply it to the academic context of postgraduate education. This sense is pertinent to the 'game' of gaining international academic credence by acquiring the appropriate currency, which might take various forms: postgraduate qualifications, especially the doctorate; publishing in prestigious journals; attaining a rating from a national or international research body; being admitted to an academy of science; and others. All of these kudos provide the scholar with a currency that is 'exchangeable' at institutional, national and international levels for various opportunities: promotion; invitations to deliver keynotes, serve on ministerial task teams, edit journals, take up scholarships and visiting appointments, and so on. This kind of currency is quantified in national and international metrics (e.g. h-index, ResearchGate score) and ratings (e.g. National Research Foundation rating in South Africa); and, at an institutional level, in national and international university rankings.

One limitation of this kind of currency is that it commodifies knowledge and producers of knowledge as marketable objects in the knowledge economy, and so operates within an economistic discourse and a neoliberal framework. An academic with a negligible 'exchange value' might nevertheless make qualitatively significant contributions to the field, for example, in teaching or community engagement, that 'do not count' (or rather 'are not counted') in the same ways as research publications. Another limitation is that the 'exchange value' is uneven across disciplines and fields (e.g. Medicine vs Arts), across publications (e.g. high impact journal articles vs 'grey literature'") and across global regions (e.g. Global North vs South) as global maps of research production indicate (Czerniewicz 2015).

Second, *currency as mobility*: Here currency refers to the flows of scholars and students as 'people currents' within the higher education landscape. Just as currents of wind and water, and flows of lava, shape the natural landscape, so people currents shape higher education. For example, many universities 'count' foreign students as an indicator of institutional attractiveness, and 'count on' their fees for financial sustainability. The ratios of international students and international academics are used as metrics of evaluation in world university rankings (QS Top Universities 2020; *THE World University Rankings* 2020). This mobility is associated with the circulation of ideas and expertise, and the widening and perhaps merging of horizons in the multinational campus environment. In different ways, local people currents also shape universities. In South Africa, the proportions of students from well-resourced and poorly resourced educational backgrounds have an impact on institutional architecture and culture in the form of policies, programmes and support services, as does the transformation of the academic staff profile regarding race, gender and generation.

Of course, the 'currents' of mobility are not evenly distributed. The movement of students and scholars from the Global South to the Global West, North and, increasingly, East, reflects global inequalities and is characterised as 'brain drain' that can negatively affect the country of origin (see, for example, Dodani & LaPorte 2005). The concepts 'brain circulation', 'brain networking' and 'brain retain' (see, for example, Ciumasu 2010; Varma & Kapur 2013) reflect other stances in this debate and how to address global inequalities. They also indicate that mobility is multi-directional and can take both digital and physical forms.

Third, *currency as immediate relevance*: This sense of currency derives from the meaning of 'current' as 'present reality' as in 'the current pandemic crisis'. The scholar gains this kind of currency when his or her work is directly relevant to a pressing social or scientific concern. For example, cutting-edge research on the development of an effective vaccine for Covid-19; on reducing the amount of plastic in the oceans; or protecting and empowering women in contexts of abuse. As the world compacts in its commonalities and connectedness, this kind of currency often has simultaneously global and local dimensions; for example, global warming manifests locally in the form of extreme weather events and changes in ecosystems. Currency in educational research might link to pressing problems in national education systems (e.g. throughput and completion rates at South African universities) or be common across various contexts (e.g. funding for higher education).

Finally, *currency as intellectual charge*: Besides the movement of people, the flow of ideas across the thought-scape of higher education is our fourth sense of currency. This sense draws metaphorically on the idea of current as a flow of electrical charge to propose the notion of currency as intellectual charge. This recognises the power of ideas to shape reality and change the world: ideas such as monotheism and democracy, and, in the current era, artificial intelligence. Arguably, 'the global' is one such idea that is becoming increasingly important as we recognise our connectedness and mutuality with the earth and its life forms, and the imperatives of 'the global' to our survival as a species.

Such currents cross national and continental boundaries to energise the intellectual life of the academy. They can spread in multiple forms: publications, guest lectures, social movements, YouTube videos, Ted Talks, blogs, colloquia and conferences are a few examples. Some currents might be spectacular but short-lived, like the fireworks of a new intellectual fad; others are more enduring, a sustained illumination that generates new centres, research projects, journals, qualifications, and even entirely new fields of inquiry. Without such currents, academics and institutions can become insular, complacent and inherently conservative. The challenge is to discern between generative and destructive currents, short-lived and enduring, progressive and reactionary, and what their implications are for institutional life and thought. Within postgraduate education, various intellectual currents shape, for example, how we understand and conduct supervision: apprenticeship models, cohort models, co- or team supervision, digital and/or face-to-face interactions. A further example is the concept of 'paradigm' (Kuhn 1962) which sheds light on how ontology, epistemology, axiology and methodology combine to inform research. The intellectual charges that inform our thinking may arise from this kind of meta-theory, but also from practice or research, or a combination of sources.

These various senses of 'currency' are connected, as Figure A.2 indicates. Academic mobility may help to 'conduct' the intellectual charge of shared ideas. Often such ideas have an immediate relevance to context at the level of theory, policy, practice and/or research. They can also contribute to an academic's exchange value, which may in turn create further opportunities and demands for mobility. The arrows in the diagram indicate that the currency of the global scholar is dynamic, adding energy to, or removing energy from his or her career trajectory (see next section). Currents and currency are also relevant to our understanding of horizon. Just as natural currents shape and transform the physical horizon and everything in it, both proximal and remote, so social currents of people and ideas shape personal, institutional and wider horizons.

INTRODUCTION • **THE GLOBAL SCHOLAR**

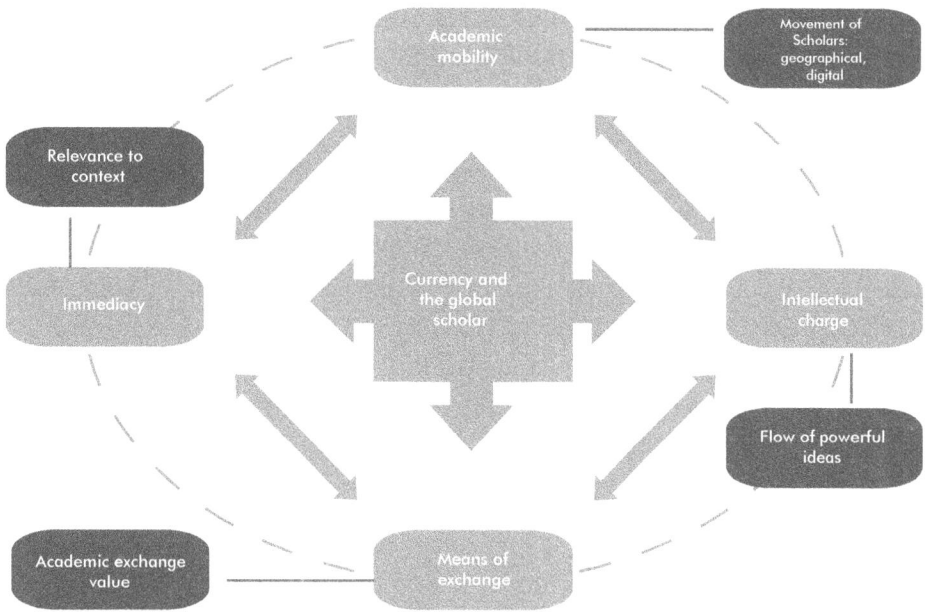

**FIGURE A.2**  Currency and the global scholar

In this volume, Jan Botha, Marc Wilde, Mike Kuria and Murat Özgören adopt a comparative approach in elaborating the standards that underpin the 'currency' of the doctorate. They compare doctoral standards arising from three contexts: the European Union, East Africa and South Africa. More than any other degree, the doctorate represents a global academic currency that symbolises internationally valued academic qualities and attributes such as originality, methodological rigour and theoretical coherence. The authors argue that formal standards are a necessary but not sufficient condition for quality doctoral education; standards need to articulate with substantive questions of implementation. The contextualisation of standards is also crucial, and finds expression in the articulation of global and local horizons.

The intellectual charge of Sioux McKenna's contribution resists the prevailing currents of human capital theory in higher education. She tackles the individualistic, meritocratic, consumerist and instrumentalist assumptions of the human capital discourse that dominates higher education. Her chapter encourages academics to be different and to act differently in their supervision work. She suggests five simple but profound steps: resist the metrics and foreground the knowledge; make space for reading; be vulnerable (take intellectual risks and acknowledge failures); be kind; and collaborate and celebrate. The charge of her critique disrupts the embedded assumptions of the system, and perhaps our complicit embeddedness with them, in a way that is both discomforting and affirming of our agency and our humanity.

Two chapters explore currency in the sense of academic mobility. Anna Morozov and Cally Guerin focus on what the intersection of mobility and digital technologies means for the supervision of research degrees. They argue that remote supervision requires a more careful structuring of supervisor-student contact, and a more deliberate approach to community building. They also point to the potentially harmful effects of mobility on supervisors' health and well-being. They raise the important question of whether, in an age of supervisor mobility, a team supervision approach may be more effective than the traditional apprenticeship model. Rebekah Smith McGloin emphasises the current of doctoral student mobility. She uses survey data to investigate the enablers and constraints for doctoral mobility among UK doctoral researchers, and the value they attach to it. Her analysis shows that mobility, far from being an abstraction, involves actual people moving from one place to another, with all the difficulties and dislocation that this entails. She calls for a careful assessment of mobile doctoral researchers' needs, and a reconsideration of the pedagogy of intercultural supervision, language support and social integration.

## TRAJECTORY

The notion of trajectory is related to mobility – and so to 'currency' in that sense – of students, supervisors and early career researchers, but is more specific. It is about the particular course that the career of an individual or group takes. For example, according to the conventional academic trajectory, the student 'climbs the ladder' to graduate and tutor to temporary appointment as lecturer all the way to tenure and professorship. Many trajectories are much less conventional: a practitioner may re-enter academia as a postgraduate student after many years of practice and/or raising children, go on to lecture, and then, after retirement, enter government or business as a consultant.

Such trajectories are intensely personal, experienced 'from within' by the individual. They are also social, determined 'from without' by the range of possibilities available given the social forces at play, just as a comet is subject to the laws of physics as it traverses the solar system. This is reflected in the etymology of the word, from the Latin *trajectorius* – of or pertaining to throwing across, from *trans* (across) and *iactere* (to throw) (Merriam-Webster 2020). While the individual's agency is a key factor in an academic career trajectory, the social push-and-pull factors that 'throw' him or her structure the trajectory.

A trajectory may be halted, delayed or diverted by various obstacles: a student drops out of university for financial reasons, pregnancy or illness, or simply loses interest and motivation. It may also be enhanced by enablers such as personal attributes (talent, perseverance, initiative, resilience), the established trajectories of others ("I followed in her footsteps"), the 'gravitational forces' of powerful bodies ("I chose to study Big Data because of the career prospects") or extrinsic boosters such as scholarships and bursaries, mentoring, fellowships, awards and placements. Trajectories are thus shaped by both intrinsic and extrinsic energies within a particular personal and social environment.

Roxana Chiappa's chapter examines the trajectories of Chilean early career doctorate holders returning from study abroad. Factors influencing their trajectories include fellowships from the Chilean government but also, in interesting and nuanced ways, the social class origins of doctorate holders. These influence how they finally secure academic positions, where (private or public, low or high prestige universities) and how long it takes. The networks of the doctorate holders, like constellations of celestial bodies, influence their career courses in the academic firmament. The chapter shows that these academic trajectories are not innocent of the forces of social class, despite the meritocratic 'promise' of education as a path to social mobility.

Karri Holley, drawing on American and British contexts, explores the interdisciplinary PhD and students' experiences of this study trajectory. Funding for interdisciplinary PhDs has increased in countries such as the USA, the UK and SA to promote new and innovative forms of knowledge production, making it a feasible doctoral trajectory. The chapter reflects the changing global horizon from a narrow and discrete view of disciplinarity with an emphasis on specialisation (characteristic of the last century) to inter- and transdisciplinary perspectives that are seen as critical for addressing the 'wicked' problems confronting us in the 21st century. Students' trajectories within and across this horizon are nevertheless complex. Navigating the interdisciplinary terrain requires cross-cutting competencies such as leadership, communication and team work, and poses challenges for supervision and interdisciplinary integration. Holley raises important questions regarding the processes and outcomes of interdisciplinary PhDs, and their trajectories in the marketplace.

Sherran Clarence observes that a typical PhD candidate (if there is such a thing) 'trajects' through difficult moments of uncertainty, paralysis, anxiety, as well as more positive moments of excitement and affirmation. The doctoral journey is not only intellectual but also, and significantly for its process and outcome, emotional. Her characterisation of herself as an 'odd bird' is suggestive of the local and global currents that influence the doctoral flightpath, its progress, direction and destination, and the nurture, nutrition and nesting that might support its trajectory. From this starting point, Clarence develops a conceptual framework for understanding the neglected role of emotion in doctoral studies. Drawing on feminist writers, she explores concepts that can contribute to understanding affect and its role in the doctorate, and how supervisors can better support students in the supervision process. Clarence's contribution has a particular currency, in the sense of immediate relevance, in the context of the global Covid-19 pandemic with its implications for student well-being.

The trajectories of students working with their supervisors after graduation, particularly on publications, form the focus of the chapter by Gina Wisker, Gillian Robinson and Shosh Leshem. Drawing on rich data from students and supervisors, they find that such collaborations can range from the productive and mutually beneficial to the non-productive, one-sided and even predatory. They use the suggestive gothic analogy of a continuum of relationships from the 'lightside' to the 'darkside'. They characterise the scholarly relationship between doctoral student and supervisor as a "long, sensitive, essential process", akin to that of dancers who have to "learn" each other in order to create their partnership of rhythm and movement in which they learn, "like dancers, to dance together" and each relationship is different.

## CONCLUSION

Our attempts to thematise the chapters in this book in relation to the three conceptual lenses of horizon, currency and trajectory, which we use as section headings, are not meant to limit the interpretation of the chapters. Indeed, several of the chapters could have fitted with more than one of the lenses and so created interesting dialogues among them. Each section includes chapters from South Africa, as well as other contexts, creating the possibility of a local-international-local dialogue (and perhaps even local-global in the comprehensive sense of the word) within the section.

The context in which we and other chapter authors wrote – that of the virulent Covid-19 pandemic that has closed campuses and forced authors into lockdown, and in some cases quarantine and isolation – poignantly illustrates the powerful formative relation between the global and the local in our global village. Even as the pandemic darkens our horizons and impedes our mobility, we rejoice in the possibilities that digital technologies afford us. More than ever, as a global community of scholars and as global citizens, we recognise our complicity and connectedness in the fate of our shared planet. The fact that we can write together, share ideas and advance scholarship collaboratively under such trying circumstances is a source of hope and celebration.

## REFERENCES

Ciumasu IM. 2010. Turning brain drain into brain networking. *Science and Public Policy*, 37(2):135-146. https://doi.org/10.3152/030234210X489572

Czerniewicz L. 2015. It's time to redraw the world's very unequal knowledge map. *The Conversation*, 8 July. https://bit.ly/3tpqfCC [Accessed 15 April 2020].

Dodani S & LaPorte RE. 2005. Brain drain from developing countries: How can brain drain be converted into wisdom gain? *Journal of the Royal Society of Medicine*, 98:487-491. https://doi.org/10.1177/014107680509801107

Gadamer Hans-Georg. 1975. *Truth and method*. London: Sheed & Ward.

Jansen J. 2019. (ed.). *Decolonisation in universities: The politics of knowledge*. Johannesburg: Wits University Press. https://doi.org/10.18772/22019083351

Kuhn TS. 1962. *The structure of scientific revolutions*. Chicago: University of Chicago Press.

Merriam-Webster. 2020. *Dictionary by Merriam-Webster: America's most trusted online dictionary*. https://bit.ly/3geu5dX [Accessed 15 April 2020].

Modell AH. 2009. Metaphor – the bridge between feelings and knowledge. *Psychoanalytic Inquiry*, 29:6-11. https://doi.org/10.1080/07351690802246890

Pimblott K. 2020. Decolonising the university: The origins and meaning of a movement. *The Political Quarterly*, 91(1):210-216. https://doi.org/10.1111/1467-923X.12784

QS Top Universities. 2020. *Methodology*. https://bit.ly/3tq6Oob [Accessed 15 April 2020].

Rule P. 2015. *Dialogue and boundary learning*. Rotterdam: Sense. https://doi.org/10.1007/978-94-6300-160-1

THE World University Rankings. 2020. *Methodology*. https://bit.ly/3acnooL [Accessed 15 April 2020].

Varma R & Kapur D. 2013. Comparative analysis of brain drain, brain circulation and brain retain: A case study of Indian institutes of technology. *Journal of Comparative Policy Analysis: Research and Practice*, 15(4):315-330. https://doi.org/10.1080/13876988.2013.810376

# PART ONE
HORIZONS

# OPPORTUNITIES AND CHALLENGES OF INTERNATIONAL RESEARCH EXPERIENCES DURING DOCTORAL STUDIES IN A GLOBALISED DOCTORAL EDUCATION WORLD

Maresi Nerad

## INTRODUCTION

Mission and vision statements of research universities around the world proclaim on their websites in no uncertain terms that their students and postgraduate students "are educated to become global citizens" (University of Washington, Seattle, USA), "teach, learn, and conduct research at international level" (Goethe University, Frankfurt, Germany), "provide opportunities for students from all cultures" (University of Melbourne, Australia), "gain their professional identity supplemented by international experience" (Bremen University, Germany), and "are a place connected to the world" (Stellenbosch University, South Africa), to cite just a few.

In line with these lofty phrases, international experiences are strongly encouraged at all levels. Why? What do we know about the effect of international experience on the learning to undertake research and on research itself? Is it all positive? Are there no pitfalls in postgraduates travelling to other countries? How do international research experiences fit into the overall picture of the state of doctoral education worldwide in the 21st century?

These questions will be addressed by presenting an overview and analysis of the changes in doctoral education worldwide during the last 30 years, a review of findings from three National Science Foundation (NSF) workshops in the USA (Blumenfield & Nerad 2012; Mitchell, Besterfield-Sacre, Bhandari & Jesiek 2019; Mitchell, Vögler & Nerad 2016), and an overview of assessment models of researching the impact of participating in international research activities. Challenges for students and their supervisors in these endeavours will be discussed and lessons learned presented. Much of the discussion is based on the international research work of the Centre for Innovation and Research (CIRGE) at the University of Washington, the Forces and Forms of Doctoral Education workshops (2005, 2007, 2009, 2019, see CIRGE website), and a workshop held during the Biennial Conference on Research into Postgraduate Supervision, organised by Stellenbosch University in March 2019, in South Africa.

## DEFINING INTERNATIONAL RESEARCH EXPERIENCES

International research experience is characterised here as any research-related activity undertaken by (post)graduate students who are enrolled in a PhD programme and who, during their doctoral studies, travel abroad, either individually or in groups. The report from the 2019 US NSF-sponsored workshop on the topic states, "These experiences are distinctly different from undergraduate credit-bearing activities, often known in the US as 'study abroad' and international activities that do not have an academic or research component such as [pure] cultural exchange" (Mitchell *et al.* 2019:2). 'International research experiences' also do not refer to the multi-year studies of international doctoral students outside their home country, or the complete postdoctoral stay in another country. Instead, the phrase refers to research stays between "at least a week or around 3-6 months," and involving "exposure to how research is conducted in an international context" (*ibid.*). Thus, simply attending an international conference does not count as an 'international research experience'.[1]

We also see the phrase 'student mobility' used, most often in Europe, as a term referring to border-crossing for the purpose of study or work. As Teichler (2015:11) explains, "often, mobility means a non-permanent border-crossing: for temporary study, for study of a whole programme, for mid-career international experience or employment in another country for a while. Mobility can be described as outward, i.e. related to the country of origin, and as inward, with reference to the country of destination." In the following I will focus mainly on the sending of advisees (and postdoctoral students) abroad rather than on the role of receiving them. I will use the term 'mobility' interchangeably with 'international academic stays' and will focus mostly on outward mobility. Similarly, I will use the following terms interchangeably:

---

1 At a follow-up meeting with NSF officers and US Graduate Deans, the 2019 workshop participants suggested replacing 'international' with 'global' research experience. For me the term 'global' conveys two aspects: It includes local and implies more than a visit to one country. Remaining true to the definition presented earlier, I will not adopt it here.

- Graduate education and postgraduate education
- Doctoral students and doctoral candidates
- Early career researchers = Advanced doctoral candidates, postdoctoral fellows, anyone after five years of the PhD (assistant professor/lecturers, researchers)
- Adviser and supervisor
- Academic department and institute[2]
- Professional competencies and generic skills

## BACKGROUND OF INTERNATIONAL RESEARCH EXPERIENCE

International research experiences are not new in the history of higher education. The medieval universities of Europe and North Africa were international centres of learning, with Latin as a common language for their international clientele of students (De Wit 2002; De Wit, Gacel-Ávila, Jones & Jooste 2017; Kerr 1994). Centuries later, promoting international research was widely discussed after the Second World War with the hope that increasing international activities would help overcome the hatred and mistrust among countries and contribute to mutual understanding and readiness to cooperate (De Wit 2002; Teichler 2015).

Since the beginning of the 21st century a global goal of national education ministries, higher education coordinating agencies, and universities has been to strive for international experiences of their future researchers. They have established special grant funding schemes that include international experiences for the participating doctoral students and postdoctoral fellows. Doctoral students are seen by governments as part of a future transnational elite, and as such are expected to create new knowledge by engaging in international research experiences that will prepare them to become a skilled labour force which circulates and contributes to the knowledge transfer.

Before delving into approaches for better preparing supervisors to prepare students for international experiences and to assess the outcomes of those experiences, it is important to review the context in which doctoral education is located and note the major changes that occurred in its education and training during the last 30 years. Globalisation and the subsequent governmental innovation policies worldwide have impacted doctoral education substantially and encouraged funding to proliferate doctoral education while also spurring the funding of international research experiences.

---

2   Mostly at German universities, the organisational unit of an Institute, i.e. Institute of Physics, or Sociology is the same as a department of physics or sociology at North American universities.

PART ONE • HORIZONS

### The global context

Doctoral programmes respond to external forces such as state and national governments, as well as to the internal dynamics of their own universities. During the past 25 years, motivated by the belief that more PhDs will increase a country's innovation potential and in turn lead to economic growth, national governments and their research funding agencies have established special funding models to ensure an increase in PhDs, and to include a focus on an international mobility experience at the education and training of doctorates and postdoctoral fellows (De Rosa 2008; Nerad 2020a:35, Ryan 2012). On the institutional side, research universities aspire to be of world-class quality, and doctoral education plays an essential part in this. For both governments and universities, the ranking of higher education institutions worldwide (Times Higher Education World University Ranking, QS World University Ranking, and Academic Ranking of World Universities) has become a notable driving force in doctoral education reforms, not only in countries of the Global North, such as the USA, Germany and the UK, but also in emerging economies like Chile, Brazil, India and China, which was also considered an emerging economy until recently. Doctoral education has moved beyond the purview of faculty and administrators in educational institutions alone. National policy makers are aware of, and are responding to, developments in higher education outside their national borders. The innovation policies of national governments have had an impact on doctoral education in every part of the world. The effects have been felt at both the system (macro) level and the university and programme (micro-) levels. In many cases, governments have pursued these policies even if the national infrastructure both inside and outside academia was not able to absorb the newly trained doctoral recipients. For example, this has been the case in China, Japan, and Chile, to name a few.

In several earlier writings, I have explained these underlying forces, as well as the connections between globalisation, governmental innovation policies, and postgraduate education (Nerad 2010, 2018, 2020b). Globalisation, defined as "intensified movement of goods, money, technology, information, people, ideas, and cultural practice across political and cultural boundaries" (Holton 2005:14), has exerted a steady influence on graduate education. One result is that doctoral education and postdoctoral training have acquired a significance that far exceeds the academic institutions through which they are carried out, and that has expanded beyond a single country's borders.

Governments have devised competitive funding schemes for the development of master's and doctoral programmes that train students for employment in multiple sectors, increase students' mobility, direct students toward problem-solving approaches to learning and research, and connect students and graduates to industry, business, and local communities. Moreover, governments, like universities, have learned that if innovations and economic growth are to emerge from new knowledge, it must be disseminated effectively through publications and patents – a reason some countries provide monetary incentives for completed PhD degrees and publications. Academic departments and doctoral programmes have followed these external and internal encouragements, monetary incentives, or policies, and included or expanded international experiences in doctoral studies and postdoctoral training.

The innovation policies of national governments have had an impact on postgraduate education in many parts of the world, at both the macro level and the micro level.

## Macro-level impacts: Growth and reform

At the macro level, the impact of governmental innovation policies is felt on many levels.

### Increase in PhD production

The most noticeable of the impact features is the proliferation of doctoral programmes and the diversification of student bodies, especially with increases in the number of international doctoral students. More women, more part-time students, and more students who are 30 and older are now enrolled in doctoral programmes. With the growth of the middle class in many Asian countries, a greater flow of students from Asia to the USA and Europe has also changed the composition of doctoral programmes. In addition, countries with low birth rates or shrinking populations – including Australia, Germany, Japan, the Scandinavian countries, and the UK – have sought to attract highly skilled workers via postgraduate education, particularly in science, engineering, mathematics, and agriculture (Nerad 2010).

### Multidisciplinary teams and translational research

The second feature is that governmental innovation policies have contributed to a change in the mode of research. Policies intend to link universities more closely to society. This has been occurring mainly in the natural sciences and engineering, but is increasingly occurring in other fields as well. Programmes are moving from what sociological and higher education experts term 'Mode 1', that is, learning from one master scholar within one discipline, to 'Mode 2', which emphasises the theory-practice relationship and translational research, whereby basic findings are given practical societal applications (Gibbons, Limoges, Nowotny, Schwartzman, Scott & Trow 1994). Examples are universities working with industry in research hubs, such as in the US Silicon Valley and in the Food Valley at Wageningen, between the university of Wageningen and the agri-business of the Netherlands (Etzkowitz 2008).

Academic staff and graduate students at research universities are increasingly facing pressure to accelerate translational research, which can be a revenue source for the universities.

*Governmental funding schemes, flagship programmes: Policy borrowing*

A third major change at the macro level is the development of competitive schemes for the allocation of government funds aimed at fostering human capital development. In addition to changes that were initiated through general top-down reforms from government ministries, federally funded competitive research grant allocations were established that directly targeted professors, doctoral students and postdoctoral fellows. The spread of these types of funding schemes is often the result of policy borrowing behaviour, whereby countries with newer doctoral programmes and emerging economies look to mimic so-called top universities located mainly in the Global North. Steiner-Khamsi (2016:382) noted several empirical research studies that demonstrated how policy borrowing helps to mobilise financial resources, "especially when it is preceded by political talk of falling behind some international standards or best practices". For example, the Malaysian government invited the German Council of Science and Humanities to advise them on developing their own excellence initiative, which resulted in the creation of a new Apex University competition in Malaysia in 2007.

Another area where policy borrowing has taken place is the creation and funding of grant programmes. National and regional research councils have implemented well-funded, competitive grant programmes that solicit innovative, collaborative, multidisciplinary and often multinational models of doctoral education, with the goal of training a globally engaged workforce. These very selective national flagship programmes are more common in the STEM (science, technology, engineering and mathematics) fields than in the humanities or the arts. Examples include the European Commission's Erasmus Mundus programmes at the master's level and the Innovative Training Networks (ITN) at the doctoral level; the National Science Foundation's National Research Traineeship (NRT) in the USA; the Cooperative Research Centres Programme in Australia; and the German Excellence Initiative Graduate Schools (see Nerad 2020b).

These new funding schemes are designed to promote innovative approaches to graduate education and hopefully spur imitation throughout universities. However, they demand intensive investments not always available outside of the targeted programmes; often other barriers to their replication exist as well. For example, programmes that require research stays in universities outside the country need trained administrative staff who understand the intricacies of international travel arrangements, such as visa requirements, currency restrictions and foreign language skills, and who can devote the time to these arrangements in addition to their existing duties. The programmes are an important way for doctoral students to acquire specialised research skills, to have access to instrumentation and new methods not available at their own programmes, to learn intercultural communication competencies, and to build connections and networks with peers and potential colleagues in other countries (Bilecen & Faist 2017). While these are important features for today's globalised world and labour market, they are not always possible to fund, support and sustain.

Many of these macro-level governmental funding schemes, be they governmental programs, individual grants, or a cluster of university collaborating and applying for supranational grant schemes, formed the background for the international experiences at the postgraduate level that will be described later.

*Accountability and data collection*

Requiring greater accountability, which has necessitated the increased collection of output and outcomes data and the setting up of accreditation agencies where they do not exist, is another shift many national governments have taken. In light of the rapid expansion of doctoral education and the increased mobility of doctoral candidates, governments and agencies have established standards and processes designed to guarantee the quality of higher education, including doctoral education and theses. For example, they may define those standards externally, and then determine whether particular programmes and dissertations comply with them. Examples of standards for doctoral education include the advice papers of the League of European Research Universities, the best practices publications and reports by individual European countries on competencies for early career research, including the UK Council of Graduate Education, the German University Association of Advanced Graduate Training, and the US Council of Graduate Schools; and the Australian Council of Graduate Research good practice guidelines. In the last 30 years, accreditation agencies have been established in Europe, Japan, and, most recently, India (2017) (see Fortes *et al.* 2014, Nerad 2020a). These agencies, very much aware of one another's findings and reports, have both standardised and homogenised expectations for doctoral training and innovation programmes, while creating pressure for government bodies to provide support at levels comparable to their international peers.

### Communication and international networks

Governments and regional organisations are encouraging and funding international collaborations in research, international network building, and degree offerings as new computing information systems make communication across vast spaces easier, faster and more widespread. Universities are actively pursuing these activities, which are now supported by national and supranational funding agencies, such as the European Commission, the German Academic Exchange Service (DAAD), governments of ASEAN countries, Mercosur countries,[3] many African countries, or the National Institute of Health in the USA, among others. Research universities are keen to get the best possible students to their campuses, and may find themselves competing for the same pool of elite students. They also connect internationally with other universities to use facilities and instrumentation they lack (De Wit et al. 2017; Nerad & Evans 2014). As a result, scholarly networks have formed rapidly, and universities have established a number of joint or dual-doctoral degrees.

### Support for the returning expatriate

The sixth macro feature is a relatively new trend in many countries. Governments have developed programmes to attract doctoral students or postdoctoral fellows who studied abroad back home in an attempt to stem the 'brain drain' of talent away from the sending country. France, Portugal and Germany, for example, sponsor gatherings in the USA and other countries, where doctoral students or postdoctoral students living abroad are informed about employment opportunities in their home countries. China grants returning doctorates the difficult-to-get status of local residents in major cities, as well as tax and monetary incentives to start their own businesses, as enticements to reside in China. More recently, China's Thousand Talents Programme (Jia 2018) has offered lucrative packages including generous housing subsidies, tuition remission for dependents, and copious amounts of research funding, in addition to internationally competitive salary packages, to lure qualified scholars back to their native country.

These system-level policy changes are expected to bring about changes at a nation's universities and their doctoral programmes. These governmental schemes and interventions have been launched in both the Global South and the Global North. Their effects and consequences have intended and positive, but also unintended and negative outcomes (Altbach 2016; Nerad 2020a).

---

3  Mercosur is an economic and political bloc comprising Argentina, Brazil, Paraguay, Uruguay and Venezuela.

### Micro-level impacts: Commonalities and competencies

At the university level, and at the programme level between doctoral candidates and their supervisors, a number of changes have occurred over the past 20 years. In some countries, these changes are still in progress, while in other countries and universities, programme-level changes have now become the norm. The most common change worldwide is the introduction of structured programmes, the move away from a single dissertation adviser to at least two, and the opening up of possibilities to study under dual or joint doctoral degrees and in an inter- or multidisciplinary and international context. The external changes and reforms discussed above demand more competencies from the increasingly larger generation of doctoral candidates than were required in the past. In addition to the traditional academic competencies – critical thinking, knowing and applying research methods and design, undertaking competent data analysis, academic writing and publishing within the rules of ethical and responsible research – doctoral students are now also expected to acquire professional competencies, as well as intercultural communication understanding and skills (Nerad 2012, 2015). Professional competencies include grant writing, presenting complicated scientific concepts and results to a diverse audience, working effectively in teams, applying for professional jobs, and managing people and budgets. Intercultural competency means working effectively with people from different classes, races/ethnicities, cultures, religions and perspectives (Deardorff 2009). It is these intercultural competencies that doctoral students hope to gain by undertaking international research experiences.

### *A paradigm shift in supervision and assessment of quality*

Given the heightened emphasis on increasing the number of doctoral degrees and on securing quality research education, funding agencies have proposed a shift away from a single supervisor to a team of two supervisors or a dissertation committee. This paradigm shift to a multilevel advising and mentoring model (Rudd, Nerad, Emory & Picciano 2008; Nerad 2015), away from the traditional apprenticeship model, tries, among other things, to reduce the doctoral candidate's dependence on a single person and broadens input to multiple sources (Nerad 2012). This model, together with a more structured learning process and a predetermined number of classes (dependent on the student's background) to be taken (e.g. in research methodology), has proved to create more academic freedom and diverse guidance for the doctoral candidate on his or her way to becoming a junior scholar. This type of supervision has been emulated by many doctoral programmes around the world, but certainly not by all. Such a paradigm shift is a slow process. It involves an attitudinal shift by professors who are no longer esteemed as the single best scholarly authority. Notably, doctoral programmes without external funding are slow to change.

In addition, quality assurance schemes are increasingly observed at the programme and university levels. These follow the common input, throughput, and output quality assurance model used in businesses (CGS 2011; Nerad 2014). They are also a tool for diminishing the migration of talented potential doctoral students. At the doctoral level, quality assurance includes four core elements. The first is a graduate programme's inputs: its admitted students, its professors who teach and advise, its research infrastructure in the form of library holdings and functioning laboratory equipment, and its research money, including students' research support. The second element is the programme's throughputs: advising or supervision, coursework, and students' development of professional competencies. The third element is the programme's outputs: its production of scholars holding valid university degrees, its production of theses and dissertations, and various forms of research publication. The final element is the programme outcomes, including the programme's production of new knowledge and the societal impact of that knowledge. Thus, tracking of graduates' careers has been introduced at the institutional, national, and international levels as an important measure of a programme's quality, along with attrition rates and time to degree completion.

## *The prevalence of English*

The exponential increase in international doctoral students has spread the use of English in doctoral education. It is now prevalent worldwide, although its use has lately come under attack in some countries, such as the Netherlands and Denmark (De Groot 2019). Nevertheless, English has become the *lingua franca* of doctoral education, and many scholarly journals are published in English. The use of a common language allows students greater mobility and provides greater visibility for their research when they are also able to publish in English journals. At the same time, the use of English as doctoral education's common language gives an advantage to students from English-speaking countries, as well as to those who have had access to English-language schooling before entering their doctoral programmes, increasing inequities in opportunities for those with weaker English language skills.

## *Admission practice and funding packages*

The expansion and internationalisation of doctoral education have led to an admission process that has become more defined and more competitive. However, even within a country and a university, a variety of admissions models still exist.

Worldwide competition for the best doctoral students has pressured doctoral programs to offer three years of funding to outstanding applicants. Depending on the country, the funding may come directly from the government, indirectly from federal research grants awarded to departments or professors, or in form of state government teaching assistantships, or from private foundations.

*Diversification of degrees and dissertation formats*

There is also greater diversification when it comes to the accepted forms of both dissertations and doctoral degrees. In some disciplines, instead of a cohesive doctoral dissertation, three journal articles with an introduction and conclusion or three already accepted first-author journal articles are being accepted.

In the UK, Australia, and the USA, a growing number of doctoral programmes have shifted toward professional and practice-based approaches, in which more weight is placed on coursework than on training in research methods, and more emphasis on applied rather than original research (Zusman 2017). These new professional degrees have to be differentiated from the long-existing professional doctoral degrees in business, education, medicine, clinical psychology and jurisprudence.

*Centralised campus-organised unit for doctoral and postdoctoral education*

Centrally coordinated postgraduate education is a new phenomenon in Europe, Africa and Latin America, but such graduate schools or graduate divisions, as they are called in North America, are an established presence in the UK, Australia, New Zealand and China. In these countries, graduate schools serve as advocates for postgraduate education and postdoc training with top university administrators, develop guidelines for the overall process of postgraduate education, provide training in professional competencies, and offer incentives for excellence in academic mentoring. Many major research universities also solicit doctoral students' evaluations regarding programme quality and the quality of professors' supervision, and lately increasingly track the careers of their graduates to collect outcome information. In addition, a US-type graduate school may establish procedures for earning a dual degree or a joint degree with another university.

*Flagship doctoral programmes*

National, well-funded, competitive flagship programmes often require certain specifications, including many of the micro-level changes just described. These national or supranational flagship programmes allow doctoral candidates to study under ideal situations: in a well-funded, highly structured setting, with a small number of committed professors attending to a carefully selected cohort of doctoral students. These programmes not only provide each doctoral student with extra research allowances but also pay attention to the theory that learning is a social act (Lave & Wenger 1991), and that social interaction boosts research.

Many of these recent systemic and programme-level changes in doctoral education – particularly the heightened attention to the learning environment and the creation of new flagship doctoral programmes – have improved the lives of doctoral candidates and the quality of their education and training. These well-funded and well-structured doctoral programmes uniformly compare favourably to traditional education. Students say they highly value the availability of resources to attend national and international conferences and to create international collaborations along common research lines (Manathunga, Pitt, Cox, Boreham, Lant & Mellick 2012; Morris, Pitt & Manathunga 2012). However, only a very small number of doctoral students get the opportunity to study in these flagship programmes. The majority end up in traditional doctoral programmes in their own countries.

## Global tension

Encouraged by increased funding during the last 30 years and sustained by a number of converging policies and practices, government innovation policies and subsequent changes at universities and in doctoral studies certainly had positive effects. But they have also created tensions. Around the world, a number of common issues are prevalent: increase in the production of doctoral education, access to doctoral education for women and minorities, and structure and quality of doctoral education, supervising and mentoring. What is new, however, is that workforce preparedness now dominates the discussion, while topics like ensuring the intellectual excitement of undertaking research and creating space for intellectual risk-taking – not to mention examples in which these two conditions were successfully created through international research experiences, providing access and quality experiences for first-generation and non-traditional doctoral students – get little attention.

### *Monetary incentives and the quality of doctoral education*

The governmental competitive grant funding that directly targeted professors, doctoral students and postdoctoral fellows was intended to entice those who wanted to make changes in the structure and research approach of doctoral education. While governments hoped that these well-funded programmes would have a 'spill-over effect' into all doctoral education at a given university, they have instead created a new stratification. On the one hand, these grant-funded initiatives have created a small group of well-funded, well-designed, project-based doctoral programmes with international components. On the other hand, there are still many less well-funded programmes – where students study under less favourable conditions – that carry the mass of doctoral education. This bifurcation exists now among universities across the globe, among universities in one country, and even within the same department at a university.

There have been other unintended effects from government policies giving universities monetary incentives for every new PhD produced and every peer-reviewed publication: the rise of institutional compliance behaviour, rather than an improvement of the quality of doctoral education. In 2012, the American Society of Cell Biology passed the San Francisco Declaration of Research Assessment to stop the abuse of the academic journal impact factor by correlating this impact index to the merits of a specific scholar's contributions. A good number of European societies signed the declaration, but it has had no impact in countries such as China, India, or South Africa, where universities and faculty members receive money for every peer-reviewed journal article. While positive changes may have occurred – it has certainly multiplied the numbers of doctorates produced – these mechanisms of quantitative monitoring have done little to encourage quality, intellectual risk-taking, and true innovation.

### *Social justice: Equity, access, affordability*

Another source of tension can be the conflict between a programme's goal of attaining world-class ranking, often on the mere basis of quantifiable outcomes, and its commitment to equity in terms of access to graduate education and the programme's affordability. Too often these two goals are in conflict with one another. With rankings in mind, departments tend to admit risk-free doctoral students from other top-ranked institutions, rather than considering promising first-generation domestic students from lower-ranked universities, who will perhaps require more faculty efforts and departmental resources to be successful and complete at similar rates (Chiappa & Perez Meijas 2019; Perez Meijas, Chiappa & Guzman-Valenzuela 2018). It is also important to note that in many countries, race, ethnicity, gender, age, class background, and/or disability are seldom discussed, and relevant data on these topics is not systematically collected.

### *Neglect of the humanities and the arts*

Unfortunately, most of the governmental funding schemes and the special financial allocations under innovation policies are focused on STEM and health fields. Doctoral programmes in STEM disciplines and biomedicine are perceived as offering the strongest local and regional economic impact. They are, therefore, the first programmes to be supported, financially and in other ways (more space, better location on campus). The humanities, the arts, and the social sciences (with the exception of business administration) have received far less governmental and university funding. As a result, their status and influence within their own institutions have diminished. This is the case not only in the USA and China, but increasingly in other countries too.

## *Workforce preparedness and a lack of intellectual risk taking*

Another source of tension involves conflict between a programme's goal of educating students to be creative and innovative – with all the false starts and learning from experience that this goal entails – and funders' demands for the shortest possible time to degree completion. The pressure on doctoral students to demonstrate efficiency by funders demanding the shortest possible time to degree completion has stifled creativity and intellectual risk taking, both necessary for innovation, which is often the emphasised goal of a research education. This overemphasis on workforce preparedness as the sole function and goal of a doctoral education has resulted in a loss of intellectual curiosity and inflamed the anxiety of current doctoral students.

It is in this context that international research activities contribute most to broaden our advisees' horizons, excite their curiosity and contribute to creative knowledge production. It is unfortunate that some supervisors do not allow their students to leave for a research visit to another country, concerned it will prolong time to doctoral completion. If national governments truly view doctorate holders as critical for innovation and discovery, then future researchers must not only be allowed but actively encouraged to cross disciplinary, institutional, national and cultural boundaries. To advance knowledge requires the willingness to pursue risky but potentially transformative research projects under the thoughtful guidance of a supervisor and ideally a dissertation committee – and to be allowed to make mistakes. It is in this spirit that I recommend universities develop programmes to train doctoral supervisors explicitly in preparing for risk recognition and for international research visits. Departments and doctoral programmes need to develop a research culture that values and rewards innovation, creativity and boundary crossing in disciplines and cultures. Every doctoral curriculum is advised to train students to be aware of the limits and strengths of their disciplines by exposing them to other fields and other cultures through international team-building opportunities (CIRGE 2009). In the following section we will learn from findings of three international workshops, about key questions to address when investigating international research experiences, about research approaches and research findings, models on structuring and assessing international research experiences during doctoral studies, and practical considerations in implementing international research visits.

## INTERNATIONAL RESEARCH ACTIVITIES

There are many ways in which postgraduate students can participate in international research activities, ranging from highly structured to no structure at all, from cohorts to individual research, or a combination of both, varying in length, in time of the year (summer programme, semester activity) and year in the doctoral programme.

Most higher education policy reports and guidelines declare international researcher mobility as uniformly desirable, without documenting empirical evidence. Given the prominence of emphasis on physical mobility connected to the goal of internationalising universities during the last two decades, it is surprising that the state of actual knowledge on border-crossing mobility is largely anecdotal (Teichler 2015).

**Results and outcomes from three workshops on investigating the international research experiences at the postgraduate level**

Recognising that a comprehensive worldwide review of the literature on research on international research experiences would go beyond the scope of this chapter, reviewing three international National Science Foundation-sponsored workshops in the USA (2011, 2016 and 2019) that explicitly set out to investigate the benefits of international research experiences can provide some important insights. The subsections below highlight the major findings in terms of relevant research questions and research approaches to assess the specific value of such experiences (Blumenfield & Nerad 2012; Mitchell Mitchell, Vögler & Nerad 2016; Mitchel, Besterfield-Sacre, Bhandari & Jesiek 2019).

*Central research questions*

One key outcome was reaching consensus on central questions as priorities for further empirical research:

- Does international collaboration lead to better science/ better scholars?
- Do current institutional and funding structures lead to missed opportunities for international collaboration? If so, how?
- How can we assess institutional preparedness for international collaborations/ experiences?
- What are the expected outcomes and goals of international experiences/collaborations? How are they established?
- What are the actual impacts, outcomes, and transformation of the international experiences/collaborations?

## Models and frameworks for impact assessment

A second major result of the workshops was the pooling of participants' knowledge and existing literature to come up with recommendations for a number of models and conceptual frameworks in undertaking research that would answer these questions.

- The first model suggests examining outcomes of the international research experience on the individual student by focusing on intercultural competencies using the Intercultural Development Inventory (Deardorff 2009). This model concentrates on subjective measures, including first-person accounts of experiences and scholarly investigations of identity and attitudes.
- A second model uses insights from intergroup psychology and social identity theory (Tajfel & Turner 1979), postulating that optimal results occur when such an experience forges a new personal and professional identity within participating students.
- A third model studies individual doctoral programmes with strong international components by using participant observation, interviews, focus groups and document analysis.
- A fourth model evaluates doctoral student participants' international research experiences and their research productivity before and after the project by comparing both sets of outcomes to a control group of students who had not participated in international experiences.
- A fifth model documents the career outcomes of doctoral recipients and compares those who participated in international research visits, exchanges and collaborations with those who did not have such experiences during their doctoral or postdoctoral phases.
- A conceptual framework assessing the entire duration of an international research experience is the 'Before-During-After' model, developed by Brent K. Jesiek, professor of Engineering at Purdue University in the USA, illustrated in Figure 1.1.
- Another framework, an outcomes-oriented logic model, includes aspects from Deardorff's (2009) model of intended and unintended outputs, outcomes, and impacts, as well as intercultural competence, technical skill acquisition, and science-oriented outcomes (see Figure 1.2, provided by BK Jesiek). (Nerad & Blumenfield 2011).

# CHAPTER 1 • OPPORTUNITIES AND CHALLENGES OF INTERNATIONAL RESEARCH EXPERIENCES ...

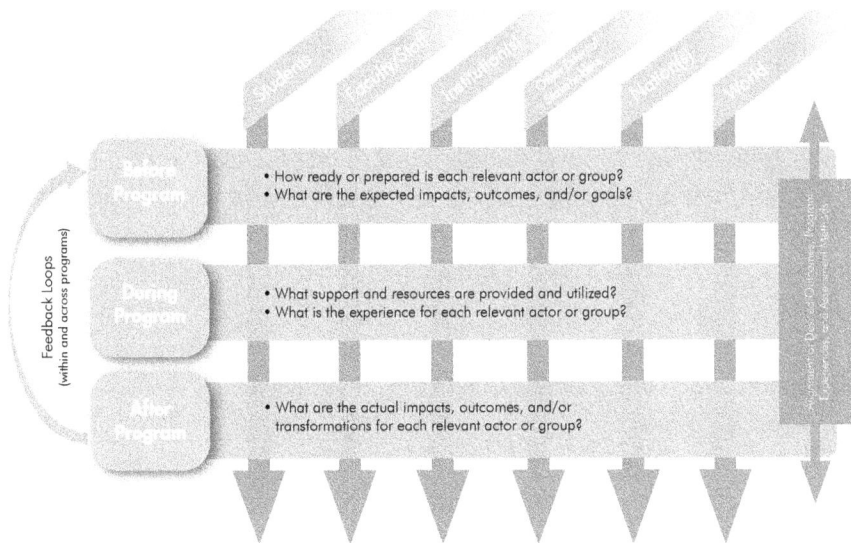

**FIGURE 1.1**  Conceptual assessment framework of Before-During-After

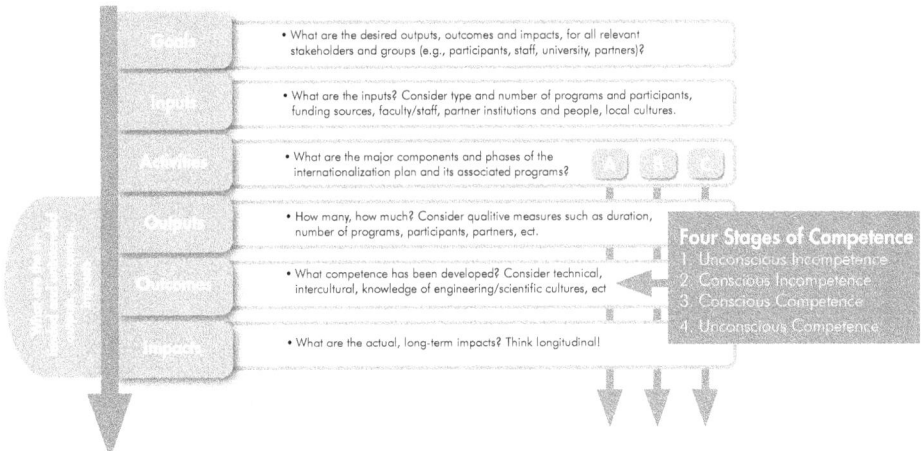

**FIGURE 1.2**  An outcomes-oriented logic model for international programmes and initiatives

*Note: A, B, and C represent 'before-during- after' the international experience

### Further findings

A number of further findings are briefly discussed below.

#### *Timing*

Decisions regarding when a doctoral student should undertake a research experience and for how long a time depends on the type of research activity and structure (individual, cohort or hybrid), funding level, family considerations and the intended outcome. Given that countries aim for different completion time to doctoral degrees (three years in most of Europe, five to seven in North America), ideal timing depends on a student's readiness for an international activity. In countries with five years, between the second and fourth year of a PhD student's tenure seems to be optimal for an extended research stay.

#### *Duration*

The duration of the international research experience is influenced not only by the student's preparedness, the type of international programme, the funding (including the level of financial and logistical support from the host institution), and family considerations, but also by the number and duration of previous research visits, language considerations, and the specifics of a disciplinary research culture. A scaffolding model, with brief introductory, observational visits (1-2 weeks) that allow students to gain insight into a new culture or research opportunity and lay the foundation for longer subsequent visits can be beneficial particularly for those students from minority backgrounds. Repeated or longer-duration visits can be used for specific research or technology development projects.

#### *Gender, race and class*

In *Women in Global Science*, Zippel (2017) found that international mobility benefits are gendered. The academic space (.edu bonus) widens professional circles for women and circumvents potentially exclusionary networks at home. By moving horizontally across borders, female early career researchers rise vertically through glass ceilings. Zippel also found that postgraduate advisers steer students from diverse cultural backgrounds and female students away from certain opportunities based on perceived fears that they may face discrimination. Further, this study found that more men than women received unsolicited invitations to engage in international work by another institution.

International experiences thus magnified inequalities. Student characteristics in these programmes highlighted the privileges with which many of the doctoral participants entered these international research experience. A number of studies found that class, gender, race and disability matter substantially, and therefore need to be urgently addressed to create fair opportunities in the participation of international research activities.

*Time to degree and productivity*

Findings from studies that compared doctoral students with international experience with a control group who had not participated in an international experience found that international mobility did not prolong time to doctoral degree and added value for the scientific, personal and career development of participants (Heidler 2015). Doctoral students with international experiences had a higher average number of annual post-award publications than their comparison group peers. They were also more likely to maintain international collaborators and travel abroad as postdoctoral fellows or in their professional careers than their peers.

*Dissertation supervisors*

The ideal role of the supervisor is to be an advocate for their advisees' international research experience and to support them in this role. Their institution should provide training on how to best facilitate their advisees' experience by leveraging institutional expertise on logistics such as health, visas and responsible conduct of research. Supervisors may also need to draw attention to institutional roadblocks that act as barriers to international experiences, and advocate for institution-wide changes that enable and facilitate these experiences.

*Data collection and participant tracking*

Consensus was reached that there need to be two levels of data collection and maintenance: the institutional and programme-level data, and cross-institutional studies that aggregate common data. The latter allows for an examination across multiple institutions; with common measures, these studies may best identify trends and provide evidence that can help institutions advocate for the value of international experiences for graduate students. These data collection efforts should be made freely and easily accessible to current and prospective doctoral students.

Together, these workshops drilled down deeper into this fairly new field, helping us better understand international research experiences and produce empirical evidence of their impact. As such, the workshop findings are valuable lessons learned for the implementation of national and supranational schemes for macro- and micro- level changes in doctoral education that speak to international research experiences.

## OVERALL RECOMMENDATIONS: PREPARE FOR CHALLENGES AND SHARE LESSONS LEARNED

Perhaps the biggest challenge for today's doctoral student is the indirect expectation as seen in the guidelines of major higher education funding agencies that today's scholar is a cosmopolitan, entrepreneurial, internationally mobile, hyper-flexible jet-setter. This expectation reflects the worldview of an unattached individual (Hannerz 2002). In reality, a doctoral student going abroad faces many logistical and academic challenges: a new language, especially challenging when venturing outside the university; finding housing and getting used to different styles of accommodation; new food; managing shopping when the language, fruits, vegetables and daily staple items are different; and learning to use new modes of transportation, to name a few. Academic challenges, especially in the fields of science and engineering, are to cope with the frustration that experimental setup takes longer time than anticipated, that one does not know how things get done in a laboratory, and that the hierarchy of publishing with professors is not openly discussed, as disciplinary, regional, national, and international conventions for publication, co-authorship, and research vary greatly. On this topic we need to plan for misunderstandings and offer compassion for the challenges encountered on all sides. And we should not forget that nearly everyone, at times, especially after work and during holidays, will miss the support networks of friends and family, and this will intensify the feelings of loneliness.

Preparing for these challenges can be best done by thinking through with the supervisor the three phases of a research visit: before the visit, preparing by drawing on existing campus resources (contacting international students and scholars from the country of proposed visit, contacting other students and academics who have previously visited the country or done research there, and connecting with the Office of Global Affairs or similar unit for health, safety and visa issues); during the visit, by ensuring regular contact and documentation (requiring periodic progress reports, blog posts, social media, Zoom or other forms of real-time conversations, fieldnote or diary entries, and surveys); and after the visit, by planning for integrating the experience into the overall doctoral training, into the department or doctoral programme and beyond.

Important lessons learned are many, but making sure that the activities build on mutual benefits and trust, ideally emerging from the bottom and not beginning from a top-down approach, then confirmed through a memorandum of understanding (MOU) by university presidents, were the most important lessons voiced on many occasions with experienced colleagues (see University of North Texas 2013).

Now in 2020 the list of recommendations is long. Many have been presented throughout the review of the three workshops findings. In summary let me highlight only the most useful lessons learned.

As supervisors and researchers interested in allowing more doctoral students to participate in such experiences, we shall engage in evaluation research that collects evidence to persuade funders, our colleagues, and our own university to support these valuable experiences in our doctoral advisees' education and training. In doing so, we know that no one model fits all purposes. We need to use a multiple lens view considering the multiple stakeholders in such an experience. We shall distinguish between individual and institutional level of analysis and contribution to the advancement of knowledge per se. We now know that intercultural competencies are outcomes that can be measured, and we shall be prepared for misunderstandings. A careful analysis of the funding structures will be wise in order to understand whether they facilitate or hinder the intended goal of an international research activity. Creating room for post-assessment and integration of the international experience into academic teaching and learning at re-entry of our advisees is extremely important.

Finally, with the 2018 emergence of the Me-Too movement, the high prevalence of sexual assault and other harassment during international fieldwork came to light. This topic is not a new one, but had previously received little attention and will certainly need to be addressed seriously, as it showed the unpreparedness of many institutions in the USA, and probably universities in other countries too, to support students assaulted or harassed during unsupervised international research experiences (Clancy, Nelson, Rutherford & Hinde 2014). Being away from support networks, and often being alone or with a small group and reliant on host institutions and supervisors makes students particularly vulnerable in ways that sending universities are only now beginning to address. All this points to institutional training of research supervisors on how to best facilitate international research experiences for their advisees

## CONCLUSION

Quality preparation of a doctoral candidate requires coordinated efforts at many levels in the university, between universities, between national and international funding agencies, and across various learning communities throughout the duration of that candidate's doctoral education inside and outside his or her own country (Nerad 2012). It is important not only to increase funding, especially for international research experiences as these have many benefits as presented in this chapter, but to assure that for many more doctoral candidates such opportunities are available. In doctoral education we can commit to questioning the norms and values that cause inequality and exclusion in society at the local, national, and global levels, and international research experiences are a powerful vehicle in accomplishing this goal.

## AFTERWORD FROM SEATTLE, WASHINGTON, IN MAY 2020

Reflecting from the vantage point of the lockdown, stay-at-home and social distancing policies due to the coronavirus will mean that many of us who educate and train doctoral candidates and postdoctoral fellows, will need to think collectively: what happens when the mobility we take for granted is no longer possible? Even under normal circumstances, when is it most valuable to recommend an international experience and then make the most out of it, knowing that we also contribute to increasing carbon footprints and thus climate change? While much can be accomplished today online, and the younger generation is used to the new technology, I still believe that an initial physical experience in another research culture under the thoughtful guidance of a supervisor and a dissertation committee is still extremely important to ignite or maintain the flame of intellectual curiosity. The crossing of institutions and national boundaries in order to enrich the research results and to add value to personal and professional growth of our advisees remains an important element of doctoral education, even if it might take on a different form.

## REFERENCES

Altbach Ph. 2016. *Global perspectives on higher education*. Baltimore: Johns Hopkins University Press.

Bilecen B & Faist Th. 2017. Wissensvermittlung in transnationalen Netzwerken. In: A Neusel & A Wolter (eds.), *Mobile wissenschaft (Mobile science)*. Frankfurt: Campus.

Blumenfield T & Nerad M. 2012. International assessment: Developing a research agenda for (post)graduate education and collaboration. *Australian Universities Review*, 54(1):72-83.

Chiappa R & Perez Mejias P. 2019. Unfolding the direct and indirect effects of social class of origin on faculty income. *Higher Education*:1-27. https://doi.org/10.1007/s10734-019-0356-4

CIRGE. 2005. *Forces and forms in doctoral education – Seattle 2005*. https://bit.ly/3tnaMTq

CIRGE. 2007. *Forces and forms in doctoral education – Melbourne 2007*. https://bitly/3e6lw23

CIRGE. 2009. *Forces and forms in doctoral education – Kassel 2009*. https://bit.ly/3dlh93Z

CIRGE. 2019. *Revisiting forces and forms in doctoral education worldwide – Hannover 2019*. https://bit.ly/2ORDQ6w

Clancy KB, Nelson R, Rutherford JN & Hinde K. 2014. Survey of academic field experiences (SAFE): Trainees report harassment and assault. *PLOS ONE*, 9(7):0102172. https://doi.org/10.1371/journal.pone.0102172

Council of Graduate Schools (CGS). 2011. *Assessment and Review of Graduate Programs*. Washington D.C: CGS publication.

De Groot A. 2019. The English Trojan horse destroying Dutch universities. *University World News*. January 25.

De Rosa A. 2008. New Forms of International Cooperation in Doctoral Training: Internationalization and the International Doctorate- One Goal, Two Distinct Models. *Higher Education in Europe*, 33(1):3-25. https://doi.org/10.1080/03797720802228084

De Wit H. 2002. *Internationalization of higher education in the United States of America and Europe: A historical, comparative, and conceptual analysis*. Westport, CT: Greenwood Press.

De Wit H, Gacel-Ávila J, Jones E & Jooste N. (eds.). 2017. *The globalization of internationalization. Emerging voices and perspectives*. London and New York: Routledge. https://doi.org/10.4324/9781315657547

Deardorff D. (ed.). 2009. *The Sage handbook of intercultural competence*. Los Angeles: Sage.

Etzkowitz H. 2008. *The triple helix: University-industry-government. Innovation in action*. New York: Routledge.

Fortes M, Kehm B & Mayekiso T. 2014. In: M Nerad & B Evans (eds.), *Globalization and its impacts on the quality of PhD education worldwide: Forces and forms of doctoral education worldwide*. Rotterdam, Netherlands: Sense Publishers. 81-110.

Gibbons M, Limoges C, Nowotny H, Schwartzman S, Scott P & Trow M. 1994. *The new production of knowledge: The dynamics of science and research in contemporary societies*. London: Sage.

Hannerz U. 2002. *Transnational connections: culture, people, places*. New York: Routledge. https://doi.org/10.4324/9780203131985

Heidler R. 2015. *Drivers of internationalisation: Results from the evaluation of international research training groups*. Bonn, BRD: Deutsche Forschungsgemeinschaft.

Holton R. 2005. *Making globalization*. New York: Palmgrave McMillan. https://doi.org/10.1007/978-0-230-80234-6

Jia H. 2018. China's plan to recruit talented researchers. *Nature*, 17 January, 553:8. https://doi.org/10.1038/d41586-018-00538-z

Kerr C. 1994. *Higher education cannot escape history*. Albany, NY: SUNY Press.

Lave J & Wenger E. 1991. *Situated learning: Legitimate peripheral participation*. New York: Cambridge University Press. https://doi.org/10.1017/CBO9780511815355

Manathunga C, Pitt R, Cox L, Boreham P, Lant P & Mellick G. 2012. Evaluating industry-based doctoral research programs: perspectives and outcomes of Australian Cooperative Research Centre graduates. *Studies in Higher Education* 37(7):843-858. https://doi.org/10.1080/03075079.2011.554607

Mitchell B, Besterfield-Sacre M, Bhandari R & Jesiek B. 2019. Final report: *Best practices in international research experiences for graduate students*. https://bit.ly/3mTYtMc

Mitchell B, Vögler M & Nerad M. 2016. *Evaluating international research experiences for graduate students*. A report from the 2016 CGS-NSF-DFG Workshop. Washington D.C: National Science Foundation.

Morris S, Pitt R & Manathunga C. 2012. Students' experiences of supervision in academic and industry settings: Results of an Australian study. *Assessment & Evaluation in Higher Education*, 37(5):619-636. https://doi.org/10.1080/02602938.2011.557715

Nerad M with June R & Miller D. (eds.). 1997. *Graduate Education in the United States*. New York: Garland Press.

Nerad M. 2010. Globalization and the internationalization of graduate education: A macro and micro view. *Canadian Journal of Higher Education*, 40(1):1-12. https://doi.org/10.47678/cjhe.v40i1.1566

Nerad M. 2012. Conceptual approaches to doctoral education: A community of practice. *Alternation*, 19(2):57-72.

Nerad M. 2014. Developing 'fit for purpose' research doctoral graduates. Increased standardization of quality measures in PhD education worldwide. In: M Nerad & B Evans (eds.), *Globalization and its impacts on the quality of PhD education worldwide: Forces and forms of doctoral education worldwide*. Rotterdam, Netherlands: Sense Publishers. 111-128. https://doi.org/10.1007/978-94-6209-569-4_6

Nerad M. 2015. Professional development for doctoral students: What is it? Why now? Who does it? *Nagoya Journal of Higher Education*, 15:285-318.

Nerad M. 2018. Graduate Education Development in an International Context. In: JC-Cheol Shin & P Teixeira (eds.), *Encyclopedia of International Higher Education Systems and Institutions*. New York, Berlin: Springer Science and Business Media. https://doi.org/10.1007/978-94-017-9553-1_259-1

Nerad M. 2020a. Doctoral education worldwide. Three decades of change. In: M Yudekevich, H de Wit & Ph Altbach (eds.), *Trends and issues in doctoral education worldwide: An international research inquiry*. Los Angeles: SAGE. 33-50. https://doi.org/10.4135/9789353885991.n2

Nerad M. 2020b. Governmental innovation policies and change in doctoral education worldwide: Are doctoral programs converging? Trends and tensions. In: S Cardoso, O Tavares, Ch Sin & T Carvalho (eds.), *Structural and institutional transformations in doctoral education*. London: Palgrave McMillan. 43-84. https://doi.org/10.1007/978-3-030-38046-5_3

Nerad M & Blumenfield T. 2011. *Investigating the International Experiences in STEM Graduate Education and Beyond*. A Report to NSF from the 2011 Workshop to Develop a Research Agenda. Seattle: CIRGE, UW.

Nerad M & Evans B. (eds.). 2014. *Globalization and its impacts on the quality of PhD education worldwide: Forces and forms of doctoral education worldwide*. Rotterdam, Netherlands: Sense Publishers. https://doi.org/10.1007/978-94-6209-569-4

Perez Mejias P, Chiappa R & Guzman-Valenzuela C. 2018. Privileging the privileged: Global university rankings' effects on a Chilean fellowship programme for postgraduate studies abroad. *Social Sciences*, 7(12):243. https://doi.org/10.3390/socsci7120243

Ryan J. 2012. Internationalization of doctoral education: Possibilities for new knowledge and understanding. *Australian Universities' Review*, 54 (1):55-63.

Rudd E, Nerad M, Emory M & Picciano J. 2008. *Professional development for PhD students: Do they really need it?* Seattle, WA: Center for Innovation and Research in Graduate Education. https://bit.ly/3wWYgwa

Steiner-Khansi G. 2016. New directions in policy borrowing research. *Asia Pacific Education Review,* 17:381-390. https://doi.org/10.1007/s12564-016-9442-9

Tajfel H & Turner JC. 1979. An integrative theory of intergroup conflict. In: WG Austin & S Worchel (eds.), *The social psychology of intergroup relations*. Monterey, CA: Brooks-Cole.

Teichler U. 2015. Academic mobility and migration: What we know and what we do not know. *European Review*, 23(1):6-37. https://doi.org/10.1017/S1062798714000787

University of North Texas. 2013. *Global research funding forum. Maximizing opportunities to build a global research portfolio*. [Conference Report] Spring, 2013.

Zippel K. 2017. Women in Global Science, Advancing Academic Careers through International Collaboration. Redwood City, CA: Stanford University Press. https://doi.org/10.1515/9781503601505

Zusman A. 2017. Changing degrees: Creation and growth of new kinds of professional doctorates. *The Journal of Higher Education*, 88 (1):33-61. https://doi.org/10.1080/00221546.2016.1243941

# DOCTORAL EDUCATION AS A FIELD OF GLOBAL SCHOLARSHIP

## AN ANALYSIS OF ANGLOPHONE PUBLISHED RESEARCH (2005-2018)

Liezel Frick and Johann Mouton

## INTRODUCTION

Doctoral education (including the supervision thereof) has gained prominence internationally as part of the global competitiveness debate, nationally as a means of promoting industrial and social innovation,[1] and within universities as a key indicator of higher education efficiency, quality, and status. But doctoral education is not merely practice rooted within (and sometimes across) disciplines – there is a growing body of scholarship that theoretically supports and empirically underscores such practice. The call in this publication to consider the concept of the 'global scholar' and its implications for postgraduate studies and supervision is thus positioned within the growing body of knowledge on postgraduate supervision in general, and doctoral education in particular. Such knowledge is not only of pedagogic importance to students and supervisors but also provides an evidence-based foundation for decision-making by university, government and funding body decision-makers.

Yet, there is a current lack of systematic consideration of the positionality of this body of knowledge both geographically and thematically. In this chapter, we report on an overview of relevant scholarship through an analysis of journal article publications focused on doctoral education for the period 2005-2018 (N=907). We specifically

---

[1] Innovation is defined as the practical application of a novel and thus original idea, but it must be an idea with a potential application. Innovation thus involves the process of transforming an invention (or something that is considered original) into practical application, and is most commonly associated with private industry and features in the in economic discourses on production processes or products – even though the notion of social innovation extends this conceptualisation (Sternberg, Pretz & Kaufman 2003). A social innovation "has the potential to improve either the quality or the quantity of life", which is not necessarily profit driven (Pol & Ville 2009).

consider the contributions the selected journals make to the field of doctoral education, the increase in number of journal articles on doctoral education per year, the geographical distribution of authorship, and noticeable collaboration trends. A more in-depth thematic analysis of these journal articles highlights global doctoral education scholarship trends.

Our analysis shows that there is indeed a growing body of knowledge on doctoral education globally, but that a limited number of countries and journals (mostly positioned within the Global North) dominates the academic discourse in this field from an Anglophone perspective. The thematic analysis highlights nine themes emerging from the studied articles: doctoral education (including doctoral pedagogies), supervisory models and approaches, doctoral supervision, socialisation, work focused on doctoral students themselves during, and beyond the doctorate; as well as studies focused on the research context, the research process, and the research product. Though the analysis has certain limitations and delimitations (in terms of journal selection, language and geographical representation), it does show that the scholarship on doctoral education emanating from particular regions (including the African continent excluding South Africa) is limited in the international Anglophone arena.

## BACKGROUND TO THE STUDY

In the Points for Debate section of the journal *Higher Education Research and Development* an article titled 'The higher education research archipelago', Macfarlane (2012:129) positions "doctoral supervision" as part of the much broader "teaching and learning island", while there is no mention of postgraduate or doctoral education in Le Grange's (2009) survey of higher education research in the second decade of South Africa's democracy (using 423 articles published in the *South African Journal of Higher Education* between 2004 and 2008 in his analysis). Although Tight's (2012) article on changing journal publication patterns in higher education research across 15 high status journals in the years 2000 (n=388 articles) and 2010 (n=567 articles) probably provides the most comprehensive synopsis of the broader field of higher education scholarship, it also does not highlight postgraduate or doctoral education as a key research area.

Yet there has been notable growth in this field of research, as the sustainability and growth of conferences such as the Biennial International Postgraduate Supervision (PGS – in 2019 hosting the seventh conference in this series, the first being in 2007) conference and the Quality in Postgraduate Research (QPR – which has been in existence since 1994), as well as the existence of specialist journals such as *Studies in Graduate and Postdoctoral Education* (which was initially established in 2008 under the name *International Journal for Researcher Development*) and the *International Journal of Doctoral Studies* (established in 2006) shows. It is also within these spaces that we find the most noteworthy contributions to scoping the field of doctoral education. Evans (2011:87) includes doctoral education in her much broader mapping of the scholarship of researcher development terrain, noting that

> ... doctoral education is now recognised as a valid field of study – or perhaps more accurately, a sub-field of what may be considered to be educational research, or research into higher education, or even professional development or situated learning research… How researchers develop during their doctoral education seems currently to constitute the greatest volume of research and scholarship within what may broadly be considered to represent the literature related to how people develop as or into researchers, or, expressed slightly differently, what the researcher process involves.

Evans (2011) continues to position the broader body of scholarship (including that on doctoral education) mainly within the social sciences, and subject to criticism for being under-theorised – a view shared by Tight (2004) on higher education research in general – calling for more research on related processes, concepts, contexts, and policy. It is thus timely that Hopwood (2018) chooses to focus on the possible link between practice, theory and doctoral education research in his conceptual analysis of over 200 articles, book chapters and books on doctoral education that were published between 1980 and 2017. He notes that many of the theoretical points of departure in doctoral education research have been borrowed from fields outside of education (mirroring education research in general), enriching the field in sometimes unexpected ways and positioning doctoral education as a distinct pedagogical practice that is enacted, plural, and interconnected. As such, doctoral education (and the research thereof) is shaped by spatial, historical and cultural factors – which means that any analysis of the field will be partial and biased in some way.

Jones's (2013) thematic analysis of 995 papers on doctoral education in 45 selected journals for the period 1971-2012 is one of the few contributions that aim to map this relatively new and expanding field of study in greater thematical depth. In his analysis, six themes are identified: teaching, doctoral programme design, writing and research, employment and career, student-supervisor relationship, and the doctoral student experience. Jones (2013) calls for further research in the areas of empirical research awareness, group supervision, supervisors' perceptions of their students, and feedback. The first two themes are not surprising considering that 26 of the 45 journals included in the analysis had North American origins, where a doctoral programme format including coursework is commonplace. These 26 journals accounted for 594 – or 59.7% – of the 995 articles reviewed (although of course not all of these articles might have had North American authors). The majority (64.52%) of the articles included in the overall analysis had authors from the USA – which suggests a distinct North American bias to the analysis and conclusions that can be drawn from it.

A comparative picture emerges when comparing the source foci of some of the above-mentioned contributions (Evans 2011; Hopwood 2018; Jones 2013; Tight 2012) as can be seen in Table 2.1 below. Only journal titles (not books, book chapters or other kinds of sources) were included in the comparison.[2]

**TABLE 2.1** Comparison of cited journals across four sources (Evans 2011; Hopwood 2018; Jones 2013; Tight 2012)

| Authors (chronologically) Journals (alphabetically) | | | Jones (2013) | Tight (2012) | Evans (2012) | Hopwood (2018) |
|---|---|---|---|---|---|---|
| | Established | Main geographical focus[3] | | | | |
| Academy of Management Learning & Education | 2002 | North America | ✓ | ✗ | ✗ | ✗ |
| Acta Academica | 2001 | Southern African | ✗ | ✗ | ✗ | ✗ |
| American Educational Research Journal | 1917 | North American | ✓ | ✗ | ✗ | ✗ |

---

2 Although we acknowledge that both empirical and non-empirical research on doctoral education gets reported in other forms of publication – such as books, book chapters, conference proceedings – that also meet the scholarly criteria of rigour and peer review, it is much more difficult to judge these contributions in terms of scholarly merit and decide what to include or exclude. The focus here thus fell on journal articles in reputable journals as cited in these sources alone.

3 The main geographical focus was determined by considering the geographical positionality of the editor, the editorial board and the publisher, as well as by looking at the geographical positioning of the majority of authors who had published in the journal over the past 13 years.

**TABLE 2.1** Comparison of cited journals across four sources (Evans 2011; Hopwood 2018; Jones 2013; Tight 2012) [continue]

| Authors (chronologically) Journals (alphabetically) | | | Jones (2013) | Tight (2012) | Evans (2012) | Hopwood (2018) |
|---|---|---|---|---|---|---|
| Assessment & Evaluation in Higher Education (formerly published as Assessment in Higher Education) | 1975 | UK / International | ✓ | ✓ | ✗ | ✗ |
| ASHE Higher Education Report | 1970 | North American | ✗ | ✗ | ✓ | ✗ |
| Diverse: Issues in Higher Education (formerly published as Black Issues in Higher Education) | 1984 | North American | ✓ | ✗ | ✗ | ✗ |
| British Educational Research Journal | 1975 | UK | ✗ | ✗ | ✓ | ✗ |
| British Journal of Educational Technology | 1970 | UK | ✓ | ✗ | ✗ | ✗ |
| Canadian Journal of Educational Administration and Policy | 1995 | North American | ✓ | ✗ | ✗ | ✗ |
| Canadian Journal of Higher Education | 1971 | North American | ✓ | ✗ | ✗ | ✗ |
| Chronicle of Higher Education | 1966 | North American | ✓ | ✗ | ✗ | ✗ |
| College Student Journal | 1966 | North American | ✓ | ✗ | ✗ | ✗ |
| Counselor Education and Supervision | 1960 | North American | ✓ | ✗ | ✗ | ✗ |
| Discourse: Studies in the Cultural Politics of Education | 1980 | International | ✗ | ✗ | ✗ | ✓ |
| Education & Training | 1959 | UK / International | ✓ | ✗ | ✗ | ✗ |
| Educational Researcher | 1971 | North American | ✓ | ✗ | ✓ | ✗ |
| Educational Studies | 1968 | UK | ✓ | ✗ | ✗ | ✗ |
| European Journal of Education | 1979 | European | ✓ | ✗ | ✗ | ✗ |
| Gender and Education | 1989 | UK | ✓ | ✗ | ✓ | ✓ |

TABLE 2.1    Comparison of cited journals across four sources (Evans, 2011; Hopwood, 2018; Jones, 2013; Tight, 2012) [continue]

| Authors (chronologically) / Journals (alphabetically) | | | Jones (2013) | Tight (2012) | Evans (2012) | Hopwood (2018) |
|---|---|---|---|---|---|---|
| Harvard Educational Review | 1931 | North American | ✓ | ✗ | ✗ | ✓ |
| Higher Education | 1972 | International | ✓ | ✓ | ✓ | ✗ |
| Higher Education in Europe | 1976 | European | ✓ | ✗ | ✗ | ✗ |
| Higher Education Management and Policy | 2002 | European | ✓ | ✓ | ✗ | ✗ |
| Higher Education Policy | 1988 | International | ✗ | ✓ | ✗ | ✗ |
| Higher Education Quarterly | 1987 | UK | ✗ | ✓ | ✓ | ✗ |
| Higher Education Research and Development | 1982 | Australasian | ✓ | ✓ | ✓ | ✓ |
| Improving College and University Teaching | 1953 | North American | ✓ | ✗ | ✗ | ✗ |
| Innovations in Education and Teaching International | 2001 | UK / International | ✗ | ✗ | ✓ | ✗ |
| Innovative Higher Education | 1984 | North American | ✓ | ✓ | ✗ | ✗ |
| International Journal for Academic Development | 1996 | UK / International | ✓ | ✗ | ✓ | ✓ |
| International Journal of Doctoral Studies | 2006 | North American | ✓ | ✗ | ✗ | ✗ |
| Internet and Higher Education | 1998 | North American / International | ✓ | ✗ | ✗ | ✗ |
| Journal of College Student Development | 1988 | North American | ✓ | ✓ | ✗ | ✗ |
| Journal of College Student Retention: Research, Theory & Practice | 1999 | North American | ✓ | ✗ | ✗ | ✗ |
| Journal of Educational Administration | 1963 | North American | ✓ | ✗ | ✗ | ✗ |
| Journal of Further and Higher Education | 1977 | UK / Australasian | ✓ | ✗ | ✗ | ✗ |

**TABLE 2.1** Comparison of cited journals across four sources (Evans, 2011; Hopwood, 2018; Jones, 2013; Tight, 2012) [continue]

| Authors (chronologically) / Journals (alphabetically) | | | Jones (2013) | Tight (2012) | Evans (2012) | Hopwood (2018) |
|---|---|---|---|---|---|---|
| Journal of Higher Education | 1930 | North American | ✗ | ✓ | ✓ | ✓ |
| Journal of Higher Education Policy and Management | 1977 | UK | ✓ | ✓ | ✗ | ✗ |
| Journal of Hispanic Higher Education | 2002 | North American | ✓ | ✗ | ✗ | ✗ |
| Journal of Negro Education | 1932 | North American | ✓ | ✗ | ✗ | ✗ |
| Journal of Research Administration | 1997 | North American | ✗ | ✗ | ✓ | ✗ |
| Journal of Sociology and Social Welfare | 1974 | North American | ✗ | ✗ | ✗ | ✓ |
| Journal of Student Affairs Research and Practice (formerly published as the NASPA Journal) | 1963 | North American | ✓ | ✗ | ✗ | ✗ |
| M/C Journal | 1998 | Australasian | ✗ | ✗ | ✗ | ✓ |
| NACADA Journal | 1981 | North American | ✓ | ✗ | ✗ | ✗ |
| New Directions for Higher Education | 1970 | North American | ✓ | ✗ | ✗ | ✗ |
| New Directions for Institutional Research | 1970 | North American | ✗ | ✗ | ✗ | ✓ |
| Quality in Higher Education | 1995 | International | ✓ | ✗ | ✗ | ✗ |
| Reflective Practice | 1995 | North American | ✗ | ✗ | ✗ | ✓ |
| Research in Higher Education | 1973 | North American | ✓ | ✓ | ✓ | ✗ |
| Research Intelligence | 1975 | UK | ✗ | ✗ | ✓ | ✗ |
| Review of Educational Research | 1931 | North American | ✓ | ✗ | ✗ | ✗ |
| Review of Higher Education | 1978 | North American | ✓ | ✓ | ✗ | ✗ |

**TABLE 2.1** Comparison of cited journals across four sources (Evans 2011; Hopwood 2018; Jones 2013; Tight 2012) [continue]

| Authors (chronologically) Journals (alphabetically) | | | Jones (2013) | Tight (2012) | Evans (2012) | Hopwood (2018) |
|---|---|---|---|---|---|---|
| Scandinavian Journal of Educational Research (formerly published as Pedagogisk Forskning) | 1957 | Scandinavian | ✓ | ✗ | ✗ | ✗ |
| Science Technology, and Human Values | 1978 | North American | ✗ | ✗ | ✓ | ✗ |
| South African Journal of Higher Education | 1987 | South African | ✗ | ✗ | ✗ | ✓ |
| Southern Review | 1935 | North American | ✗ | ✗ | ✗ | ✓ |
| Studies in Continuing Education | 1978 | UK | ✓ | ✗ | ✓ | ✗ |
| Studies in Graduate and Postdoctoral Education (formerly published as the International Journal for Researcher Development) | 2008 | North American / UK | ✗ | ✗ | ✓ | ✓ |
| Studies in Higher Education | 1976 | UK | ✓ | ✓ | ✓ | ✓ |
| Teaching in Higher Education | 1996 | UK | ✓ | ✓ | ✗ | ✓ |
| Tertiary Education and Management | 1995 | European | ✗ | ✓ | ✗ | ✗ |

Table 2.1 indicates the broad array of journals within which scholars interested in doctoral education publish – 64 journals were cited just across these four articles. Only two journals were cited in all four articles – *Higher Education Research and Development*, and *Studies in Higher Education*. Such information also indicates a strong Global North citation bias, and in particular North American. Though bias is inevitable in some ways in such analyses given the limitations of accessibility and language of publication, it may be timely to consider a somewhat wider playing field at least in terms of geography and associated journal selection, and in the light of recent developments since the above-mentioned articles were published.

In this chapter we therefore report on an overview of relevant scholarship through an analysis of journal article publications focused on doctoral education in 11 selected journals for the period 2005-2018. We specifically focused on the contributions the selected journals make to the field of doctoral education, the increase in the number of journal articles on doctoral education per year, the geographical distribution of authorship, and noticeable collaboration trends. A more in-depth thematic analysis of these journal articles highlights global doctoral education scholarship trends.

## METHODOLOGY

Eleven journals were purposively selected for inclusion in this analysis according to a three-pronged selection approach. Firstly, journals listed in the $^{CA}$Web of Science that had published substantive literature on doctoral education over the period 2005-2018 were included – including *Studies in Higher Education* (SHE, n=155), *Higher Education Research and Development* (HERD, n=113), *Innovations on Education and Teaching International* (IETI, n=86), *Teaching in Higher Education* (THE, n=76), *Higher Education* (HE, n=60), *Journal of Higher Education* (JHE, n=38), and *Research in Higher Education* (Res HE, n=26). Secondly, the above analysis of existing literature suggested that two journals focused on postgraduate education also merited inclusion: the *International Journal of Doctoral Studies* (IJDS, n=154) and the journal *Studies in Graduate and Postdoctoral Education* (SGPE, n=101). Thirdly, two journals with a focus on higher education in the African context were also included in the analysis to provide a more nuanced view, even though they do not appear on the CA Web of Science databases – the *Journal of Higher Education in Africa* (JHEA, n=3), and the *South African Journal of Higher Education* (SAJHE, n=95). Thus, a total of 907 articles were included in the analysis. We acknowledge that this selection still has an Anglophone bias, thus potentially excluding publications on doctoral education in regions such as South and Central America, Asia, Africa and Europe where other languages may be predominant. Favouring journals listed on the $^{CA}$Web of Science in our selection may furthermore exclude journals and authors that significantly contribute to the scholarship on doctoral education but who do not necessarily publish in these journals. However, we believe that our selection and the ensuing analysis offers a more regionally diverse and thematically inclusive analysis and current international snapshot than that offered in any previously published analysis and conceptualisation of doctoral education research.

The analysis focused on the number of articles per journal (as indicated above), the overall publication trends per year, as well as the number of authors per article, their geographical distribution, and trends in collaboration among authors. A more in-depth thematic analysis of these journal articles was done to highlight global doctoral education scholarship trends. Summative content analysis of all relevant articles (N=907) for the period 2005-2018 were conducted. Hsieh and Shannon

(2005) describe summative content analysis as, firstly, the identification and quantification of specific words in text in order to understand the contextual use of these words and explore their usage (rather than infer meaning to them). The analysis then, secondly, proceeds beyond merely word counts to interpreting the content to uncover the underlying meaning of the words. Summative content analysis allows for the interpretation of the context associated with the use of a word or phrase.

## RESULTS AND DISCUSSION

Our starting point for the analysis was to consider to what extent each of the journals in our selected sample contributed to the overall scholarship on doctoral education covered by the sample, as can be seen in Figure 2.1 below.

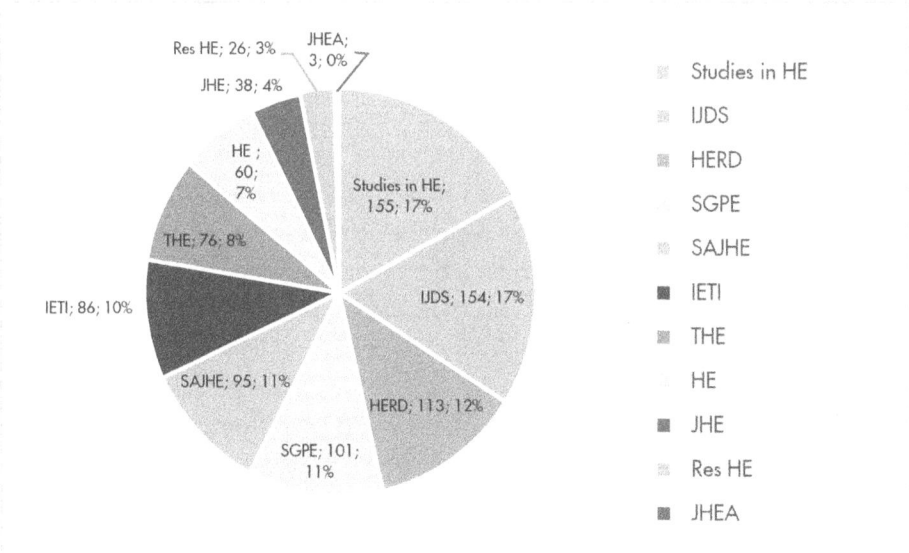

**FIGURE 2.1**   Contributions to the scholarship on doctoral education per journal (N=907)

Figure 2.1 shows that two journals – SHE (n=155) and the IJDS (n=154) – collectively published more than a third (34%) of the total scholarship on doctoral education in the sampled journals. Even though SHE has been in existence since 1976, it has a much wider focus than only doctoral education. It is one of the truly international journals, with contributors on doctoral education from 25 countries within the studied time period (even though the majority of contributions [72.7%] originated from three countries – Australia, the UK and the USA). In contrast, IJDS has a singular focus on doctoral education and was only established in 2006. Here too there is an international representation in terms of authorship with 29 countries included, although the USA is represented in 57.8% of these contributions. There is a relatively even contribution distribution amongst the journals HERD (n=113), SGPE (n=101), SAJHE (n=95), and IETI (n=86), showing the importance of including regional journals (such as SAJHE) in these kinds of analyses. However, the negligible contribution in this field by the JHEA shows that much still needs to be done either to develop the field of doctoral education research in certain regions (such as the broader African continent), or to achieve broader prominence and recognition for what is already being done (but which is not currently internationally easily accessible). The analysis furthermore showed an overall growth in the number of articles on doctoral education produced between 2005 and 2018, as can be seen in Figure 2.2.

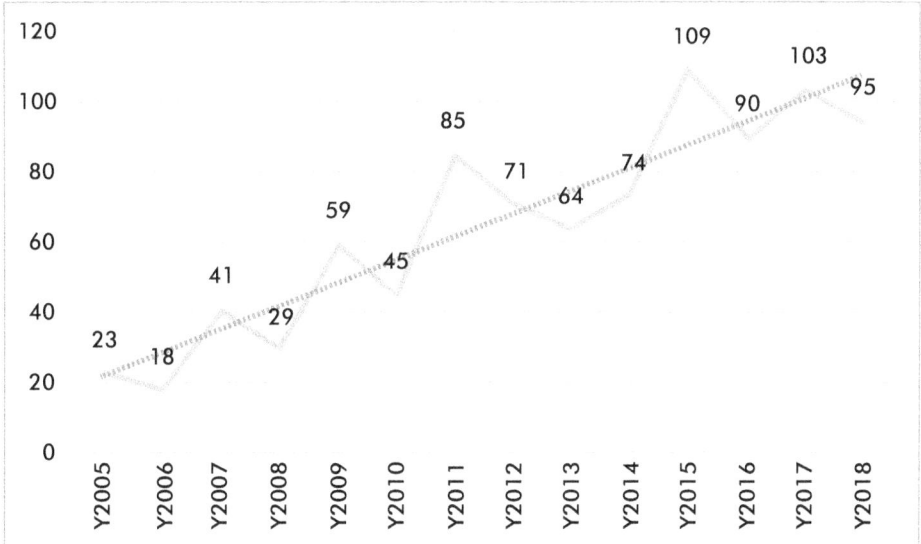

**FIGURE 2.2**  Number of articles per year overall (2005-2018)

Figure 2.2 supports the literature that describes doctoral education as a growing field of interest for scholars (see for example, Evans 2011; Hopwood 2018; Jones 2013). Observing this evident growth, and taking into account the inherent bias in our own selection of journals and that of others noted above, we were also curious about the extent to which different countries contributed to the existing body of scholarship (see Figure 2.3).

## PART ONE • HORIZONS

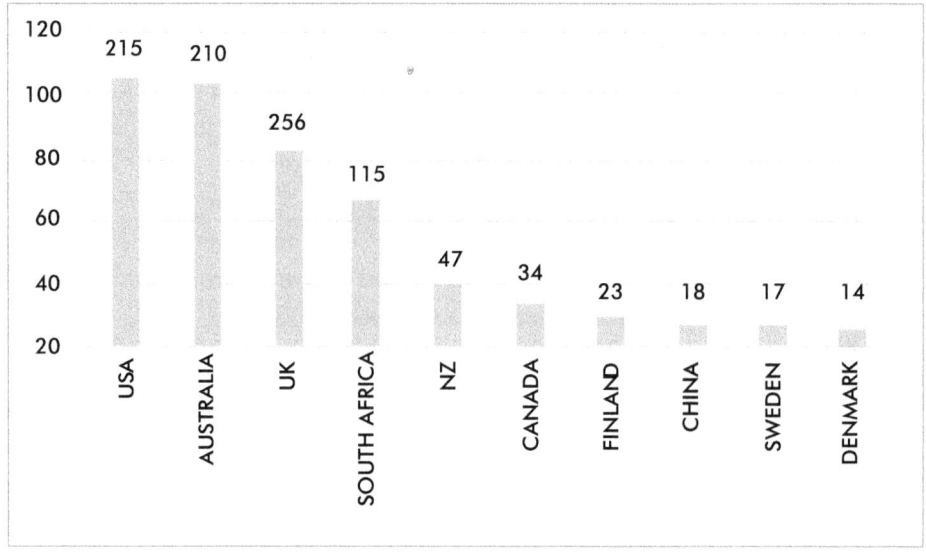

**FIGURE 2.3**   Contributions per country in overall sample (N=907)[4]

It was not surprising that the USA, Australia and the UK accounted for the majority of the articles in our sample (64,1%), seeing that the international Anglophone journal selection tends to favour these countries. However, the 12,7% that South Africa contributed is noteworthy (taking into account that SAJHE does not only focus on doctoral education research, and that this percentage of the overall South African contribution to the scholarship is also distributed across the other journals included in the sample). This contribution should also be seen against the background that South Africa is lagging behind many of these countries in terms of doctoral production rates (Cloete et al. 2015), and South African authors are often systemically disadvantaged in terms of potential publication outlets as a result of the national publication subsidy system within which many of the journals in our sample (including IJDS and SGDE) are not listed for subsidy purposes (and doctoral education researchers may thus be discouraged by their institutions to publish in these journals). The contribution by Scandinavian countries (particularly Finland, Sweden and Denmark) is also noteworthy – especially since these countries are not primarily English-speaking. The emergence of China as a site of doctoral research published in Anglophone journals is still small by comparison, but noteworthy. The

---

4   The contributions depicted here do not add up to the total number of articles in the sample (N=907), as some articles had multiple authors from different countries. If an article had multiple authors from the same country, the country contribution was only counted once.

absence of published research on doctoral education in these journals from African countries beyond South Africa is furthermore significant.[5]

We extended our country-specific analysis to look at the contributions per region, also taking into account that doctoral education systems tend to differ on a regional basis – for example, in the United States of America and Canada doctoral programmes more commonly contain coursework components, whereas in Europe (including the United Kingdom), Australasia, and South Africa the doctorate through research only has been more common.[6] Figure 2.4 provides an overview of the contributions per region.[7]

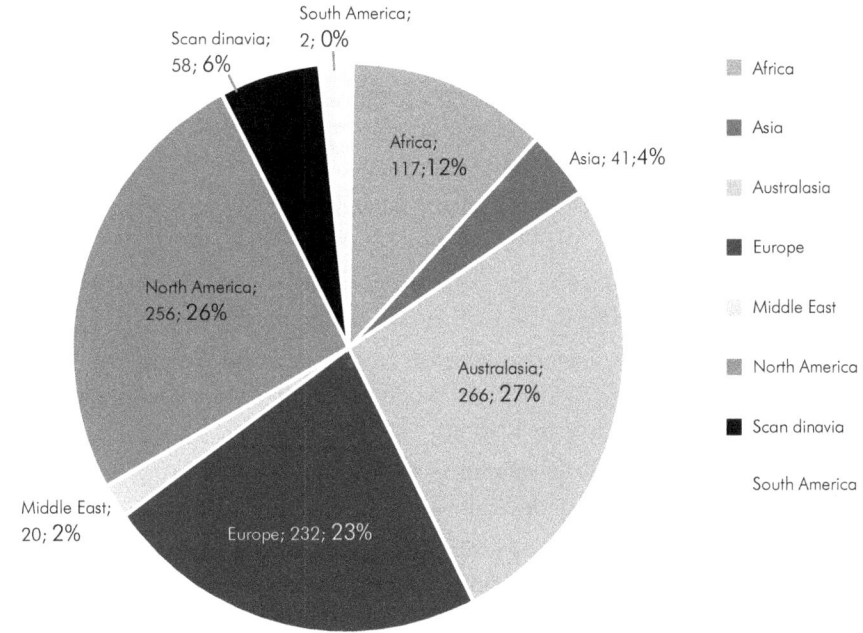

**FIGURE 2.4**  Article contributions per region

The regional contributions, of course, mirror the country contributions. But this analysis does provide us with an entry point into looking at authorship trends. On

---

5   We are not implying that there is no research on doctoral education being done in these countries, but that the scholars in this area do not significantly contribute to current international Anglophone debates through publication.

6   This trend is, however, changing with the introduction of professional doctorates as recognised doctoral qualifications across the world.

7   Again, the contributions noted here do not add up to the total sample of 907 articles, as some articles were produced by multiple authors from more than one region. Regional affiliations were only counted once per article, regardless of the number of associated authors within that region.

average, our sample had 2.21 authors per article.[8] In terms of how truly international these collaborations were, the data shows that the majority of authors were situated within one region only (n=827; 91.2%), whereas only 8% of the sampled articles included authors distributed across two regions (n=73), and only 0.8% had authors distributed across three regions (n=7). The figures indicate how doctoral education is often a situated practice, even though the qualification is often deemed to be internationally recognised and comparable. It also shows just how difficult it is for researchers to establish and sustain collaborations across multiple regions.

Our analysis furthermore included a thematic analysis of all the articles included in our sample. Based on this analysis, we identified eight main themes, each consisting of a number of sub-themes. The main themes identified were:

- *education*, including doctoral education, pedagogy, curriculum, learning, models or approaches to doctoral education, doctoral cohorts, professional doctorates, and distance or online education;
- *supervision*, including articles on doctoral supervision, the supervisor's experience, feedback, and support;
- *socialisation*, with reference to the student-supervisor relationship, communities of practice, and power within these relationships or communities;
- a *student focus*, which included articles on the doctoral experience, doctoral identity, student diversity, international students, part-time doctoral study, gender issues, and doctoral student well-being;
- *beyond the doctorate*, with reference to careers, employability, postdoctoral fellowships, and professional development;
- *the research context*, that included studies focused on particular disciplinary views, policy, history, cross-national studies, the role of industry within the doctorate, quality, retention and/or throughput, and funding issues;
- *the research process*, with particular reference to preparation for the doctorate, or developing research knowledge, doctoral writing, creativity, research ethics, reflection, research skills, or teaching competencies; and
- *the research product*, including the dissertation,[9] knowledge production, publication, innovation, generic outcomes, assessment, and doctorateness.

---

[8] With a median of 2.00. The minimum number of authors was 1, and the maximum 10.

[9] We use 'dissertation' here in reference to the product a doctoral student produces, conscious that it may take on a variety of forms and is referred to by different names (including 'thesis'). However, 'dissertation' was found to be the most commonly used term used in the literature.

Figures 2.5-2.7 below provide an overview of the summative content analysis process.

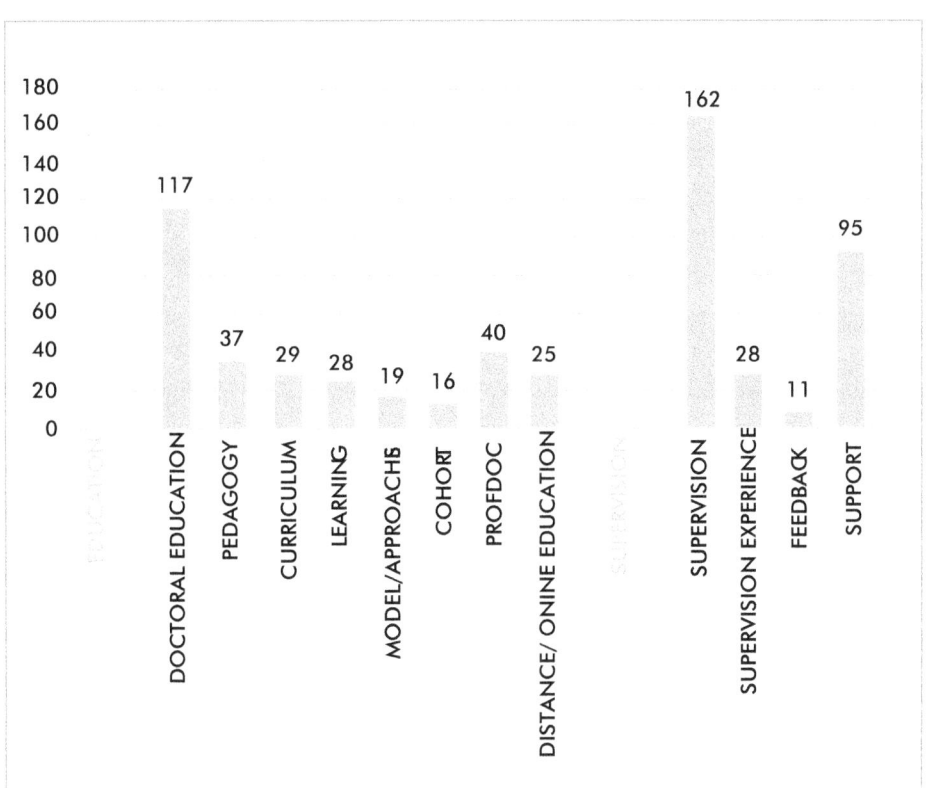

**FIGURE 2.5**   Themes related to doctoral education scholarship (1)

When comparing our findings to the themes Jones (2013) generated (including *teaching, doctoral programme design, writing and research, employment and career* – with a focus on the postdoctoral experience, *student-supervisor relationship*, and *doctoral student experiences*), we see both similarities and differences appear.

As did Jones (2013), we noted a student focus within the sampled literature, particularly the doctoral student experience, as well as a notable emphasis on what happens to students beyond the doctorate. We also saw a growing body of knowledge on the research process, including doctoral research knowledge and writing.

There was less emphasis in our analysis on doctoral programme design than that noted by Jones (2013), which may be attributed to the difference in journal selection (with less of a North American bias in our selection). The same argument may hold in terms of our emphasis on teaching in our analysis as a sub-theme in the broader research process. Our analysis shows a notable research interest in issues of doctoral retention and/or throughput, and support, which are global concerns. We also noted disciplinary diversity in our sample, which was not an aspect noted by Jones (2013) but on which Hopwood (2018) did indeed comment. This is an aspect we believe warrants further interrogation – both in terms of the disciplinary focus of the articles and the disciplinary affiliations of the authors (which are not always the same).

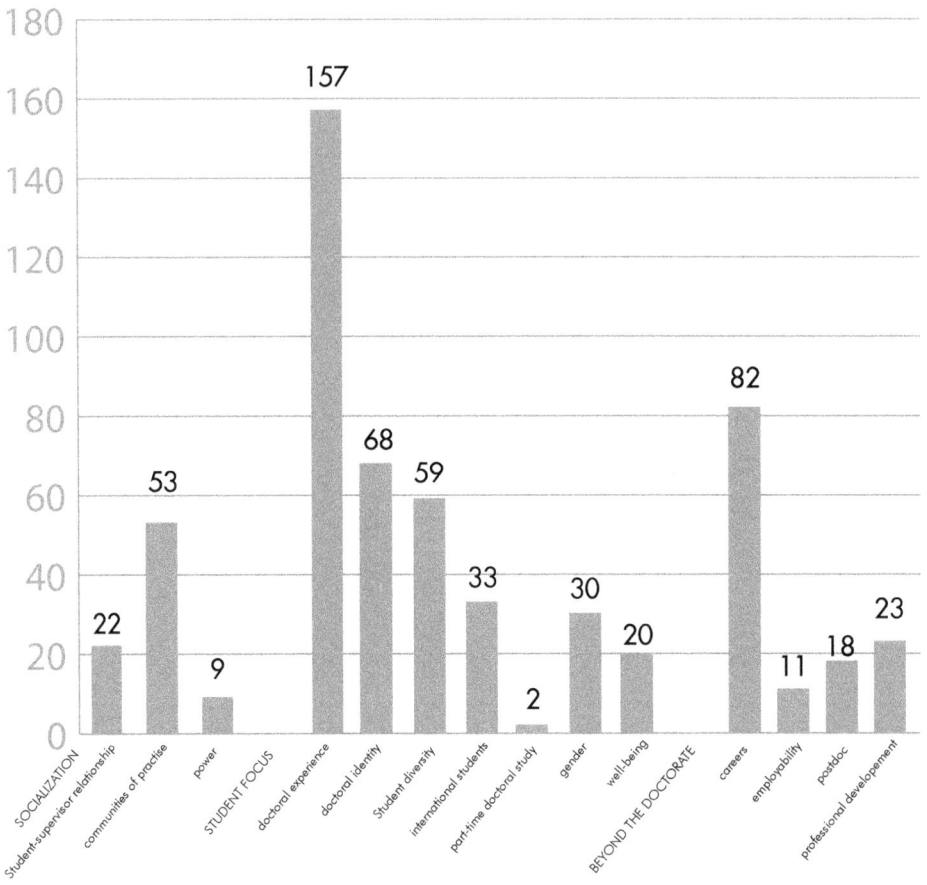

**FIGURE 2.6** Themes related to doctoral education scholarship (2)

CHAPTER 2 • **DOCTORAL EDUACTION AS A FIELD OF GLOBAL SCHOLARSHIP**

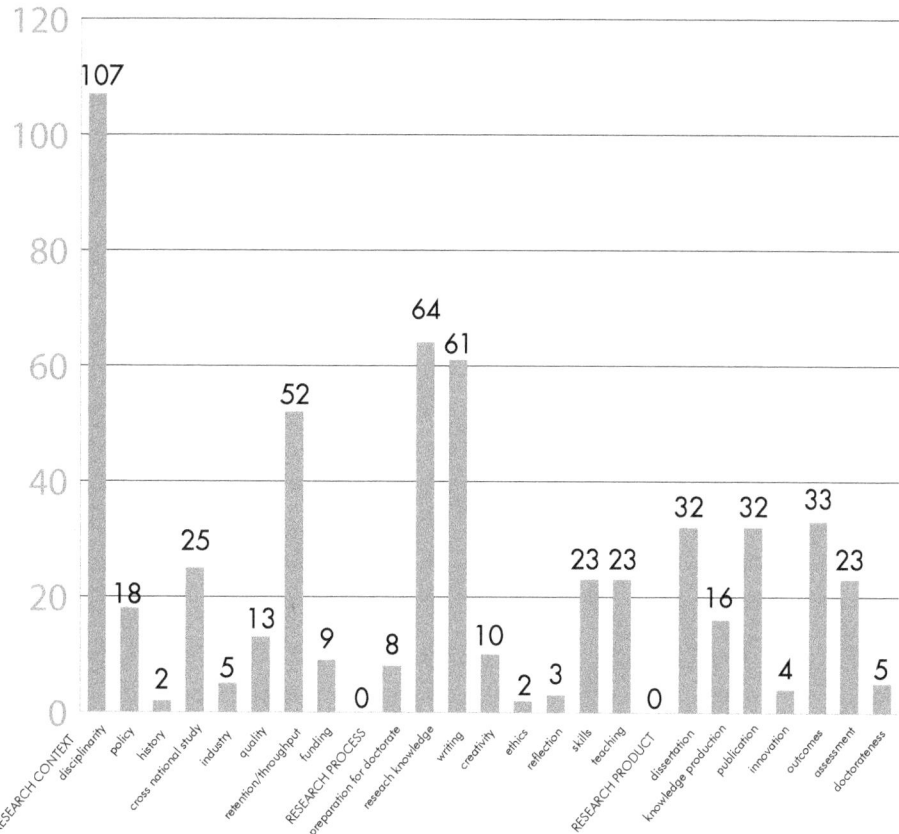

**FIGURE 2.7**   Themes related to doctoral education scholarship (3)

## CONCLUSIONS

Our analysis shows that there is indeed a growing body of knowledge on doctoral education globally, but that a limited number of countries and journals (mostly positioned within the global North) dominate the academic discourse in this field. Though there is evidence of collaboration based on co-publication trends, collaboration amongst researchers across global regions is still limited. Though the analysis has certain limitations and delimitations (in terms of journal selection, language and geographical representation), it does show that the scholarship on doctoral education emanating from the African continent (excluding South Africa) is limited in the international Anglophone arena.

The thematic analysis highlighted eight themes emerging from the studied articles: doctoral education as a field of study, supervision, socialisation, work focused on doctoral students themselves during, and beyond the doctorate; as well as studies focused on the research context, the research process, and the research product.

Even though these findings might appear familiar to those well-aquainted with the scholarship related to doctoral education, our analysis provides a unique systematic perspective that moves beyond an anecdotal overview and understanding of the existing literature. As such, the contribution lies in providing all those involved in doctoral education (students, supervisors, scholars and decision-makers) with a point of departure to understanding the trajectory of research in the field and the forces that shape the course of such research. This enables us to gain a better understanding of the currency of doctoral education research (as elaborated in Chapter 1) – in terms of *exchange value* (for example, how a neoliberal agenda may have shaped the field in terms of growth, regionality and thematically), *mobility* (for instance how researchers from different parts of the world collaborate, or don't), *immediate relevance* (as an illustration, the thematic foci of researchers in the field, how these foci might have changed over time, and what is still lacking), and *intellectual charge* (thinking about how ideas have moved and continue to shape and change the reality of doctoral education). Looking towards the horizon, the chapter helps us to consider existing gaps and limitations (particularly from an African perspective).

Finally, our findings create the scope for further analysis, including exploring the multidisciplinary nature of the scholarship produced on doctoral education in greater depth. We also propose a more in-depth analysis of the theoretical foundations within which these articles are rooted, thus exploring whether Tight's (2004) claim holds that the broader higher education research community is indeed a-theoretical. We also wish to take a more in-depth look at the research designs, methodologies and methods employed in this particular sub-set of higher education research.

## REFERENCES

Cloete N, Mouton J & Sheppard C. 2015. *Doctoral education in South Africa*. Cape Town: African Minds. https://doi.org/10.47622/9781928331001

Evans L. 2011. The scholarship of researcher development: mapping the terrain and pushing back boundaries. *International Journal for Researcher Development*, 2(2):75-98. https://doi.org/10.1108/17597511111212691

Hopwood N. 2018. Practice, theory and doctoral education research. In: E Bitzer, L Frick, M Fourie-Malherbe & K Pyhältö (eds.), *Spaces, journeys and new horizons for postgraduate supervision*. Stellenbosch: African Sun Media. 9-25.

Hsieh HF & Shannon SE. 2005. Three approaches to qualitative content analysis. *Qualitative Health Research*, 15(9):1277-1288. https://doi.org/10.1177/1049732305276687

Jones M. 2013. Issues in doctoral studies – Forty years of journal discussion: Where have we been and where are we going? *International Journal of Doctoral Studies*, 8:83-104. https://doi.org/10.28945/1871

Le Grange L. 2009. A survey of educational research in the second decade of South Africa's democracy: A focus on higher education. *South African Journal of Higher Education*, 23(6):1115-1125. https://doi.org/10.4314/sajhe.v23i4.51052

Macfarlane B. 2012. The higher education research archipelago. *Higher Education Research and Development*, 31(1):129-131. https://doi.org/10.1080/07294360.2012.642846

Pol E & Ville S. 2009. Social innovation: Buzz word or enduring term? *The Journal of socio-economics*, 38(6):878-885. https://doi.org/10.1016/j.socec.2009.02.011

Sternberg R, Pretz J & Kaufman J. 2003. Types of Innovations. In: LV Shavinina (ed.), *The International Handbook on Innovation*. Oxford: Elsevier. 158-169. https://doi.org/10.1016/B978-008044198-6/50011-5

Tight M. 2004. Research into higher education: An a-theoretical community of practice? *Higher Education Research and Development*, 23(4):395-411. https://doi.org/10.1080/0729436042000276431

Tight M. 2012. Higher education research 2000-2010: Changing journal publication patterns. *Higher Education Research and Development*, 31(5):723-740. https://doi.org/10.1080/07294360.2012.692361

# THE VITAE RESEARCHER DEVELOPMENT FRAMEWORK IN SOUTH AFRICAN POSTGRADUATE EDUCATION

Pia Lamberti and Moyra Keane

## INTRODUCTION

The focus of this chapter is the applicability of the Researcher Development Framework (RDF) (Vitae 2010) to inform postgraduate researcher education[1] in South Africa. We explore this issue from the perspective of academic development professionals working in a centralised postgraduate school at a time when we are called on to interrogate our thinking and practice in the aftermath of student protests, epitomised by the 'Rhodes Must Fall' movement, about the persistence of often outdated and irrelevant Eurocentric values in South African universities. In our discussion of the RDF, we ask:

- How relevant are the researcher competencies of the RDF for researcher development planning in South African higher education?
- In what ways could the RDF be used, taking into account the South African context and worldview?

We are interested in what learning from the global arena we can draw on, given the need to be sensitive and responsive to the local context. The challenge, as we see it, is to facilitate global engagement but also address contextual imperatives. Mastering imported theory that truncates learning has the "unfortunate outcome ... [of producing] high-cost caricatures" Jansen (2019:26). Jansen goes on

---

[1] While the term 'doctoral education' is often used interchangeably with 'research(er) education' in the international literature, we use the term 'postgraduate researcher education' in this chapter to signal that we are including for consideration master's studies, as in the South African context many students exit postgraduate study with a master's degree.

to challenge us "to rethink our aspiration, not just to import theory from outside as another developmental initiative, but to aim differently and not just higher: to theorise our own reality".

In this chapter we discuss the challenge of including global perspectives while valuing local knowledge and being sensitive to our immediate context at one South African higher education institution. We believe that it offers insights that can be used to promote discussion in other higher education institutions in similar South African contexts who might be looking for guiding principles, or a framework, to inform postgraduate researcher development activities or programmes.

We start by sketching in relevant aspects of the global and national context for postgraduate studies, and outline some of the challenges in South African postgraduate education, including the need to be responsive to calls for cognitive justice and to decolonise curricula. We then consider the national structures and policies that guide postgraduate education, focusing on new developments which need to inform strategy and future practice. Next, we outline relevant literature on researcher development and discuss the strengths and limitations of the RDF. In the last part of the chapter we describe how we have used it in the Postgraduate School at the University of Johannesburg, and consider the applicability of the RDF in the South African postgraduate education context.

## THE BROAD SOUTH AFRICAN POSTGRADUATE EDUCATION CONTEXT

As a starting point, we acknowledge that South Africa is subject to global forces. Many of the changes in postgraduate education that have taken place internationally over the last three decades are also manifesting in this country[2] (Taylor 2012:120). However, there are vast differences in the outcomes of postgraduate education in South Africa compared to other countries. South Africa fares poorly among countries producing doctorates, with a consequent need to increase the number in order to be globally competitive (Cloete, Mouton & Sheppard 2015:56). There is pressure on South African higher education institutions (HEIs) to improve throughput and time to completion rates for postgraduate studies (Herman 2014:45). In particular, there is concern about coursework master's students, who struggle with the research component of the degree (O'Neil & Dos Santos 2018), resulting in slow time to completion or even non-completion (Grant 2014:110). The majority of doctoral students work part-time, and many are underprepared for postgraduate study (Cloete,

---

2 Taylor provides a comprehensive discussion of these changes, summed up as massification, internationalisation, diversification, commodification, McDonaldisation, regulation, proliferation, capitalisation, casualisation, dislocation, augmentation, and cross-fertilisation.

Mouton & Sheppard 2015:108-109). The poor quality of PhD candidates has been lamented, with academic discourse being a particular concern (Louw & Godsell 2015:138-139). Also, the quality of postgraduate output has been called into question (Cloete, Mouton & Sheppard 2015:101-102). Given that nationally only 39% of university staff have doctorates, and that many of those with doctorates are therefore overburdened with postgraduate supervision, there is also a concern about supervisory capacity (Cloete, Mouton & Sheppard 2015:112-114). Consequently, higher education institutions are becoming more focused on increasing supervisory capacity and improving efficiency and quality in postgraduate studies.

Following on studies on how to increase the number of PhDs in South Africa (ASSAf 2010; Cloete, Mouton & Sheppard 2015), the last 10 years have seen a greater focus in HEIs on supporting postgraduate students to succeed. More structured support in specific doctoral programmes has been introduced, and special units dedicated to postgraduate development have been established. These 'postgraduate' offices, academies, centres or schools, which are generally centralised, but which are in some instances faculty-specific or school-specific, are tasked with implementing researcher development activities such as research skills workshops and writing retreats. Online support that postgraduates can access in their own time has also become a greater focus.[3] Generally, postgraduate centres or schools serve only registered students in their own universities, but some are income-generating and draw students from other universities. The African Doctoral Academy, based at Stellenbosch University, attracts students from universities across Africa,[4] which suggests that there is a real need for such support on the African continent, and that South Africa is seen as a leader in researcher development in Africa despite its own under-performance in global comparisons. Part of the reason for this anomaly is the unequal provision and opportunities across the country's higher education sector. While there are some excellent programmes and supervisors, and high-achieving postgraduates, many postgraduates are unable to complete in minimum time, and some take much longer than maximum time.[5]

---

3   See, for example, Enhancing Postgraduate Environments: https://bit.ly/3uXAv5d

4   https://bit.ly/3drAmBm

5   The national minimum time for completion of a master's degree is one year and for a doctoral degree it is two years (DHET 2013). There is no fixed national maximum time to completion. The University of Johannesburg allows two years for completion of a full-time master's and three years for part-time study. For a doctoral degree it is four years for full-time and five years for part-time studies.

## DECOLONISING RESEARCH AND RESEARCHER DEVELOPMENT

Consideration of an imported researcher framework cannot take place while pretending the knowledge creation space is neutral. The imperative to redress the marginalisation of indigenous knowledge systems, and the exclusion of local cultural contexts has been increasingly pressing in the past decades in many countries, and particularly in South African higher education. Significant efforts and resources have been directed to curriculum change and research foci, as well as all university spaces – both physical and symbolic – since the advent of democracy in 1994. Government policy[6] and funding supports knowledge reform projects and indigenous knowledge research – and indeed projects that contribute to social justice and community participation. Policy imperatives include the development of localised content and the accommodation of different ways of learning (DoE 2002). This is not to say there is an envisaged change from colonised education, entrenched knowledge production norms and Western knowledge status to an alternative knowledge system that values indigenous knowledge and rejects Western canon and discoveries: a move from A to B, A being a fixed knowledge paradigm and B being the desired alternative. Rather, as Jansen (2019:4) points out, Western knowledge has itself been contested for centuries – as part of knowledge progression through research and argument. Western knowledge is, of course, not 'one thing'. It would be simplistic to essentialise knowledge traditions into static stereotypes. However, we acknowledge that knowing is not neutral, but culturally and contextually situated. It is this nexus of knowledge relating to power, worldviews, values, status, currency, politics and history that contributes to contestation of whose knowledge is dominant. Knowledge and power are reciprocally legitimated and universities are often complicit in the politics of knowledge. It is perhaps due to the failure of universities to make significant changes to the entrenched 'powerful knowledge' extant for decades (if not centuries) that students targeted the symbolic representations of Western knowledge dominion in what started as the 'Rhodes Must Fall' movement of 2015.[7] The violent rejecting of usurped knowledge traditions and manifestation is one step in transformation, but does not provide a clear guide on how to offer Afrocentric curricula or an authentic plurality of knowledge systems in higher education. We centre our reflections and assessment of the RDF on these debates, policy imperatives and rethinking of Western knowledge traditions in mind.

---

6   See NRF Indigenous Knowledge Systems: Knowledge Fields Development (KFD) Framework Document. June 2014.

7   https://bit.ly/3edpvKb

It is also moot to consider the tensions between global knowledge communities and disciplinary discourses while rejecting a colonised entrenchment of research practice. While our aim is to review the relevance of the RDF for the South African context, it would be insufficient and even tokenistic to 'include bits that fit' in a revised framework – a step that Morrow (1989:72) might say is an example of "decolonisation lite". It is, incidentally, sobering to note that his critique of trivialised reform efforts was made over 30 years ago. We still grapple with the problem of how to authentically decolonise our education and research practices. One view of a framework that is pertinent here is Sen's defining of capabilities: "Capabilities are opportunities to flourish or achieve well-being in the form of functionings, which means to be and to do what a person has reason to value" (Sen, cited in Leibowitz 2012:60). A number of points arise from this definition: the focus on opportunities, well-being and values. Well-being and values can lead to a rethinking of researcher development using the concept of Ubuntu. Ubuntu is expressed in isiZulu as *Umuntu ngumuntu ngabantu* – I am a person through other people. "[Ubuntu] speaks of the very essence of being human," being generous, hospitable, friendly, caring and compassionate (Tutu 1999:34). It also means "… my humanity is caught up, is inextricably bound up, in theirs" (Tutu 1999:34). Hence, emphasis on individual achievement could be reconsidered through foregrounding collegiality, community, or disrupting the notion of the individual altogether. Kenyan philosopher, John Mbiti, in his seminal work on the African view of man (sic) explained, "Whatever happens to the individual happens to the whole group. Individuals exist through community" (Mbiti 1969:106). This does not mean a rejection of metropolitan theory but a recentring of Africa.

To return to the role of researchers and researcher development, it is axiomatic that researchers contribute (almost exclusively) to the validation of a Western scientific mode of knowledge production in their publications and student supervision. As researcher developers, we would be culpable in re-entrenching such practices without considering the moral, political, and cognitive justice debates. One of the questions to ask in such development work is how to interface with other knowledge systems (Mosimege 2005). Apart from the social justice imperative, the benefits of harmonising and acknowledging different knowledge systems have been argued for decades. A prominent Canadian educationalist and indigenous knowledge researcher, Glen Aikenhead, speaks to the development of professionals:

> A programme framed by different cultural perspectives promises to improve the quality of future scientists – those not imprisoned by Eurocentric mono-culturalism. A programme framed by different cultural

perspectives aims to develop responsible, savvy professionals capable of dealing with … their everyday lives – locally and globally.

(Aikenhead 2006:1)

As educationalists we agree that there is an intrinsic value in exploring diverse ways of knowing and unlearning entrenched assumptions about knowledge production. Considering indigenous knowledges in research and education assists in highlighting Eurocentric assumptions inherent in conventional ideas about creating and validating knowledge (Breidlid & Botha 2015:320). New Zealand provides significant examples of inclusion of indigenous knowledges in postgraduate supervision (see Carter, Laurs, Chant & Wolfgramm-Foliaki 2017), as well as of emphasising the education purposes, connections and worlds indigenous students may bring to their research and doctoral journeys (McKinley, Middleton, Grant, Irwin, & Williams 2011). We acknowledge the depth of reflection and critique required in this. Reviewing knowledge dimensions needs to include ontological, epistemological and axiological domains (Chilisa 2012).

## THE POLICY FRAMEWORK FOR SOUTH AFRICAN POSTGRADUATE EDUCATION

As in other parts of the world, in South Africa national education policy guides thinking about postgraduate qualification outcomes and expectations of postgraduate students' knowledge and skills. The document that maps out postgraduate education and guides curriculum at postgraduate level is The Higher Education Qualifications Sub-framework (DHET 2013), which is linked to the overarching National Qualifications Framework that guides all formal learning, with descriptions of learning achievement, referred to as 'level descriptors', on 10 levels, with master's and doctoral qualifications on levels 9 and 10 respectively.[8] The level descriptors describe expected levels of achievement in 10 areas: scope of knowledge; knowledge literacy; method and procedure; problem-solving; ethics and professional practice; accessing, processing and managing information; producing and communicating information; context and systems; management of learning; and accountability (SAQA 2012). As descriptions of postgraduate outcomes are limited to the same generic 10 areas used in the descriptors for all levels of education, the descriptors are necessarily generic, and therefore refer to very broad learning outcomes.[9]

The National Research Foundation (NRF), the national government's research funding agency, has recently initiated a National Doctoral Review, which requires higher education institutions to self-evaluate their doctoral programmes in terms

---

8   https://bit.ly/3e9X3sS

9   https://bit.ly/32nl9JX

of their quality and also the development of doctoral graduate attributes (CHE 2019). Consequently, the Council on Higher Education (CHE), the national quality assurance body which accredits higher education programmes has produced a new document, the Qualification Standard for Doctoral Degrees (CHE,2018), to guide judgements about the quality of doctoral qualifications. The stated intention of this "standards" statement is that it be "beneficial" to higher education institutions, as well as to "the students and graduates of those qualifications" and "prospective employers" (CHE 2018:4), so one might expect clearer guidelines and more detail on the attributes and skills expected of candidates on completion of the degree.

Although there is a section headed "Graduate attributes", it confounds expectations of what will be addressed, as there is almost no reference to skills or attributes that might be considered generic or transferable to work contexts outside academia. There is a sub-section headed "Knowledge", which outlines research project-specific and discipline-specific knowledge the graduate should have, and a very brief section headed "Skills", which lists and briefly elaborates on four skills in terms very similar to those of the level descriptors (SAQA 2012) and the Higher Education Qualifications Sub-Framework (CHE 2013). The first skill, listed "Evaluation, selection and application of appropriate research approaches, methodologies, and processes in the pursuit of a research objective", is also exclusively related to academic research. The other three skills are more generic: "Reflection and autonomy", "Communication skills, including relevant information and digital literacy skills", and "Critical and analytical thinking for problem-solving" (CHE 2018:14), but even one of these is glossed exclusively in terms of communication of research. The strong focus in the "Qualification standard for doctoral degrees" (CHE 2018) on the doctorate as preparation for an academic career where research and supervision will be the focus, rather than for the workplace, can be understood in terms of the need to grow the professoriate and increase the number of supervisors with doctorates. In this respect South Africa differs markedly from other countries, such as the USA, the UK and Australia, where there is strong competition for academic posts (Bhakta & Boeren 2016) and over 50% of those who graduate with a PhD find work outside of the university (Barnacle, Cuthbert & Schmidt 2019). Consequently, in those countries there is far more emphasis in policy guidelines (ACGR, 2018b) and researcher education literature (Hinchcliffe, Bromley & Hutchinson 2007) on developing transferable or generic skills in order to make graduates attractive to employers outside of the university.

Another recent macro-level policy initiative, also driven by the NRF, gives testament to the concern about the efficiency and quality of postgraduate studies. The NRF has presented a new funding policy for postgraduate students that will require higher education institutions to implement and record developmental support for grant-funded students[10] (NRF 2019). The policy is explicit about expectations of universities, proposing the broadest possible scope for NRF-funded students' training, which must encompass research skills, academic capabilities and life skills. The expectation is that students will receive "wrap-around support", which includes knowledge about research ethics, intellectual property, and publishing, mentoring and networking skills, scientific writing and presentation skills, science engagement and communication, as well as personal and professional skills, such as managing conflict, stress and finances. Interestingly, the emphasis on holistic development, which encompasses both research and personal and professional skills, is very similar to the trend in the UK and Australia, and at odds with the strong emphasis on research skills only in the Higher Education Qualifications Sub-Framework (CHE 2013) and the "Qualification standard for doctoral degrees" (CHE 2018).

The implications of this aspect of the NRF funding policy will place local institutions under even more strain to provide resources in a period of severe funding constraints in the postgraduate realm[11] (Motala & Sinha 2019). Furthermore, it can be argued that in the interests of fairness and social justice, where university funds are used, the support proposed for NRF-funded students should be extended to all postgraduate students. The implications of this are discussed in the second-last section of the chapter.

## POSTGRADUATE RESEARCHER DEVELOPMENT

What emerges when looking at some of the international literature on postgraduate researcher development produced in the last 20 years, is that the global forces, referred to earlier in the chapter, had an impact on postgraduate education by calling into question the traditional mode of one-to-one master-apprentice learning, resulting in more structured and collaborative learning processes being implemented. A result of this is that the generic aspects of postgraduate learning are increasingly offered under the umbrella of 'researcher development' in courses or workshops, some of which are facilitated by academic development practitioners or learning professionals instead of disciplinary experts or supervisors (Ayers, Hawkins, Jones, Kiley & McDermott 2018; Hinchcliffe, Bromley & Hutchinson 2007). Also, researcher development is considered to include "both 'personal' and 'professional' development", the components of which are "behavioural", "attitudinal" and "intellectual" development (Evans 2011:83).

---

10 https://bit.ly/3dpseRG

11 https://bit.ly/3x2AbnM

In the interests of keeping this section a brief overview, we focus on these trends as they manifested in the UK. With the benefit of hindsight, it is interesting to trace the lively debates about generic or transferable skills that were brought into the spotlight with the publication of the Roberts Report in 2002 (Hinchcliffe, Bromley & Hutchinson 2007). The report found that employers were dissatisfied with graduates' skills, resulting in the recommendation that all full-time doctoral candidates receive two weeks of training each year of their studies, and the provision of funding for implementation (Hinchcliffe, Bromley & Hutchinson 2007). Some of the initial objections to generic skills training were that it would detract from the time students needed to focus on research, that it was too unacademic, and that universities should not have to prepare graduates for the workplace (Hinchcliffe 2007:8). Nevertheless, the 'skills agenda', as it came to be referred to, led to the development of the RDF (Vitae 2010), which became entrenched in the UK as part of the research policy framework (Evans 2011:78). At this point it is worth noting that in the literature on researcher development, the terms 'skills' and 'competencies' are used interchangeably, and in many cases, they serve as an umbrella term for a much wider range of human attributes or qualities, which include attitudes and dispositions. While the RDF was enthusiastically taken up by some, for example Bray and Boon (2011), later opposition came primarily from educational theorists. In a very detailed analysis of just one of the RDF descriptors, 'Collaboration', which falls under 'Working with others' in Domain D, a strong critique of the framework as a whole emerges. The argument is that the "narrow focus on individual competency" results in crucial situational, relational and social networked aspects of professional development being ignored (Kahn, Petichakis & Walsh 2012:56). The RDF has also been criticised for the decontextualisation of learning (Crossouard 2013).

A Google Scholar search with the topic 'researcher development frameworks' generates thousands of references, but surprisingly few are references to generally applicable frameworks that address the development of postgraduate researchers. One such framework is the Researcher Skill Development Framework (Willison & O'Regan 2015), which was initially developed in Australia to conceptualise researcher development at undergraduate level (Willison & O'Regan 2007). It has been adapted to include seven levels of research activity[12] (Willison & O'Regan 2015), and is represented in a one-page table that outlines the different expectations of researchers, from the novice at school or undergraduate level engaged in 'prescribed research', to the internationally-acknowledged research leader who is

---

12 https://bit.ly/3ajCGlz

'enlarging research'.[13] This framework is particularly useful for indicating the degree of support from teachers or supervisors that are needed at each of level, and realistic expectations of research for each level, but the focus is on research processes and their results rather than on the skills and dispositions that researchers develop in the process of engaging in research.

We are aware of other national frameworks that guide postgraduate skills development, such as the guidelines developed by the Australian Council for Graduate Research (ACGR 2018a) and the Irish Universities' PhD Graduate Skills Statement[14] (IUA 2015), as well as institution-specific skills statements (Ayers, Hawkins, Jones, Kiley & McDermott 2018; Hinchcliffe, Bromley & Hutchinson, 2007). However, it appears that the most extensively used framework currently in use is the Researcher Development Framework (Vitae 2010), which we examine more closely in the next section.

## THE VITAE RESEARCHER DEVELOPMENT FRAMEWORK

The RDF[15] (Vitae 2010) was developed in the UK through a process of wide consultation with research councils and higher education institutions. It is intended to provide overall guiding principles for entities which plan and implement researcher development activities, as well as practical support for research students and early career researchers (as well as their supervisors) for planning and evaluating the novice researchers' current skills, training opportunities and skills development over time.

---

13 The six different 'facets of research', the cognitive or practical processes involved in research, are listed on the far left of the diagram. They are: 'embark & clarify' (curious), 'find & generate' (determined), 'evaluate & reflect' (discerning), 'organise & manage' (harmonising), 'analyse & synthesise' (creative) and 'communicate & apply' (constructive). The words in brackets, which appear as perpendicular text on the diagram, are the personal qualities or attributes associated with the processes relating to each of the facets of research.

14 https://bit.ly/32nIKLH

15 https://bit.ly/2OZO0Cg

# CHAPTER 3 • THE VITAE RESEARCHER DEVELOPMENT FRAMEWORK IN SOUTH AFRICAN ...

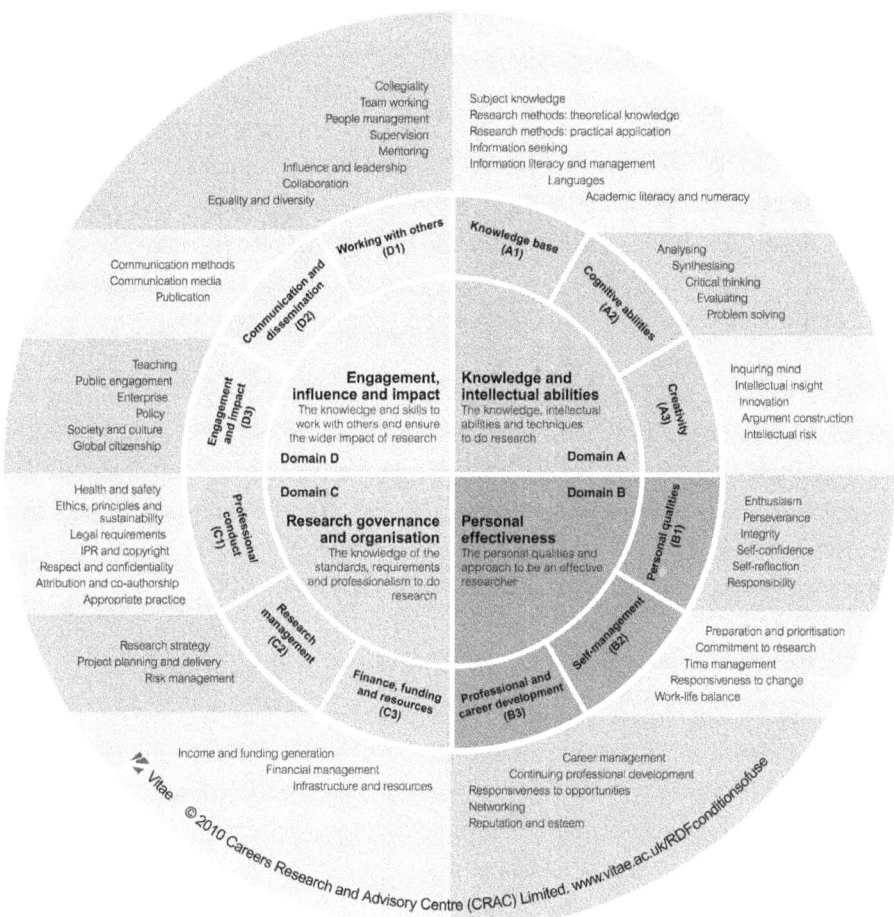

**FIGURE 3.1** The RDF domains and sub-domains

The RDF (see Figure 3.1 above) identifies four distinct broad areas, or domains, for researcher development, which are represented in a circle divided into quadrants: 'Knowledge and intellectual abilities' (Domain A), 'Personal effectiveness' (Domain B), 'Research governance and organisation' (Domain C), and 'Engagement, influence and impact' (Domain D). Each of the domains is further sub-divided into three sub-domains. Three to eight skills or attributes are identified for each sub-domain. For example, in the Domain D sub-domain designated 'Working with others', the areas of focus listed are collegiality, team working, people management, supervision, mentoring, influence and leadership, collaboration, and equality and diversity. The RDF identifies 63 attributes or skill areas that characterise an effective researcher, and describes five different levels of development, from novice to research leader, so that it is possible for an individual to plot exactly which stage of development they are at for each of the attributes or areas. The itemisation of all the areas that make researchers effective, encapsulated in either a word or a short phrase, is useful for processes of planning on the part of the researcher developer or for reflection and discussion between supervisor and postgraduate student. The RDF's comprehensiveness accommodates the great variation in skills required by researchers, and points to researchers' training needs across diverse fields and programmes. Another strength of the RDF, and an aspect that makes it more comprehensive and widely applicable than the Researcher Skill Development Framework (Willison & O'Regan 2015), is that it addresses qualities and dispositions that constitute professionalism – the generic skills and qualities which might be expected of graduates by employers, whether they are within universities or external to them. Thus, using the RDF to guide areas for development should enable postgraduates not only to complete their research projects and postgraduate studies successfully, but also to develop and be aware of transferable skills they can take into their professional lives after they have left university, or when they take up academic positions. It also lends itself to application in personal development plans, as is evident from the RDF Professional Development Planner that developed out of the RDF (Bray & Boon 2011:100).

## USING THE RDF: THE UNIVERSITY OF JOHANNESBURG EXPERIENCE

The RDF proved particularly useful for the planning of the development activities that are offered from a centralised unit that does not lie in any particular faculty, and therefore is not involved directly in students' disciplinary learning. When the University of Johannesburg's Postgraduate School was established in 2016, having looked to international best practice, we chose the RDF as the point of departure for guiding researcher development.[16] Since we found little to guide our activities in the national policy document (SAQA 2012), we looked to the RDF for two main reasons. It is sufficiently comprehensive to address the needs of all the fields of postgraduate study, and it includes professional and personal dimensions for development, which was in keeping with the stated aim of the school to provide holistic support, rather than focusing narrowly on the academic skills needed for completion of postgraduate studies.

Initially, we used the RDF to inform the range of researcher development activities. The annual programme of generic workshops and events was offered in the following categories: Research writing, Research design and methodology, Personal and professional development, Research management and governance, and Science

---

16 The Postgraduate School is charged with supporting master's students and doctoral candidates, and supervisors, in an institution that is explicitly focused on achieving 'global excellence' while being anchored in Africa. The greater proportion of UJ's postgraduates are master's students, more than half of whom do coursework and a minor dissertation.

communication. These categories have a clear relationship with the RDF domains, with the first two categories aligning with Domain A, and the other three aligning with Domains B, C and D respectively. By far the most popular workshops run at our Postgraduate School are those that can be categorised under the 'Knowledge base' aspect of Domain A. These include workshops on writing literature reviews, journal articles and the research design and methodology chapters, as well as on using software for quantitative and qualitative data analysis and for reference management.

We also introduced the RDF in workshops that focused specifically on the skills and qualities that postgraduates need to develop in order to succeed. In such workshops, where postgraduates could choose which domain to focus on for their own reflection and development planning, the majority elected to work on Domain A. This was the case even with mixed discipline groups of master's students and doctoral candidates at all stages of the postgraduate journey. On probing why they did not choose to work in the other domains, it emerged that participants did not believe that Domains C and D were relevant to their current experience and status as novice researchers. Their feedback also revealed that, while they acknowledged the importance of personal and professional development, this was not as strong a priority as the development of the knowledge and skills required for degree completion. On consideration of our experience over the last five years, which has consistently shown the greatest interest lies in activities related to the development of the postgraduates' knowledge base, it seems those students who elect to participate in the voluntary workshops feel underprepared for postgraduate studies and have a strong need to develop their capacity to engage in research and to write about it. This would suggest that the RDF as it is now is more suited to early- and mid-career researchers than to those who are still engaged in their postgraduate studies. The RDF offers an idealised vision of the well-rounded multi-skilled researcher. While this vision serves to orientate postgraduates to the wider research world, and to inspire those who will become lifetime researchers, it could be overwhelming for those who engage in limited scale research at master's level.

The postgraduates' interest in knowledge dimensions raises the issue again of the critique of Western knowledge traditions. How will cognitive justice be addressed? We cannot so soon forget the unresolved call for decolonisation that the nation-wide student protests brought to the fore in 2015, and which was subsequently also articulated by leading scholars such as Mbembe (2016). We are concerned to avoid uncritical acceptance of an imported framework: in addition to ethical, political, philosophical, and ontological reasons, there are, of course, major differences between the research contexts of the UK and South Africa. For these reasons, while we continue to use the RDF for planning, as well as for a topic of discussion in workshops, we embark on a process of investigating its value from the perspective of colleagues and our postgraduate students.

## REFLECTIONS ON THE APPLICABILITY OF THE RDF FOR POSTGRADUATE RESEARCHER DEVELOPMENT IN SOUTH AFRICA

In light of the new funding policy in South Africa that requires that postgraduates should have holistic 'wrap-around' development opportunities that are reported on annually, the role of centralised postgraduate schools and centres is likely to grow in importance. As it is not feasible that already overburdened supervisors be expected to be solely responsible for such all-encompassing development for their students, it can be anticipated that postgraduate support entities, some of which may be cross-institutional, will take on aspects of the support role, and that more such entities will be established to take some of the additional supervisory load from supervisors.

While we acknowledge that much postgraduate researcher learning needs to take place in the supervisory relationship, the departmental context, or cohorts (Samuel & Vithal 2011; Wisker, Robinson, Trafford, Lilly & Warnes 2004) in order that discipline-specific knowledge and skills can be achieved (Crossouard 2013), many of the skills and attributes required to complete postgraduate research successfully are relatively generic. The professional and personal, or 'life' skills that are expected in the new NRF funding policy are clearly generic. Given that there is little guidance in any of the South African policy documents on the development of postgraduates' personal and professional skills, the RDF could be used to inspire a list of the kinds of learning outcomes that could be developed as part of general skills training from extra-faculty units.

Despite the valid critique of skills 'training', we believe that there is a place for 'skills' development in postgraduate learning, particularly because it can raise awareness of the kinds of learning that take place in postgraduate research. Postgraduates appear to lack awareness of the skills they have developed during their studies (Cryer 1998:213), and a focus on skills can play a useful role in the development of postgraduates' metacognition, while also increasing their confidence. However, following on from Crossouard's critique of generic skills training for doctoral candidates (2013:82), we concede that such training would be best offered from a critical positioning where students are invited to reflect on their own plans and aspirations, and the possibilities of developing specific skills and qualities, given contextual realities such as their access to resources, their relationships with their supervisors and their disciplinary and institutional contexts.

The new impetus to provide more extensive support to postgraduates in South African higher education institutions highlights the importance of capacity development initiatives, and makes the question of what kind of development or training opportunities should be offered even more pressing, especially given that it is essential to make optimal use of necessarily limited funds, but also, importantly, to consider and design for decolonisation of regnant structures and disruption of hegemonic knowledge paradigms. Consequently, thoughtful design needs to underpin postgraduate researcher training. It also needs to inform supervisor education to ensure that supervisors are not only aware of relevant postgraduate competencies, but are also equipped to play an active role in postgraduate researcher development. It therefore makes sense to have a sound framework, or guiding principles, for postgraduate researcher development that can inform supervision and structured development programmes, as well as extracurricular informal ad hoc development, such as that offered from a centralised postgraduate centre. Since the RDF is comprehensive, has been implemented and tested over the last 10 years (albeit in other national contexts), and exposes South African scholars to widely accepted expectations of researchers in the global community, it could serve as a benchmarked generic set of competencies to consider in researcher development. It could be used productively as the base for a simplified framework that is more suited to the limited scope of research at master's level, and for students who are based in the workplace and unlikely to become researchers. In this respect, we are also considering what can be learned from a more recent framework, designed for "researching professionals", that draws from theories of "learning as participation" and "learning as becoming" (Lindsay, Kerawalla & Floyd 2018:2321-2323).

We need to consider the effects of presenting the RDF capabilities as unquestionably what is most important for developing researchers. Measuring competencies against individual criteria, including competitiveness, presents an underlying notion of the importance of individual achievement. The critique of the RDF from those who promote researcher development within research networks and communities of practice (Crossouard 2013; Kahn, Petichakis & Walsh 2012) is pertinent in this regard. Furthermore, the framework is based on an idealised context, which does not reflect the everyday realities that researchers in under-resourced situations face. The RDF's set of individual competencies may be criticised for being at odds with contextual realities and also the concept of Ubuntu. More appropriate qualities and competencies for African contexts might include respect, role of intuition, aesthetics, and contribution to community (see for example Chin 2007; Goduka, Madolo, Rozani, Notsi & Talen 2013; Khupe & Keane 2017; Seehawer 2018). These reflections offer a rationale and an impetus for further exploration for researcher development in the South African context. Consequently, we've embarked on empirical research that we hope will result in a reimagined framework for postgraduate researcher development.

## CONCLUSION

"'[D]oing decolonisation' as a radical act means thinking differently about the university and what is taught beyond the formal curriculum" (Jansen, 2019:9). Indeed, the value of a researcher development framework may well be as a tool to 'think differently' about researcher skills and aspirations rather than a fixed framework to guide development interventions. While the RDF may be a useful guide and starting point for (especially) early career researchers and their supervisors and mentors to consider, the individual configuration of competencies is at odds with a more community-centred research and education focus. There is a tension here between self-advancement and community benefit or, as Wahid (2004:528, cited in Solomons & Fataar, 2010:29) declares: "[I]individuals cannot simply pursue their own self-interest without regard for the common good." While the RDF has been used to promote and evaluate the development of individual researchers, it might be used more meaningfully with research teams wishing to reflect on their skills, qualities and competence as a community.

## REFERENCES

ACGR (Australian Council for Graduate Research). 2018a. *Good Practice Framework for Research Training*. https://bit.ly/3x6NNhF [Accessed 20 May 2020].

ACGR (Australian Council for Graduate Research). 2018b. *Good Practice Guidelines for Transferable Skill Development*. https://bit.ly/2RzBvy2 [Accessed 20 May 2020].

Aikenhead G. 2006. *Science and technology education from different cultural perspectives*. Keynote paper presented to the 12th Symposium of the International Organization for Science and Technology Education, Batu Ferringghi, Penang, Malaysia, 30 July-4 August 2006.

ASSAf (Academy of Science of South Africa). 2010. *The PhD study: An evidence-based study of how to meet the demands for high level skills in an emerging economy*. Pretoria: ASSAf.

Ayers NL, Hawkins M, Jones N, Kiley M & McDermott M. 2018. Using learning plans to support doctoral candidates. *Innovations in Education and Teaching International*, 55(3):248-256. https://doi.org/10.1080/14703297.2016.1233074

Barnacle R, Cuthbert D & Schmidt C. 2019. HASS PhD graduate careers and knowledge transfer: A conduit for enduring multi-sector networks. *Arts and Humanities in Higher Education*, 0(0):1-22. https://bit.ly/3sy5Z0s [Accessed 5 June 2020].

Bhakta D & Boeren E. 2016 Training needs of early career researchers in research-intensive universities. *International Journal for Researcher Development*, 7(1):84-102. https://doi.org/10.1108/IJRD-06-2015-0017

Bray R & Boon S. 2011. Towards a framework for research career development: An evaluation of the UK's Vitae Researcher Development Framework. *International Journal for Researcher Development*, 2(2):99-116. https://doi.org/10.1108/17597511111212709

Breidlid A & Botha LR. 2015. Indigenous knowledges in education: Anticolonial struggles in a monocultural arena with reference to cases from the Global South. In: W Jacob, S Cheng & M Porter (eds.), *Indigenous Education*. Dordrecht: Springer. 319-339. https://doi.org/10.1007/978-94-017-9355-1_16

Carter S, Laurs D, Chant L & Wolfgramm-Foliaki E. 2011. Indigenous knowledges and supervision: Changing the lens. *Innovations in Education and Teaching International*, 55(3):384-93. https://doi.org/10.1080/14703297.2017.1403941

CHE (Council on Higher Education). 2013. *National Qualifications Act (No. 67 of 2008)*. Department of Higher Education and Training. The Higher Education Qualifications Sub-Framework. Pretoria: CHE.

CHE (Council on Higher Education). 2018. *Qualification standard for doctoral degrees*. Pretoria: CHE.

CHE (Council on Higher Education). 2019. *National review manual: Doctoral qualifications*. Pretoria: CHE.

Chilisa B. 2012. *Indigenous research methodologies*. London: Sage.

Cloete N, Mouton J & Sheppard C. 2015. *The doctorate in South Africa: Policy, discourse, data and data*. Cape Town: African Minds. https://doi.org/10.47622/9781928331001

Croussouard B. 2013. Conceptualising doctoral researcher training through Bernstein's theoretical frameworks. *International Journal for Researcher Development*, 4(2):72-85. https://doi.org/10.1108/IJRD-05-2013-0007

Cryer P. 1998. Transferable skills, marketability and lifelong learning: The particular case of postgraduate research students. *Studies in Higher Education*, 23(2):207-216. https://doi.org/10.1080/03075079812331380394

DHET (Department of Higher Education and Training). 2013. *The Higher Education Qualifications Sub-framework*. Pretoria: DHET.

DoE (Department of Education). 2002. Transformation and Restructuring: A New Institutional Landscape for Higher Education Ministry of Education. *Government Gazette,* 23549(855), Pretoria. https://bit.ly/3gjiDxS [Accessed 15 January 2020].

DST (Department: Science and Technology). *World Intellectual Property Organization*. March 2006. Republic of South Africa: Indigenous Knowledge Systems Policy.

Evans L. 2011. The scholarship of researcher development: Mapping the terrain and pushing back boundaries. *International Journal for Researcher Development*, 2(2):75-98. https://doi.org/10.1108/17597511111212691

Goduka N, Madolo Y, Rozani C, Notsi L & Talen V. 2013. Creating spaces for eZiko Sipheka Sisophula theoretical framework for teaching and researching in higher education: A philosophical exposition. *Indilinga: African Journal of Indigenous Knowledge Systems*, 12(1):1-12.

Grant C. 2014. Pushing the boundaries of postgraduate supervision: Theorising research learning in community. In: E Bitzer, R Albertyn, L Frick, B Grant & F Kelly (eds.), *Pushing boundaries in postgraduate supervision*. Stellenbosch: African Sun Media. https://doi.org/10.18820/9781920689162/08

Herman, C. 2014. The South African doctorate: Where to now? In: E Bitzer, R Albertyn, L Frick, B Grant & F Kelly (eds.), *Pushing boundaries in postgraduate supervision*. Stellenbosch: African Sun Media. https://doi.org/10.18820/9781920689162/04

Hinchcliffe R. 2007. Can generic skills training change academic culture? In: R Hinchcliffe, T Bromley & S Hutchinson (eds.), *Skills training in research degree programmes: Politics and practice*. Maidenhead: Open University Press.

Hinchcliffe R, Bromley T & Hutchinson S. 2007. *Skills training in research degree programmes: Politics and practice*. Maidenhead: Open University Press.

IUA (Irish Universities Association). 2015. *Irish Universities' PhD Graduate Skills Statement*. Dublin: IUA. https://bit.ly/32lijq0 [Accessed 15 January 2020].

Jansen J. (ed.). 2019. *Decolonisation in Universities: The politics of knowledge*. Johannesburg: Wits University Press. https://doi.org/10.18772/22019083351

Kahn PE, Petichakis C & Walsh L. 2012. Developing the capacity of researchers for collaborative working. *International Journal of Researcher Development*, 3(1):49-63. https://doi.org/10.1108/17597511211278643

Khupe C & Keane M. 2017. Towards an African education research methodology: Decolonising new knowledge. *Educational Research for Social Change*, 6(1):25-37. https://doi.org/10.17159/2221-4070/2017/v6i1a3

Leibowitz B. (ed.). 2012. *Higher education for the public good; Views from the South*. Stoke on Trent, UK: Trentham Books.

Lindsay H, Kerawalla L & Floyd A. 2018. Supporting researching professionals: EdD students' perceptions of their development needs. *Studies in Higher Education*, 43(12):2321-2335. https://doi.org/10.1080/03075079.2017.1326025

Louw J & Godsell G. 2015. Multiple paths to success. In: N Cloete, J Mouton & C Sheppard, *Doctoral education in South Africa: Policy, discourse and data*. Cape Town: African Minds. 94-109.

Mbembe A. 2016. Decolonizing the university: New directions. *Arts and Humanities in Higher Education*, 15(1):29-45. https://doi.org/10.1177/1474022215618513

Mbiti JS. 1990. *African religions and philosophy* (2nd revised and enlarged ed). Gaborone: Heinemann.

McKinley E, Grant B, Middleton S, Irwin K & Williams LRT. 2011. Working at the interface: Indigenous students' experience of undertaking doctoral studies in Aotearoa New Zealand. *Equity & Excellence in Education*, 44(1):115-132. https://doi.org/10.1080/10665684.2010.540972

Morrow W. 1989. *Chains of thought*. Johannesburg: Southern Book Publishers.

Mosimege M. 2005. National priorities in indigenous knowledge systems: Implications for research and curriculum development. *Indilinga African Journal of Indigenous Knowledge Systems*, 4:31-37.

Motala S. & Sinha S. 2019. Postgraduate funding needs a boost. *Mail & Guardian*, 27 September 2019.

NRF (National Research Foundation). 2019. *Statement of expectations for NRF postgraduate student funding*. https://bit.ly/3dpseRG [Accessed 19 January 2020].

O'Neil S & Dos Santos C. 2018. Factors affecting time to completion of master's mini-dissertations. In: E Bitzer, L Frick, M Fourie-Malherbe, K Pyhältö (eds.), *Spaces, journeys and new horizons for postgraduate supervision*. Stellenbosch: African Sun Media. 177-193.

Samuel, M. & R. Vithal. 2011. Emergent frameworks of research teaching and learning in a cohort-based doctoral programme. *Perspectives in Education*, 29(3):76-86.

SAQA (South African Qualifications Authority). 2012. *Level descriptors for the South African National Qualifications Framework*. https://bit.ly/32nhdKj [Accessed 18 January 2020].

Seehawer MK. 2018. Decolonising research in a Sub-Saharan African context: Exploring Ubuntu as a foundation for research methodology, ethics and agenda. *International Journal of Social Research Methodology*, 21(4):453-466. https://doi.org/10.1080/13645579.2018.1432404

Solomons I & Fataar A. 2010. A conceptual exploration of values in education in the context of schooling in South Africa. *South African Journal of Education*, 31:224-232. https://bit.ly/2QzpUPf [Accessed 16 January 2020]. https://doi.org/10.15700/saje.v31n2a482

Tayor SE. 2012. Changes in doctoral education: Implications for supervisors in developing early career researchers. *International Journal for Researcher Development*, 3(2):118-138. https://doi.org/10.1108/17597511311316973

Tutu D. 1999. *No future without forgiveness*. London: Rider. https://doi.org/10.1111/j.1540-5842.1999.tb00012.x

Vitae 2010. *About the Vitae researcher development framework*. Cambridge: Vitae. https://bit.ly/2OZO0Cg [Accessed 6 March 2019].

Willison J & O'Regan K. 2007. Commonly known, commonly not known, totally unknown: A framework for students becoming researchers. *Higher Education Research & Development*, 26(4):393-409. https://doi.org/10.1111/j.1540-5842.1999.tb00012.x

Willison J & O'Regan K. 2015. *The Research Skill Development Framework*. https://bit.ly/3ajCGlz [Accessed 20 March 2019].

Wisker G, Robinson G, Trafford V, Lilly J & Warnes M. 2004. Achieving a doctorate: Metalearning and research development programmes supporting success for international distance students. *Innovations in Education and Teaching International*, 41(4):473-489. https://doi.org/10.1080/1470329042000277048

# IS INTERNATIONAL BENCHMARKING APPROPRIATE FOR IMPROVING THE QUALITY OF THESIS EXAMINATION?

Margaret Kiley

## INTRODUCTION

Doctoral examinations are important to universities in the sense that they are often considered by peers as quality measures and seen as representing international benchmarks of doctoral outcomes. However, how one might approach such an issue of benchmarking for quality remains difficult, as universities, higher education systems and countries differ in how their doctoral programmes are offered and how knowledge might be viewed and understood at a global level. Nevertheless, questions can be posed in terms of what (doctoral) benchmarking means, what doctoral indicators are examined, what criteria prevail and who the examiners are. Therefore, in this chapter I pose a series of questions related to doctoral examination as a means of coming to terms with some problematic key issues, leading, I hope, to some tentative responses.

## THE RESEARCH

There has been considerable international research on various aspects of doctoral examination. For example, work by Golding, Sharmini and Lazorovitch (2014) and Clement, Lovat, Holbrook, Kiley, Bourke, Paltridge, Starfield, Fairbairn and McInerney (2015) addresses ways in which examiners make judgements about the thesis. On a related topic Lovitts (2007) and Prins, De Kleijn and Van Tartwijk (2015) share insights into issues related to the qualities of a thesis. There is also helpful research on examining theses with published papers (Mason 2018; Sharmini, Spronken-Smith, Golding & Harland 2014) and the role of an oral component in the thesis examination process (Lovat, Holbrook, Bourke, Fairbairn, Kiley, Paltridge, Starfield 2015; Mezek & Swales 2016; Share 2016; Trafford 2003). Furthermore, there is research on the processes of examination (Alexander & Davis 2019; McKenna, Quinn & Vorster 2018).

However, other than the two examples discussed below, much of the research does not specifically address the idea of using examination to benchmark the quality of… well what? Is it doctoral education, the thesis, the candidate, the outcomes, the supervisor, or…? But perhaps, before moving onto the questions and issues that would need to be addressed, it might be worth examining the concept of benchmarking.

## WHAT IS BENCHMARKING?

A general definition of benchmarking states that it "is used to measure performance using a specific indicator… resulting in a metric of performance that is then compared to others" (Wikipedia). This definition suggests that benchmarking involves the components of measurement, indicators, metrics and comparison.

For example, using higher education as a context, a component of measurement might be employment following graduation. Indicators might include types of employment, salaries, and level of security in terms of permanency. The metrics could include gender, nationality and disciplinary area of study. But, does this address issues of quality?

Also, as the definition above suggests, a key to benchmarking is with whom one is benchmarking. For example, a small regional university specialising in environmental programmes might like to choose to benchmark the graduates of those programmes with a number of other regional universities and/or other national universities that have similar environment programmes. But it might not be helpful for them to benchmark all of their programmes with all universities in the country. This is not to say it is not possible, but the usefulness of such an activity might be questionable.

One form of national benchmarking in higher education is through the use of various frameworks. For example, in Australia the *Australian Qualifications Framework* (Australian Qualifications Framework Council 2013) works through various levels of educational awards with doctoral degrees at Level 10. However, a critical component here is how the various practices are evaluated and reported in a way that can allow benchmarking and institutional learning. If each institution does not report the same data in the same ways then benchmarking is difficult, if not impossible.

An attempt to benchmark at the doctoral level was the Australian Postgraduate Research Experience Questionnaire (PREQ) which was used to evaluate candidate satisfaction with various aspects of their experience. However, when Marsh, Rowe and Martin (2002) evaluated its usefulness in benchmarking across universities they found that the "results did not support the usefulness of PhD students' evaluations for benchmarking universities" (2002:342).

One doctoral level benchmarking project that was reported to be successful was the work done early in the 2000s through the Universitas 21 and the Forces and Forms of Doctoral Education Worldwide networks. The project involved the Canadian Deans of Graduate Studies, the US Council of Graduate Schools and the Australian Deans and Directors of Graduate Studies. The representatives were trying to develop a meaningful international instrument to benchmark many PhD practices and outcomes. While they initially concentrated on time to completion, which varies greatly because of the different enrolment systems, the group became particularly interested in evaluating completion rates and what they could then share with the various countries and universities. The instrument developed by the University of Melbourne for Australian use was based on the UK HEFCE[1] doctoral guidelines at the time and so that it was initially considered 'international'. It was then modified to accommodate North American doctoral practices. The benchmarking was carried out across a number of international groups with both practices and outcomes being effectively benchmarked (Personal communication, B Evans, 2019). Further benchmarking by some members of this original group looked at examination practices between Canada and Australia with issues such as the use of the oral examination in Canada, but not in Australia. As Hall (2006:49) argued, a key feature of the comparative exercise was that the – "population, land area and number of universities – have a bearing on the ways in which it might be feasible to examine doctoral theses and/or candidates", thereby enabling the two countries to "benefit from knowing what the other is doing" (Hall 2006:52).

While higher education quality is an important issue in many countries only a few have attempted to benchmark the quality of theses through examination. For example, in Norway (Thune, Kyvik, Sörlin, Olsen, Vabø & Tømte 2012) the international member of the doctoral examining committee was invited to comment on the quality of the thesis they had examined against seven criteria. Similarly in Denmark (Danish Ministry of Higher Education and Science 2017:41) the "foreign assessors have been asked to assess the quality of the Danish PhD students compared with the international leading universities in the research area".

While it is possible to find various projects where national groups of universities with similar backgrounds might benchmark for some specific issues of common interest, or even international groups, using examination as an international benchmark poses a considerable number of implicit and explicit issues as discussed below.

---

1   The Higher Education Funding Council for England (HEFCE) "ceased to exist as of 1 April 2018, when its duties were divided between the newly created Office for Students and Research England" (Wikipedia).

## POSSIBLE QUALITY INDICATORS IN EXAMINATION

What might be some of the benchmarking indicators that could be used in the examination of doctoral theses at an international level?

### Quality of the written thesis

One indicator might be the quality of the research, such as its originality, the presentation and quality of writing, the use of appropriate methods, or relevance of the study. But returning to the title of this chapter: what might be some of the criteria that could or should be used for benchmarking at an international level and across all disciplines? Furthermore, are the examiners who are making these decisions all coming from similar levels of experience in examination? Some countries have developed the means of doing this at a national level, for example France and Germany, but could this system be applied internationally? While it might be possible to develop rubrics, as for example Lovitts (2007), do such methods apply to all disciplines and all styles of doctorate, not to mention all countries and universities?

### The country

There are different frameworks for doctoral education across the globe, and the outcomes may not necessarily be comparable between countries. Therefore, would it be wise, possible or even helpful to benchmark aspects of thesis examination across all countries and universities offering a doctorate? Would the doctorate from North America, Asia and Africa provide relevant and helpful quality benchmarking information to the different participants?

One might think that this should be possible given that the PhD, as a particular form of the doctorate, is often considered to be an international award resulting in the title 'Dr', but is this really the case? And if we were to benchmark, on which specific aspects might we focus: perhaps originality or time to completion? The latter aspect might be easier to identify, but will the various calculations be broadly recognised and based on the same types of programmes or does one include additional time for coursework and perhaps additional time for examination? Or does one address issues such as maternity leave, or time to engage in internships? Furthermore, what might be the links between time to completion and quality?

### The university

While there are a number of university ranking systems, for example the Times Higher Education (THE) and the Shanghai Jiao Tong Academic Ranking of World Universities, given the variation in methods of calculating the various rankings, as well as the number of universities world-wide, would benchmarking the PhD thesis from all universities offering the doctoral programme be at all useful or reliable? Perhaps one could consider benchmarking the top 20, the top 50, or perhaps the top 100 universities with one another, and then benchmarking those from 101-200 and so on. But again one must return to the question, what factors would we be benchmarking and what would be the quality criteria? Of course, even asking this begs the question of the validity and reliability of such rankings at the specific level of doctoral education. Furthermore, is it likely that examiners might approach examination differently depending on the ranking or reputation of the university? In other words, will they expect a higher quality thesis from a university that is in the top 10 of, for example the THE rankings, compared with one that is ranked about 500? How would this be reflected in the reports in a way that might allow benchmarking? Moreover, would it make any difference if the examiner came from a substantially lower ranked university than the one submitting the thesis, or vice versa?

### The type of doctoral programme

Another consideration is the type of doctoral programme. There are different types of doctorates and their various outputs may not be comparable. Here we might consider the PhD, the Professional Doctorate, the Industry Doctorate and the Practice Doctorate. In addition, we might include the thesis by published papers or compilation and a doctoral programme where coursework is an assessed aspect of the overall result with perhaps a comprehensive examination before beginning the research component.

If we were to use thesis examination as a benchmark of quality, would we need to have quite different processes for different types of doctorates, for example professional and practice doctorates and the various programme designs, for example those where coursework is an assessable component and those where coursework is integrated into the overall programme?

Where the thesis includes published papers (that might be multi-authored), is examination approached in the same way as for the monograph? One question to be posed is: Would it make it easier to benchmark if all theses included published papers (or none of them did)? Or, if only single-authored papers, by the candidate, could be included? (Clearly, in some disciplines this is virtually an impossibility.)

### Disciplinary or multidisciplinary research

Doctorates vary considerably between disciplines and may not be comparable across them. Also, doctorates may be interdisciplinary, which again raises issues of comparability and identifying examiners (Kiley 2004, 2009). If we were thinking of benchmarking the thesis examination, we might need to be aware of any 'implicit' or 'acceptable' standards within disciplines which suggest that examination is more of a disciplinary 'thing'. Another issue with multidisciplinary theses was reported in Kiley (2009:894) where respondents suggested:

> In many cases it was not possible to find examiners knowledgeable across more than one of the content areas addressed, and hence supervisors had to resort to an examiner from each of two or more different fields. Experienced supervisors recognised that there was a serious risk attached to doing so, as their experience suggested that each of the examiners will address the dissertation from their own disciplinary perspective, and expect it to address all the issues of that disciplinary approach.

### Approaches to research

The consideration of different approaches to research can cover two very different and important issues, particularly in terms of benchmarking thesis examination. The first relates to indigenous and other cultural approaches to research, including theses written in indigenous languages. For example, there may be very few examiners who are able to assess theses within particular indigenous languages. Additionally, there is the issue of methodologies. While there are the obvious differences between qualitative and quantitative research methods, some examiners are very forthright about their views on methodology whereas others might not be so overt and yet their views maybe coloured by the methodological approaches taken in the study.

As one interviewee in the study by Kiley (2009:894) suggested: "You might find yourself sending it to an examiner who has some sort of prejudice against the methodology or the particular reading style in the thesis, and you would never want to do that unwittingly."

Adding further complexity is the issue of indigenous and culturally specific research methodologies. It is likely that there will be relatively few examiners who can address culturally specific methodological approaches for some indigenous research.

### The method of examination and what is examined

Another consideration relates to the examination method. While in most countries an oral examination is a standard part of the PhD examination process, this approach is not universal. So, we need to ask, does it make a difference if there is an oral examination or not? Could we benchmark across different ways of examining? Furthermore, does it matter which kind of oral component it is? For example, is it a public oral as in parts of Europe and Scandinavia, or a private viva voce as in Britain? On the other hand, it might be the Committee Defense as in the USA, or the Practice Doctorate where the candidate addresses various creative outputs. This has not even addressed the doctoral programme where there is not an oral component, for example as at the time of writing, in most South African and many Australian universities.

One of the arguments for an oral component in the doctoral examination process is that this is one way of assessing the researcher, not just their research. Is this important in benchmarking at an international level and across all systems? Or, would benchmarking require that all universities in the process have similar examination processes?

### The examiners

If we were to consider the PhD thesis examination report as a form of international benchmarking then it is likely that we would need to consider the examiners themselves. For example, who nominates examiners, and does that matter? Might it be that the selection process in some situations causes the benchmarking process to be invalid? Secondly, does it make a difference if the university requires at least one of the examiners to be from outside the country; furthermore, does the country location of the examiner have any particular significance in relation to benchmarking? And thirdly, what about using examiners from within the university and even the department? Is that likely to influence the reports and the legitimacy and reliability of benchmarking?

### Background of the candidate

In addition to the many considerations listed above, another one might relate to the background of the candidate. Should (or do) examiners take into account whether candidates are undertaking their research degree in their home country or in a different country and probably in a language that is not their home language? Additionally, should examiners consider whether the candidate might have physical, mental or personal issues and whether that might have influenced their research (and so the examiner's approach)? Might this be why some universities suggest that candidates do not provide personal information in the Acknowledgements that the examiner can read before assessing the candidate and their work (Kumar & Sanderson 2019)?

**Purposes of the programme**

The final consideration addressed here relates to the proposed purpose of the PhD. For example, when examining, do all examiners have a shared view of the purpose of the doctorate so that they can have agreed assessment outcomes? It is likely that one examiner might be seeking the magnus opus, whereas others are seeking indicators that the candidate has learned how to undertake research and then develop over the following years as a highly regarded researcher with 'the habits of mind' of a researcher (Walker 2012). Are there agreed indicators that could be used for international benchmarking in terms of what makes a quality PhD or graduate?

Therefore, in light of the above, any benchmarking exercise would have to control for these variables to allow for helpful and realistic comparisons to be made.

## DISCUSSION: WHAT MIGHT ALL THIS MEAN?

It may well be that this issue is 'purely academic', that is, it is something that we can discuss at conferences and committees but is outside daily practical consideration. But why would this be the case when we live in a globalised world with academic mobility being widely prevalent?

Another thought is that perhaps such benchmarking is already occurring tacitly and there is no need to make it overt. For example, by using international examiners are we not already using a form of international benchmarking? And by encouraging candidates to present at international conferences or publish in international journals, might that be considered a form of international benchmarking at the doctoral level?

Another thought is that the idea of using PhD thesis examination as an international benchmark is close to impossible and so too difficult to pursue.

## CONCLUSION

Given that the focus of this book is the 'global scholar', one might think that thesis examination was an appropriate method of approaching the issue of international benchmarking. However, as the discussion above suggests, it is extraordinarily complex.

Furthermore, there are some other, more general issues that need to be addressed. For example, can we benchmark and still leave room for change and development in doctoral education? It might well be that by benchmarking too tightly with potential competitors, that is, similar universities, programmes become too rigid and uniform. Alternatively, perhaps with competition arising from benchmarking, doctoral programmes become so fluid that they lose their focus.

Another thought relates to mobility and ease of transport. While it might have been important to set up benchmarking processes at the international level for doctoral outcomes when travel was severely limited, this is to a large extent no longer the case, partly because of developments in travel but also in technology. For example, given that we can be in communication with people across the planet with programs such as Zoom and Skype, is there considerable benchmarking occurring already?

Another issue is the use of technology in relation to the doctoral research itself. For example, what might be the issues related to alternative forms of doctoral theses in light of technical strategies?

As a concluding comment I pose the following, deliberately 'tongue in cheek' question: Could we avoid all this by training robots, using artificial intelligence, to examine theses based on internationally agreed criteria? On the one hand this is not as extreme as it sounds: robots can (or so I understand) be trained to do this sort of work, but, then we would have to address all the above issues in developing algorithms and criteria by which examiner roborts could be trained as 'benchmark' setters. Good luck!

## ACKNOWLEDGEMENT

I acknowledge the helpful advice provide by colleagues Professor Stan Taylor and Nigel Palmer.

## REFERENCES

Alexander D & Davis I. 2019. The PhD system under pressure: An examiner's viewpoint. *Quality Assurance in Education*, 27(1):2-12. https://doi.org/10.1108/QAE-04-2018-0033

Australian Qualifications Framework Council. 2013. *Australian Qualifications Framework*. (2nd Edition) https://www.aqf.edu.au/ [Accessed 28 February 2013].

Clement N, Lovat TL, Holbrook A, Kiley M, Bourke S, Paltridge B, Stafield S, Fairbairn H, & McInerney D. 2015. Exploring doctoral examiner judgements though the lenses of Habermas and epistemic congnition. *Theory and Method in Higher Education Research*, 1:213-233. https://doi.org/10.1108/S2056-375220150000001010

Danish Ministry of Higher Education and Science. 2017. *The quality and relevance of the Danish PhD program*. https://bit.ly/3swVo5z [Accessed 2 December 2019].

Golding C, Sharmini S & Lazorovitch A. 2014. What examiners do: What thesis students should know. *Assessment and Evaluation in Higher Education*, 39(5):563-576. https://doi.org/10.1080/02602938.2013.859230

Hall F. 2006. Canadian practices related to the examination of PhD theses. In: M Kiley & G Mullins (eds.), *Quality in postgraduate research: Knowledge creation in testing times – Part 1: Refereed papers*. Canberra: CEDAM. 41-54.

Kiley M. 2004. What examiners' comments can tell us about the postgraduate learning environment. In: C Rust (ed.), *Improving student learning: Theory, research and scholarship*. Hinckley, Leicestershire: The Oxford Centre for Staff and Learning Development. 213-222. https://doi.org/10.1080/03075070802713112

Kiley M. 2009. You don't want a smart alec: Selecting examiners to assess doctoral dissertations. *Studies in Higher Education*, 34(8):889-903.

Kumar V & Sanderson L. 2019. The effects of acknowledgements in doctoral theses on examiners. *Innovations in Education and Teaching International*, 1-11.

Lovat T, Holbrook A, Bourke S, Fairbairn H, Kiley M, Paltridge B & Starfield S. 2015. Examining doctoral examination and the question of the viva. *Higher Education Review*, 47(3):5-23.

Lovitts B. 2007. *Making the Implicit Explicit: Creating Performance Expectations for the Dissertation*. Sterling, Va: Stylus.

Marsh H, Rowe K & Martin A. 2002. PhD students' evaluations of research supervision: Issues, complexities, and challenges in a nationwide Australian experiment in benchmarking universities. *The Journal of Higher Education*, 73(3):313-348. https://doi.org/10.1353/jhe.2002.0028

Mason S. 2018. Publications in the doctoral thesis: Challenges for doctoral candidates, supervisors, examiners and administrators. *Higher Education Research and Development*. https://doi.org/10.1080/07294360.2018.1462307

McKenna S, Quinn L & Vorster J-A. 2018. Mapping the field of higher education research using PhD examination reports. *Higher Education Research and Development*, 1-14. https://doi.org/10.1080/07294360.2018.1428178

Mežek S, & Swales J. 2016. *PhD defences and vivas from: The Routledge Handbook of English for Academic Purposes Routledge*. https://bit.ly/3txPtyE [Accessed 27 June 2017]

Prins F, De Kleijn R & Van Tartwijk J. 2015. Students' use of a rubric for research theses. *Assessment & Evaluation in Higher Education*, 1-23. https://doi.org/10.1080/02602938.2015.1085954

Share M. 2016. The PhD viva: A space for academic development. *International Journal for Academic Development*, 21(3):178-193. https://doi.org/10.1080/1360144X.2015.1095759

Sharmini S, Spronken-Smith R, Golding C & Harland T. 2014. Assessing the doctoral thesis when it includes published work. *Assessment & Evaluation in Higher Education*. https://doi.org/10.1080/02602938.2014.888535

Thune T, Kyvik S, Sorlin S, Olsen TB, Vabø A & Tømte C. 2012. *PhD Education in a Knowledge Society: An evaluation of PhD education in Norway*. Oslo, Nordic Institute for Studies in Innovation, Research and Education. https://bit.ly/3ssyxYX [Accessed 2 December 2019].

Trafford V. 2003. Questions in doctoral vivas: Views from the inside. *Quality Assurance in Education*, 11(2):114-122. https://doi.org/10.1108/09684880310471542

Walker G. 2012. Lessons from the Carnegie Initiative on the Doctorate. In: M Kiley (ed.), *Quality in Postgraduate Research conference: Narratives of Transition: Perspectives of Research Leaders, Educators and Postgraduates*. Adelaide: The Centre for Higher Education, Learning and Teaching. The Australian National University. Canberra. 7-20.

Wikipedia Benchmarking. https://bit.ly/3giGzBt [Accessed15 August 2019].

Wikipedia Higher Education Funding Council for England. https://bit.ly/3v23C7o [Accessed15 August 2019].

# PART TWO
CURRENTS AND CURRENCIES

# THE POLITICS OF POSTGRADUATE EDUCATION

## SUPERVISING IN A TROUBLED WORLD

Sioux McKenna

## INTRODUCTION

The postgraduate scholars build knowledge at the very frontiers of the field (Council on Higher Education 2013). To succeed, they need to be aware of the most recent advancements on their topic taking place all across the globe. While this is daunting, it is still not enough. In this chapter, I argue that today's scholars are undertaking their research on a troubled planet and they need to do far more than just contribute to knowledge. Postgraduate students, regardless of their discipline or topic, need to grapple in some way with their context of crass consumerism and the accumulation of wealth amid environmental ills. They need to consider the implications of their contributions, for knowledge is never neutral, and they need to act in ethical and responsible ways with the responsibilities that come with being critical citizens. Sadly, such a conception of the global postgraduate scholar is not only lacking in many conversations in the sector, it is often actively undermined. In the first half of the chapter, I look at the ways in which dominant conceptions of postgraduate scholarship can turn what ought to be a public good into a public bad. In the second half, I offer a few personal reflections on supervising within this context.

## THE RELATIONSHIP BETWEEN SKILLS, THE ECONOMY AND EDUCATION

Higher education has been captured by a particular way of thinking about the relationship between skills, the economy and education. The dominant understanding is so accessible as to feel self-evident, making it really rather alluring. Simply put, the 'knowledge economy' is the idea that the economy grows through knowledge development. This notion suggests that a country's wealth rests on its ability to produce and use information, rather than to produce goods. In contrast to an agrarian economy, where the key basis of the economy is farming, or an industrial economy, where the economy rests on the production of goods reliant on a significant portion of semi-skilled labour, a knowledge economy is seen to rely on sophisticated use of intellectual capital. Absolutely key to the idea of the knowledge economy is that knowledge and education are productive assets that can be leveraged for a high return. A country that wants to build its place within the knowledge economy should therefore invest in education. Furthermore, the education should be directed at a very particular purpose: to develop the kinds of skills that can drive the economy. Greater levels of education lead to greater levels of skill, and postgraduate education, in particular, is seen to be a means of ensuring that the country has the kind of high-level skills that can translate into job creation and development. This formula is known as human capital theory (see Mincer 1993; Romer 1989; Schultz 1963) and it is based on the idea of return on rates of investment. For every dollar invested by the individual, there should be a return of social mobility and financial security for the individual. For every dollar invested by industry, there should emerge measurable profits for owners and shareholders. And for every dollar invested by the State, there should be a benefit for the national economy.

This understanding of the role of higher education as a driver of economic development is at times presented as a public good, given that a healthy national economy can bring significant positive consequences for its citizens. But I would argue that the human capital theory of higher education in general, and postgraduate education in particular, does not provide us with higher education as something that is good for the public and this is because it privileges the private good nature of higher education. The focus is not on the role of higher education as something that is good for society at large or for the ailing planet on which we live. Human capital theory sees higher education as mainly or exclusively something for the benefit of those industries that employ this skilled capital and those students who achieve social mobility through skills which they can use to negotiate better jobs and incomes. In the instrumentalist approach of human capital theory, economic growth becomes the raison d'être of the university. Vally and Motala (2014) argue that the power of this theory emerges in part because many thousands of students worldwide are fed a daily diet of nothing but human capital theory.

Human capital theory is a resilient conceptualisation of the purpose of higher education despite consistent evidence of its shortcomings. In South Africa, for example, despite a doubling of graduates in the last 20 years, we continue to see increases in unemployment and sluggish economic growth. But the theory itself is not questioned in the light of such refutation, instead we are told that the problem is that higher education is hopelessly out of tune with the relevant skills that lead to employment and economic growth. Feedback from industry is that universities are failing to provide the precise kind of labour that can hit the ground running when they enter the workplace. And so, our universities rush to greater and greater evidence of 'skills training' and 'employability attributes'.

There is no evidence that levels of unemployment are related to education's supposed inability to provide the particular workplace skills required by industry. Unemployment emerges from a number of complex structural conditions over which education has little or no control – globalisation, shifts in the labour market, tax avoidance, technological advancements and so on. It is impossible for education alone to address slow economic growth. Ironically, some argue that a focus on workplace skills in the curriculum makes it less rather than more likely for graduates to impact in any meaningful way on the economy given that skills so rapidly become redundant (Grubb & Lazerson 2005; Wheelahan 2009). Instead of challenging the assumptions that universities should become more efficient at skilling labour, universities continue to elevate the skills discourse across their processes and practices. Postgraduate studies seen through the lens of human capital theory are expected to be underpinned by what is known in the literature as vocationalism. This means that postgraduate studies are expected to always have immediate utilitarian outcomes in service of industry and the economy and where possible this should lead to intellectual property, patents and marketable products. Treat (2014) argues that it is only once universities dismiss the notion of a "skills gap" that we can begin to get focused on "socially useful work".

Another shortcoming of human capital theory lies in its promises of a graduate premium. The graduate premium is a measure of the extent to which obtaining a particular qualification increases an individual's chances of employment, increased salary and promotion. South Africa has a very small participation rate in higher education and an even smaller participation in postgraduate education (Council on Higher Education 2019), which in part explains the relatively high graduate premium in South Africa (Cloete & Maassen 2015).[1] Internationally, however, the graduate premium is no longer seen to be the reward it once was. The combination of increased graduate unemployment and staggering student debt elsewhere in the world has meant that the private rewards of higher education have started to decrease. The graduate premium in the UK (Mason, Williams & Cranmer 2009; O'Leary & Sloane 2016) and the USA (Bennet & Wilezol 2013) for example, are now far less certain than they once were.

---

1 Graduate unemployment, for example, is far lower than the national unemployment rate, though it is uneven by institution and race group (Van der Berg & Van Broekhuizen 2012).

Even in the current South African context of a strong graduate premium, we need to ask whether social mobility can be the core educational goal for all our students and the system as a whole. Extrapolating from a few individuals who have enjoyed social mobility through obtaining a qualification to making claims about this being the purpose of the entire system of higher education is problematic.

## HUMAN CAPITAL THEORY ASSUMES A MERITOCRACY

The promise of a graduate premium, which is embedded in the human capital theory account of higher education, rests on the premise that with hard work anyone can 'Achieve the dream' and go 'From rags to riches'. Because human capital theory promises that education leads to a better life for the individual, or, to use the language of the theory, because it promises a high rate of return on investment, it has to promote the idea of education as a meritocracy where everyone who invests in education has an equal chance of success. The common-sense idea of how skills relate to employment places responsibility on the individual in two ways: firstly, it places the responsibility on them to have the necessary inherent attributes to succeed, and secondly, it places the responsibility on the student to pay the costs of their education.

### Human capital theory assumes that inherent attributes lead to success

Alongside making it seem sensible that individuals pay for their own studies, human capital theory rests on the idea that higher education success is determined by the student. If the individual fails and does not obtain the marketable skills designed to provide them with the goods of society, then they have clearly made poor choices (Shumar 2013). It is not the structures of society that have constrained them, it is their own deficits that account for their failure. Chrissie Boughey and I have called this the "discourse of the decontextualised learner" (Boughey & McKenna 2016:2017), whereby the student's success or failure is understood to emerge entirely from attributes inherent in the individual, be it their levels of intelligence or motivation or language competence, rather than acknowledging that higher education success correlates with and reinforces large social structures, particularly social class (Case, Marshall, McKenna & Mogashana 2018). Taking on the knowledge-making practices of a discipline is a far more complex process that the meritocratic account underpinning human capital theory allows for.

Academic literacy practices (or the practices of engaging with and communicating knowledge) differ significantly from discipline to discipline. By postgraduate level, students should have grappled with the foundational concepts on which the particular field builds knowledge. They should also have been inducted into many of the practices necessary for the field, such as where and why we reference in philosophy, or how we construct an argument in politics, or what counts as evidence in physics. And yet much of this remains mysterious as students make the move to postgraduate level. At postgraduate level, they move from being knowledge-tellers, displaying their engagement with the field, to becoming knowledge-creators, actively involved alongside those who are already fully-fledged members (Bartholomae 1985), and this transition is a complex one that is more readily navigated by some than by others. While hard work and intelligence play an important role in postgraduate achievement, these mechanisms work in concert with numerous other structural constraints and enablements.

Allais and Nathan (2014) argue that the overemphasis on the agency of the individual in discourses about the relationship between skills, education and the economy allows an under-emphasis on structural constraints. Human capital theory is generally silent on issues of social structures of race, gender and so on. In our research, we found that the discourse of the decontextualised learner was the most dominant explanation within South African universities for success and failure and that the myth of the meritocracy is alive and well in our universities despite ample research to the contrary (Boughey & McKenna 2016:2017; McKenna & Boughey 2014; Sobuwa & McKenna 2019).

### Human capital theory drives the user-pays model of education

It's very easy to see why governments around the world have cut funding within a human capital theory conception of higher education. Why should taxes from all people in the country be used to subsidise the studies that will benefit just a few? It is this logic that led to the massive increases in student fees in South Africa and ultimately to the #FeesMustFall protests.

Spending cuts by the State on higher education are not peculiar to South Africa. The idea that higher education is a private good whereby it is the individual graduate who benefits is strongly tied to capitalist values of individualism and choice in a free market. With Reagan and Thatcher's acceptance of Friedman's neoliberalism, practically the entire world's higher education system went down a particular path that is playing out in various ways across the planet. The effects of human capital theory are evident everywhere: from the rapid increase in for-profit privatised higher education, to the unbundling of our public institutions whereby tasks previously considered to be core to the academic project are outsourced to private consultants, to the deskilling and casualisation of academics whereby 65% of academics in South

Africa are now employed on a contract basis (Council on Higher Education 2019). These are all effects of human capital theory where the academy is increasingly understood as a high-level training centre requiring efficient management.

What Barnett refers to as the "entrepreneurial university" has emerged in response to the related ideas of a global knowledge economy, human capital theory, marketisation and neoliberalism or free-market economics. The entrepreneurial university allows ecological imperatives to be subsumed by intellectual property rights and it lacks ideas that are "critical in tone, positive in spirit, and [which bring] an awareness of the deep and global structures that underpin institutions" (Barnett 2013:1).

If the human being is understood to take the form of capital that has more value in the marketplace as a result of their education, then they should be responsible for paying for that education. But this responsibility for the student to fund their own process of becoming marketable capital assumes that they have the means to do so and it is self-evident that in an economically uneven and racially divided country such as South Africa, there are enormous constraints on students' capacity to self-fund their studies.

The instrumentalist linking of education to a graduate premium also assumes a particular kind of workplace, whereby the graduate's credentialing by the academy acts as a ticket to secure employment. But the nature of employment has changed significantly in the last decade or two. Wedekind (2014) shows that employability discourses underpinning human capital theory rely on older notions of work that brought access to benefits, a strong career path, autonomy and so on, whereas in the current context, employability is often reduced to zero-hour contracts in an ongoing cycle of short-term gigs, where people are having to constantly hustle to make a living. All those who believe the central role of the university is the production of skilled labour for employment and economic growth need to take a hard look at the nature of employment and the impact of current models of economic growth.

This is an international phenomenon. Globalisation has privileged multinational corporations over nation states, and nation states have responded by looking to maximise profits and positions of power within this globalised world. This often leads to fierce nationalism, competition, and a desperate bid for all national structures, including the higher education system, to perform within the global arena, such as through the institutional rankings game. The role of the State in protecting the commons for its people and taking care of its most vulnerable has been subsumed by its role to support big business in this global competition.

## ECONOMIC RATHER THAN SOCIAL AND ENVIRONMENTAL DEVELOPMENT

When Nussbaum (1998) makes the plea for integrating humanities education across our universities — something that is side-lined by human capital theory — she states that the acquisition of high-level skills and factual knowledge without a humanistic and critical perspective is not only technicist and limited, but it privileges economic interests over social and environmental ones. If high-level skills do indeed function to strengthen the economy and lead to individual social mobility — and I have thus far argued that this is far too simplistic an understanding of the relationship between students, employment and the economy — we would need to acknowledge that it does so in a context of inhumane arrangements of poverty and wealth. Producing graduates to serve the economy does not seem to have tempered such inequalities and it is probably time to accept that economic growth in global corporate capitalism is not in the business of supporting high levels of labour participation and wide-scale economic stability. The logic of economic growth in the era of late-capitalism is individual wealth creation for corporate owners and shareholders. Is this then what we are producing postgraduate scholars for?

Many postgraduates have attained enormous wealth and steered major corporations to great financial success — which would seem to illustrate the success of the human capital theory — but under the watch of these graduates we have seen an increase in environmental disasters and the normalising of inhumane working conditions. Human capital theory does not account for the ethical aspects of roles played by the most educated citizens. Nor does it insist that universities reflect on how they have enabled graduates' acquisition of skills that allowed such behaviours.

If we construct higher education's purpose as driving the relationship between education, skills and the economy, we need to accept that we are complicit in the environmental degradation and social inequality that have emerged from such skills. We have to ask ourselves: Do our education processes undermine or reinforce underlying socio-economic and environmental pathologies? Is postgraduate education good for the public, many of whom will never venture onto university premises? Or is it at times a public bad?

Alongside the often uncritical adoption of human capital theory in many of our universities has been the rhetoric about the Fourth Industrial Revolution. The innovative leaps that technology provides are exciting but the current Fourth Industrial Revolution discourse seems once again to flatten postgraduate education to skills acquisition. As we face the merging of technology with everyday processes there is less and less need for large numbers of skilled labour as graduate level jobs are increasingly undertaken by automation. Rather than competing to lead the Fourth Industrial Revolution, our universities should be striving to consider how we can ensure a more humane society within this technological era.

## THE NATURE OF HUMANITY IN HUMAN CAPITAL THEORY

Thus far, this chapter has critiqued the idea that education's central role is to provide skills that can be traded for salaries at the individual level and economic growth at a national scale. This theory assumes that humans can be conceived of as capital and it is this conception to which I now turn. Citizenship is largely framed in human capital theory discourse as the ability to participate as an active consumer rather than as the flourishing of human freedoms and capabilities. Social visions of equity are overshadowed by the notion that all individuals are driven by brutal self-interest. Hyper-capitalism may drive many of us to live in constant desire for 'stuff' and in constant dread of debt, but the focus on competition and pitting each of us against each other in the name of efficiency has thankfully not been entirely successful. Most of us care and connect. We remain compassionate and we continue to seek justice in the world. Freire (1985) argued that the whole notion of *homo economicus* is oppressive and alienating and at odds with our basic nature to become more human.

We are more than a "bundle of technical skills" (Block 1990, cited in Vally & Motala 2014). We are not expensive machines. We are lovers and fighters and parents and children and builders and midwives and artists and communities and ancestors and animals. Understanding ourselves primarily in terms of the skills we can peddle in the marketplace ignores the complex realities of being human. The notion of the university as a provider of generic skills decontextualises us from our histories and it absolves us from responsibility for the structural inequalities that surround us.

## KNOWLEDGE AS SKILLS

Increasingly we are seeing postgraduate studies being funded by industry and briefed as to what kind of knowledge should be the focus of such studies (Frick, McKenna & Muthama 2017). Wedekind (2014) points out that vocationalism can increase the chances of direct funding to increase skills development. This is the allure of the discourse. If we are willing to agree with the unproven relationship between education, skills development and economic growth, then we can get access to funding from industry and the State to develop these skills.

Neville Alexander (2014), in a piece published after his death in 2012, warns us about the increasingly close relationships between knowledge creation in the university and transnational corporations: "Is it morally and politically defensible to use public revenues, dispensed via government and universities to maximise profits for corporate entities, which appropriate profits for their shareholders?" (Alexander 2014:51). We need postgraduate education that provokes individuals to think about who they are and what they are doing: to create, to challenge, to champion – this is unlikely to occur in studies that are driven by industry's need for profit. Funding comes at a cost: it often comes at the cost of carving out the humanistic purposes of postgraduate education; it can entail disregarding the social function of knowledge creation; and it can come at the cost of more abstract knowledge which is replaced with more immediate vocational knowledge.

A significant body of work indicates how it is that a focus on 'relevant skills' undermines access to powerful knowledge (Maton 2013; Wheelahan 2012; Young & Muller 2013). The powerful knowledge offered by the academy is abstracted, theoretical and specialised. It allows us to make sense across multiple current and future contexts. If instead of access to this, students are provided access to immediate 'work-ready' skills demanded by industry, they are severely limited. We have to challenge narrow, reductive and economic determinist positions on knowledge.

Unfortunately, there is a dearth of language about the nature of knowledge. We seem to suffer from a knowledge blindness that assumes that all knowledge is equal and is unrelated to where it comes from. The White Paper 3 (Department of Education 1997) included an understanding of the role of universities to provide powerful knowledge necessary for imaginative responses to complex problems, and it called for the nurturing of a critical citizenry and the fostering of social cohesion in the new democracy. But such discourses sat with some degree of tension alongside nascent human capital theory discourses also evident in the 1997 White Paper, and increasingly evident in subsequent policies that say little about the emancipatory role of education and its responsibilities to provide access to powerful knowledge.

We need to ask of our postgraduate education system: Who gets access to it and what is it that is accessed? And we need to ensure that the answers to these questions are in the interests of the planet rather than whether or not they are likely to make money. This entails taking a close look at context. While skills development should indeed be central in many kinds of postgraduate curricula, it cannot be skills development simply in terms of technical, industrial practices; we need political, social, cultural, and environmental skills development too. While market fundamentalism and neoliberalism may increasingly be taking hold of our universities, we need to insist on a consideration of the social context within which postgraduate education takes place – a context of poverty, low wages, landlessness, social inequality, and environmental catastrophe. An explicitly articulated commitment within our postgraduate curricula to a just and sustainable world is our only inoculation against the drift of our universities towards serving corporate interests.

Human capital theory gets away with ignoring the broader context through the notion of trickle-down economics. If our universities produce more skilled labour, the story goes, they will produce more jobs and the poor will thus eventually be taken care of. But we have not seen evidence of this. We have seen the reduction of labour through technology and the export of labour to sweatshops, and we have seen the crass accumulation of wealth by the few. If we fail to challenge the ways in which human capital theory frames postgraduate education, and higher education more generally, we not only neglect this reality, we actively reinforce it.

Kate Raworth's excellent *Doughnut Economics* (2017) provides a far more nuanced (and yet readily accessible) account of the relationship between economic development and what she terms "social foundation" and the "ecological ceiling". Growth that falls short on providing a social foundation for all or which overshoots the ecological ceiling of the planet's resources, is toxic growth. This could be extended to argue that education that ignores the social foundation and exploits the ecological ceiling is toxic education.

The obsession with skills development in a cult of efficiency provides significant obstacles to critical thinking, so we really need to build intentional spaces to connect and share in our immediate institutional contexts. Thornton (2009:392) suggests that the corporate university has severely constrained its spaces of critique: "Since it is primarily as neoliberal subjects that academics are now generally valued, feminist scholars, like their peers, are expected to serve the new knowledge economy rather than to critique it." I would argue that the effects on decolonial scholars and others are similarly positioned. We need to overtly claim the value of critical and creative thinking (Frick & Brodin 2014).

## WHAT CAN BE DONE? I'M JUST A POSTGRADUATE SUPERVISOR

It would be easy to sink into a morass of despair when we consider the ways in which our universities have been captured by human capital theory and have implemented managerialist structures to keep us all efficient or at least compliant. But such despair is only a sensible response if we are without agency. And one thing about argumentative academics (McKenna & Boughey 2014) is that we exercise agency.

In the remainder of this chapter, I change direction somewhat by reflecting on five things I try to do to protect postgraduate education against the assumptions of human capital theory. This is a practical list with seemingly simple, everyday ways of being. But taking on these practices is not straightforward and requires vigilance. The responsibility for ensuring that postgraduate education stewards powerful knowledge and contributes to the common good rests on all of us working in higher education. Some of us may have the institutional influence and energy needed to directly address institutional structures emerging from human capital theory's limiting of postgraduate education to skills for capital, but many of us may feel overwhelmed. The aim of this list is to illustrate that there are actions that we can take in our day-to-day life as supervisors that can enable a conception of postgraduate education that is more generous, creative, and connected to people and the planet. This is by no means an exhaustive list, and I hope the reader will bring to it their own examples of how we can provide meaningful supervision in a troubled world.

### Resist the metrics and foreground the knowledge

We need to actively try to think of our work in terms of cognitive engagement and intellectual pleasure rather than in terms of productivity and outputs. As we shift the focus from the product to the process of understanding that underpins it, so this makes for a more meaningful and more rewarding intellectual process. Our language models this for our postgraduate scholars. While the thesis must get written, the key is the activity of thinking and meaning-making rather than the production of the next chapter.

We need to judge scholarship, not measure it. We need to ask of our own work and that of others: What contribution does this make? What ways of thinking or knowledge does this scholarship provide? We need to ask this question of our postgraduate scholars. We need to look at the topics and theories our students are addressing. We need to ask them to confront the challenging ethical dilemmas inherent in designing a bridge or developing a new drug or understanding the views of a particular community.

Collini (2012) tells us that it is difficult to push back when neoliberalism in the university has the power to "colonise the mind". Berg and Seeber (2016:ix) argue that we need to claim a counter-identity to the "beleaguered, managed, frantic, stressed and demoralised professor who is the product of the corporatisation of higher education". Those with institutional power need to resist the reduction of knowledge creation to the ideology of human capital and the related moulding of our universities into efficient training centres. We need to model another way of being. We need to model the professor who is insatiably curious and consistently compassionate. Someone who cares far more about understanding and creating knowledge than about output. Someone who is a stalwart champion of her postgraduate students, their loudest cheerleader and their greatest support.

### Make space for reading

I have not seen any performance management systems allocate reading time for academics. Time allocated to 'Research' on such systems is generally conceived of as performance and production, but we need to read for non-utilitarian purposes. Reading is absolutely fundamental to our job descriptions as academics and central to our work as postgraduate supervisors. We may find ourselves so busy that the only reading we do is reviewing journal articles or commenting on student work. In the rushed managerialist university where we are encouraged to focus on what is counted rather than on what counts, we rarely read for the activity of thinking. It seems indulgent to read for the purpose of thinking, just as it does to write for the purpose of thinking, and yet this should be fundamental to what we do. Reading and writing for thinking about the knowledge of our field rather than for the next research output becomes a radical act.

### Be vulnerable

We have to consistently demonstrate to those around us that "[n]ot everything that counts can be counted" as Collini (2012:240) reminds us. We have to make explicit to our postgraduate students those things that can and do count even if our systems fail to count them. We have to show the pleasure of taking intellectual risks and we have to demonstrate how we expect and sometimes even welcome failure for the lessons it provides. We need to be vulnerable and open about these failures. Berg and Seeber (2016) speak of the "shadow CV" – the resumé that includes the list of rejected articles and unsuccessful grant applications.

If the postgraduate scholars we are welcoming into the discipline only see our successes, no wonder they feel overwhelmed by their own failures. It is only when those of us with institutional security and power behave in these ways of compassion and vulnerability that novice academics and students will see that it is okay for them to be fully human too. As we do so, we need to ask questions about whose interests are being served by the taken-for-granted practices of our institutions. "If we ask academics to hold students in a space of vulnerability and uncertainty in which they can embrace their own beings, it is necessary that we create the kind of environment where academics can explore their own vulnerability and uncertainty" (Blackie, Case & Jawitz 2010:643).

### Be kind

This is not the same as being nice. Being nice is being polite and compliant and reinforcing the social norms that uphold the status quo. Being kind is about caring and being compassionate and being collegial. There are lots of ways of being kind, many of which are the antithesis of the managerialist university rushing to measure postgraduate output.

For example, the writing groups run by and for our postgraduate scholars have become a powerful anti-hierarchical space (Achadu, Asfour, Chakona, Mason, Mataruse, McKenna & Oluwole 2018; Wilmot & McKenna 2018) with an explicitly stated ethos of collaboration and critical kindness. Being kind can take the form of continuing to support and mentor students after the university has excluded them for slow progress or introducing our students to the keynote speaker at a conference by referring to the students' work. Giving feedback to students is another key place for kindness. We are often pushed by institutional cultures to see feedback in terms of correction rather than as a means of making the knowledge creation processes explicit. We need to use feedback on students' work as a dialogical space of engagement for epistemological access rather than a place of power play. Are we using our feedback to welcome our postgraduate students into the knowledge community? Are we using our feedback to give students access to understandings that challenge their assumptions and provide them with powerful knowledge? There are so many ways of supervising with generosity and kindness that I am taught new examples all the time.

We need to be open to having our own assumptions challenged by our students' thinking. We need to take seriously our responsibility to learn, unlearn and re-learn from our students and from those with whom we disagree. Listening is another radical act of kindness. Often listening means being quiet and opening the spaces of privilege for others to speak – others who may be used to having their views silenced and side-lined.

Being kind includes being kind to ourselves. This is not about going easy on ourselves or settling for mediocrity. Being kind to ourselves means understanding that we have to have spaces to read and think if we are to produce anything meaningful. And being kind to ourselves means being willing to take risks and to tackle failure when it inevitably comes as part of our knowledge creation activity.

### Collaborate and celebrate

In just the last few months I have come across a master's student who didn't want to discuss her research in a seminar lest someone 'steals her ideas', a doctoral student whose supervisor reprimanded her for talking about her study with another supervisor, and an honours student who was very excited about an article she had come across but didn't want to share the bibliographic details with her class as then "everyone will quote it". If we want to break this competitive individualism, we have to model it in our own departments and in our own supervision relationships.

When a colleague's success gives us a jolt of competitive unhappiness even as we are congratulating them, we need to pause and reflect on how we have been turned into the competitive neoliberal subject even though knowledge creation is inherently collaborative. One of the best ways to resist individualised competition so lauded by the neoliberal project is to celebrate one another. We need to take genuine pleasure in one another's successes. We need to be generous in our support of one another. When the system pushes us to compete and score points, we can choose to collaborate instead.

## CONCLUSION

In this chapter I have argued that postgraduate supervisors have the daunting challenge of creating pedagogical spaces of hope. Holding on to hope is key – this is not about optimism that blinds us to the challenges ahead but hope is a necessary antidote to paralysing despair. Resisting the corporatisation of our universities in service of the highly problematic and reductionist conceptualisation of postgraduate education within human capital theory has to be matched by a clearly articulated sense of the academic endeavour as a democratic project.

We have to nurture the development of ethical responses to current crises of environmental degradation and social injustice. We have to foster supervision practices that enable recognition, mutual learning, risk-taking, kindness and critical citizenship, all while ensuring a deep commitment to the common good.

## REFERENCES

Achadu O, Asfour F, Chakona G, Mason P, Mataruse P, McKenna S & Oluwole DO. 2018. Postgraduate writing groups as spaces of agency development. *South African Journal of Higher Education*, 32(6):370-381. https://doi.org/10.20853/32-6-2963

Alexander N. 2014. Universities and the 'Knowledge Economy'. In: S Vally & E Motala (eds.), *Education, economy and society*. Pretoria: Unisa Press. 48-56.

Allais S & Nathan O. 2014. Skills? What Skills? Jobs? What Jobs? An overview of research into education/labour market relationships. In: S Vally & E. Motala (eds.), *Education, economy and society*. Pretoria: Unisa Press. 103-124.

Barnett, R. 2013. *Imagining the University*. London: Routledge. https://doi.org/10.4324/9780203072103

Bartholomae D. 1985. Inventing the university. In: M Rose (ed.), *When a writer can't write: Studies in writer's block and other composing-process problems*. New York: Guildford. 134-165.

Bennet W & Wilezol D. 2013. *Is college worth it? A former United States Secretary of Education and a liberal arts graduate expose the broken promise of higher education.* Nashville, TN: Thomas Neilson.

Berg M & Seeber BK. 2016. *The slow professor: challenging the culture of speed in the academy.* Toronto: University of Toronto Press. https://doi.org/10.3138/9781442663091

Blackie MAL, Case JM & Jawitz J. 2010. Student-centredness: the link between transforming students and transforming ourselves. *Teaching in Higher Education*, 15(6):637-646. https://doi.org/10.1080/13562517.2010.491910

Boughey C & McKenna S. 2016. Academic literacy and the decontextualised learner. *Critical Studies in Teaching and Learning*, 4(2):1-9.

Boughey C & McKenna S. 2017. Analysing an audit cycle: A critical realist account. *Studies in Higher Education*, 42(6):963-975. https://doi.org/10.1080/03075079.2015.1072148

Case J, Marshall D, McKenna S & Mogashana D. 2018. *Going to university: the influence of higher education on the lives of young South Africans.* Cape Town: African Minds. https://doi.org/10.47622/9781928331698

Cloete N & Maassen P. 2015. *Knowledge production and contradictory functions in African higher education.* Cape Town: African Minds. https://doi.org/10.47622/978-1-920677-85-5

Collini S. 2012. *What are universities for?* London: Penguin Books.

Council on Higher Education. 2013. *The higher education qualifications sub-framework.* Pretoria: Council on Higher Education.

Council on Higher Education. 2019. *Vital stats public higher education 2017.* Pretoria: Council on Higher Education.

Department of Education. 1997. *White Paper 3: A programme for the transformation of higher education.* Pretoria: Government Printing Works.

Freire P. 1985. *Pedagogy of the Oppressed.* London: Penguin Books.

Frick L & Brodin E. (2014). Developing expert scholars: The role of reflection in creative learning. In: E. Shiu (ed.), *Creativity Research: An Inter-Disciplinary and Multi-Disciplinary Research Handbook.* Abingdon, Oxon: Routledge. 312-333

Frick L, McKenna S & Muthama E. 2017. Death of the PhD: When industry partners determine doctoral outcomes. *Higher Education Research & Development*, 36(2):444-447. https://doi.org/10.1080/07294360.2017.1263467

Grubb WN & Lazerson M. 2005. Vocationalism in higher education: The triumph of the education gospel. *The Journal of Higher Education*, 76(1):1-25. https://doi.org/10.1353/jhe.2005.0007

Mason G, Williams G & Cranmer S. 2009. Employability skills initiatives in higher education: What effects do they have on graduate labour market outcomes? *Education Economics*, 17(1):1-30. https://doi.org/10.1080/09645290802028315

Maton K. 2013. *Knowledge and knowers: Towards a realist sociology of education.* Abingdon, Oxon: Routledge. https://doi.org/10.4324/9780203885734

McKenna S & Boughey C. 2014. Argumentative and trustworthy scholars: The construction of academic staff at research-intensive universities. *Teaching in Higher Education*, 19(7):825-834. https://doi.org/10.1080/13562517.2014.934351

Mincer J. 1993. *Studies in human capital: Collected essays of Jacob Mincer.* Volume 1. Vermont: Edward Elgar.

Nussbaum MC. 1998. *Cultivating humanity*. Cambridge, Mass: Harvard University Press. https://doi.org/10.2307/j.ctvjghth8

O'Leary N & Sloane P. 2016. Too many graduates? An application of the Gottschalk-Hansen model to young British graduates between 2001-2010. *Oxford Economic Papers*, 68(4):945-967. https://doi.org/10.1093/oep/gpw027

Raworth K. 2017. *Doughnut economics: Seven ways to think like a 21st century economist.* Vermont: Chelsea Green Publishing.

Romer P. 1989. *Human capital and growth: Theory and evidence.* Occasional Paper from National Bureau of Economic Research, United States of America. https://doi.org/10.3386/w3173

Schultz T. 1963. *The economic value of education.* New York: Columbia University Press.

Shumar W. 2013. *College for sale: A critique of the commodification of higher education.* New York: Routledge. https://doi.org/10.4324/9781315043142

Sobuwa S & McKenna S. 2019. The obstinate notion that higher education is a meritocracy. *Critical Studies in Teaching and Learning*, 7(2):13-28. https://doi.org/10.14426/cristal.v7i2.184

Thornton M. 2009. Universities upside down: The impact of the new knowledge economy. *Canadian Journal of Women and the Law Revue Juridique La Femme et Le Droit*, 21(2):375-393. https://doi.org/10.3138/cjwl.21.2.375

Treat J. 2014. On the use and abuse of education: Reflections on unemployment, the 'skills gap' and 'zombie economics'. In: S Vally & E Motala (eds.), *Education, economy and society.* Pretoria: Unisa Press. 171-189.

Vally S & Motala E. 2014. *Education, economy & society.* Pretoria: Unisa Press.

Van der Berg S & Van Broekhuizen H. 2012. *Graduate unemployment in South Africa: A much exaggerated problem.* Stellenbosch Economic Working Papers 22/12. Stellenbosch: University of Stellenbosch.

Wedekind V. 2014. Going around in circles: Employability, responsiveness and reform of the college sector. In: S Vally & E Motala (eds.), *Education, economy and society.* Pretoria: Unisa Press. 57-80.

Wheelahan L. 2009. The problem with CBT (and why constructivism makes things worse). *Journal of Education and Work*, 22(3):227-242. https://doi.org/10.1080/13639080902957913

Wheelahan L. 2012. *Why knowledge matters in curriculum: A social realist argument.* Abingdon, Oxon: Routledge. https://doi.org/10.4324/9780203860236

Wilmot K & McKenna S. 2018. Writing groups as transformative spaces. *Higher Education Research and Development*, 37(4):868-882. https://doi.org/10.1080/07294360.2018.1450361

Young M & Muller J. 2013. On the powers of powerful knowledge. *Review of Educational Research*, 1(3):229-250. https://doi.org/10.1002/rev3.3017

# ACADEMIC MOBILITY IN THE DIGITAL ACADEMY

QUESTIONS FOR SUPERVISION

Anna Morozov and Cally Guerin

## INTRODUCTION

Universities and academics are increasingly positioned within a global environment that is marked by academic mobility and digital technologies that enhance the connections between institutions and individuals around the world. Universities in many countries actively recruit international students. In Australia, for example, this has become a major concern as universities' heavy reliance on the income from international student fees becomes clear (see, for example, Universities Australia 2019) and academics actively build on their personal and institutional relationships to create opportunities for research collaboration. There is clearly much to be gained from this swirl of circulation and digitally networked connection at all levels of academia, which in turn has implications for the supervision of doctoral candidates.

This chapter explores issues surrounding academic mobility in the digital academy from the perspective of supervision. Theoretical frameworks from migration studies are used to help us understand contemporary patterns of mobility. We are interested in what this intersection of mobility and digital technologies means for the supervision of research degrees; hence, we contribute to the conceptual understanding of research supervision for global scholars.

## ACADEMIC MOBILITY

The concept and practice of 'academic mobility' is not new. It can imply permanent, temporary and circular relocation, referring to both students and staff as they move between institutions and countries to pursue their academic work (Bauder 2012;

Dervin 2011; Hugo 2009; Kim 2017; Kim & Brooks 2012; Teichler 2015). This section briefly outlines the history of academic mobility and the types of mobility relevant to academia from the perspective of migration studies.

Historically, academics have been mobile for centuries: they travelled between cultural centres in Ancient Greece, between European and Arab countries in the Middle Ages, between Europe and its colonies in the 15th-19th centuries, and from the 20th century until now this movement has been global (Bauder 2012; Kim 2009, 2010; Taylor, Hoyler & Evans 2008). Over time, the concept of academic mobility has developed from the 'wandering scholar' (Pietsch 2010) phenomenon to recently becoming part of the complex set of interdependencies between (and social consequences of) a number of diverse mobilities of people, objects, images, and information (Elliott & Urry 2010). Therefore, it is not surprising that many universities are competing not only for international students, but also for talented, reputable and highly skilled researchers and lecturers in the hope that they will facilitate innovation and contribute to the knowledge-based economic growth of the particular university and, theoretically, of the host country. Universities all over the world promote mobility of staff and students as a critical aspect of their learning and professional development experience (Altbach, Androushchak, Kuzminov, Yudkevich & Reisberg 2013; De Wit 2019; Robertson 2010; Yudkevich, Altbach & Rumbley 2016). Academic mobility is currently measured in some of the most influential global ranking systems for universities (see, for example, https://bit.ly/3tq60ob), where the ratio of international staff and international students is used as a metric demonstrating an institution's global outlook and multinational environment. Indeed, the phenomenon of academic mobility is often seen as the most important dimension of internationalisation of higher education in the global knowledge society of today (Egron-Polak 2017; Egron-Polak & Hudson 2014; Rumbley & De Wit 2019).

### Academic mobility types

Academic mobility has a range of dimensions and its typology and terminology might vary, depending on the research agendas at different times. Some of the common types of academic mobility are: conventional, lateral, vertical/spatial, and generational (Hoffman 2009). Conventional mobility is usually associated with short-term academic staff movements and with information and technology-based mobility; it is often limited to academic circulation within a narrow geographical range (such as study visits or guest lecturing) or even virtual mobility conducted online (Hoffman 2009; Schreurs, Verjans & Van Petegem 2006). In contrast, lateral mobility is related to the crossing of national borders for academic work or study for over a year, which often leads to subsequent migration (Dekker, De Grip &

Heijke 2002; Varghese 2008). Both vertical (Hoffman 2009) and spatial (Christie 2007) academic mobility are associated with social mobility, that is, moving up or down the socio-economic scale (Bilecen & Van Mol 2017; Haveman & Smeeding 2006; Marginson 2016). Academic mobility and migration can also be described as generational (Blanden, Gregg & Machin 2005), seen in repeated migration experiences and practices of switching countries and cultures over several generations (Hoffman 2009; Hugo 2013); this is sometimes labelled as 'circular' to indicate frequent movements between the origin and destination countries (Hugo 2013; Kim 2009, 2010; Vertovec 2007). Return migration is usually distinguished from circular migration, though there is in reality little difference between them (Hugo 2013; Lee & Kuzhabekova 2018); even 'permanent' migration can include continued movement between countries for prolonged periods. The directions of academic mobility flows often depend not only on political and economic forces, but also on the academics' agency and their professional networks (Kim 2008, 2009). Kim (2009, 2010) explains further that the practices of return and circular migration are becoming typical patterns of transnational academic mobility.

### Brain drain vs brain circulation

The effect of 'brain drain', 'brain gain', and 'brain circulation' on the performance and quality of scholarship is important for universities (Nunn & Price 2005; Kim 2010). Brain drain occurs when well-educated, talented citizens leave their home country for extended (possibly permanent) periods abroad for improved conditions of living and professional development, including further research and/or academic work opportunities. The number of people leaving their country of residence greatly depends on the sending and hosting countries' political, economic and social profile (Bentley, Coates, Dobson, Goedegebuure, & Meek 2013; Fahey & Kenway 2010; Robertson 2006): most often developing countries or those with repressive regimes lose their most educated people to more industrialised Western countries. Therefore, brain drain may threaten the stability of some countries as it often contributes to slowing their growth by making already wealthy economies richer at the expense of the poorer countries (Saxenian 2005; Tanner 2005; Todaro 1985). It is thus often assumed that brain drain benefits only the host country, while the source country is left to deal with the loss of highly skilled human resources and economic losses (Lee & Kuzhabekova 2018; Saxenian 2002, 2005; Tanner 2005). In contrast, a concept of 'brain gain' has been used to describe the benefits that highly skilled migration brings to the host country. A number of studies in academic mobility emphasise either a brain drain or gain (Froese 2012; Kim 2016; Richardson & McKenna 2003); however, in an era of universal labour mobility and global changes, the concept of 'brain drain' is being progressively replaced by the concepts of 'brain circulation' and 'talent flow' (Carr, Inkson & Thorn 2005), as the old pattern of one-way flows of people, goods and knowledge is replaced by more complex and decentralised two-way transnational flows of skills, knowledge and technology (Bentley *et al.* 2013; Kim 2009, 2010; Saxenian 2005). More than that: while some scholars argue that academic mobility is one of the factors intensifying brain drain (Carr *et al.* 2005), other scholars suggest that brain drain could be reduced by transnational academic mobility and circular migration (Hugo 2013).

Universities and academic disciplines are profoundly affected by all of these types of mobility. There is a perception that it is easy for highly educated and professionally successful people to move across borders because they possess the relevant competencies for cross-border communication and exchange (Faist 2013), so that "now academe is one of the most internationally mobile of all professions" (Bentley *et al.* 2013:9). However, not every academic or student is able or wants to become mobile, as academic mobility is influenced not only by national and international political and economic relations of power (Kim 2009), but also by personal and professional constraints that potentially limit individual agency (Lee & Kuzabekhova 2018; Kuzhabekova & Lee 2018). Nevertheless, every year thousands of students and academics move between cities and countries, with a range of push and pull factors stimulating this process. As a result of all this movement, we see more and more academics and students who regard themselves as global citizens. Regardless of where research students and supervisors are located, their academic work is necessarily global in that, however specifically local the topic, the project must engage with the theories and discourses circulating in its discipline internationally.

An important factor in facilitating academic mobility has been the advancement in digital technologies that allow for communication across time and space. As academics take up opportunities for mobility, whether they are pushed or pulled into the various types of mobility outlined above, the digital academy both promotes and demands their continuing connections at a distance. The affordances of digital technology open up possibilities for undertaking research from different geographic locations whilst maintaining communication with collaborators in other parts of the globe. Conversely, this opportunity also seems to bring with it the obligation to use the available technology and maintain existing connections while developing new relationships too, regardless of whether academics are engaged in temporary or long-term migration, brain drain, gain or circulation.

## WHAT DO THESE TWO INFLUENCES MEAN FOR SUPERVISION?

What does the intersection of mobility and the digital mean for the supervision of research degrees? Is remote supervision an increasingly attractive (that is, cheaper, less disruptive) proposition, or does it result in a minimal learning experience? What new challenges face supervisors and students in terms of their mobility within the digital academy? This is not a new concern in doctoral education. In 1995, Evans and Green articulated their concerns regarding the intersection of postgraduate pedagogy and distance education. By approaching this pedagogy from the perspective of 'performance', they highlight that the 'teaching' that occurs at doctoral level is not simply instructional; rather, there is a whole level of mentoring and facilitation that relies on how supervisors conduct themselves, how they 'say and do' being a researcher or an academic – that is, they demonstrate the disposition of being 'a researcher' (Evans & Green 1995). However, the 'absent presence' of the supervisor who is not physically co-located with the candidate requires some further mediation if this transformative aspect of doctoral education is to be achieved.

The range of technologies available and their level of sophistication have improved dramatically since Evans and Green first explored this aspect of doctoral education. Much of the literature on remote supervision focuses on the student experience and assumes this situation arises because PhD candidates study off-campus. However, by attending to the extra dimension of supervisor mobility, we see the challenges and solutions posed by supervisors themselves also being off campus. When supervisors move to new universities, sometimes in other countries, doctoral students can feel abandoned, even 'orphaned' (Wisker & Robinson 2013); often, though, supervisors maintain contact with students, acting as external co-supervisors from a distance. Thus, supervisors are not necessarily the stable point at the centre of the compass with students orbiting about them – they too may be on the move.

The following section considers what remains much the same and what is new and different for the supervision of doctoral candidates in today's mobile, digital environment, testing the contention that "the qualities of an effective supervisor remain the same regardless of whether the student is on or off campus" (Gray & Crosta 2018:10); it appears that 'the dancers have changed, but the drums are the same'.

### Standard supervision practice includes digital communication

Maor and Currie (2017) detail the range of digital technologies commonly used in supervision. It is clear from their study that many of the practices of contemporary supervision are already conducted online: email communication is used to arrange meetings and to pass on useful information, such as links to relevant websites and blogs, between face-to-face meetings; candidates often record supervision meetings on their smart phones; research groups and individuals share EndNote libraries; topics are debated and relevant information and links are circulated via Twitter; research data and documents are held in Google Drive, Dropbox or a university's equivalent cloud-based storage; Google docs and SharePoint are frequently used for collaborative research writing; online forums and discussion boards are established for communication between members of a postgraduate cohort. With the appearance of Covid-19 and the consequent *restriction* of mobility experienced by many researchers in 2020, we have seen how remote supervision relies on these technologies – and how effective they can be in many cases. Thus, it would seem that the blended learning practices recommended by De Beer and Mason (2009) are by now well entrenched for many supervisors, regardless of their geographic distance from doctoral candidates.

Some of this communication between supervisors and candidates is conducted via spoken word, but much is written, often asynchronously. In this respect, it offers a useful record of conversations and developing ideas (Andrew 2012). But such written communication also requires skilful execution to minimise the misunderstandings that can arise in the absence of tone of voice and body language to support the message. We know how valuable it is for supervisors to provide both written and verbal feedback on writing (Can & Walker 2011; Lee & Murray 2015; Paré 2011). This would suggest, then, that both supervisors and candidates need to attune their writing skills carefully to accommodate the affective aspects of research communication and organisation. It also draws attention to the importance of including synchronous verbal communication in supervision pedagogy, such as video-facilitated meetings. Nevertheless, regular written communication online can provide valuable opportunities for candidates to practise articulating their ideas, reflecting on argument structure and word choice, revising and editing for clarity. This practice also has the potential to break down reluctance to write about research for the thesis – writing, in this way, can become normalised.

### Relationship with supervisor

Until now, much of the literature on doctoral supervision has focused on the importance of the candidate's relationship with their supervisor as key to successful outcomes (see Gray & Crosta 2018, for an overview of the literature on this topic). Establishing and maintaining that relationship is likely to take more active work at a distance than it does in person, when the possibility of popping into the office or enjoying informal chats in the tea room is removed from the equation. Distance supervision requires deliberate and conscious efforts in "negotiation, interpretation and reciprocity" (Andrew 2012:51).

We see a shift in the supervisor-candidate relationship when conducted online. Importantly, the digital environment promotes a more participatory approach to supervision (Maor & Currie 2017:3), including candidates training supervisors in the use of digital technologies. Such moves towards less hierarchical, more reciprocal relationships between supervisors and candidates (Andrew 2012) are to be encouraged in an environment where candidates bring enormously diverse work and life experience to their projects (Harbon & England 2006; Hutchings 2017).

### Absent supervisor

When faced with the physical absence of the supervisor, two critical elements come into play: firstly, the contact between supervisor and candidate requires much more active structuring; and secondly, more active community building is needed.

#### Structure

The doctoral education literature reports on the introduction of structured programmes for PhD candidates in situations where the focus had previously been only on the research project. This innovation stems from some of the professional doctorates, particularly the EdD (Lai 2015; McKenna 2017). While some of these structures require specific coursework, others focus on meeting milestones; many require regular meetings between candidate and supervisor to ensure continual monitoring and input into the research. Such measures are designed partly to address attrition rates (Lai 2015) and partly in recognition of the diverse educational and research backgrounds of today's PhD candidates.

A danger in distance supervision is the temptation for supervisors to ignore their candidates' needs when not directly in front of them; more pressing and immediate concerns are likely to take centre stage when supervisors have moved into new institutions, possibly in different time zones and with many new demands and responsibilities. In these cases, supervision needs to be much more organised and planned (Andrew 2012). Meeting times must be scheduled ahead and can't be left to the more random chance that corridor and tearoom conversations can rely on.

#### Belonging vs isolation/disconnection

For some time now, digital communication has been employed to build connections between PhD candidates and their supervisors, as well as between candidates themselves (see, for example, Crossouard 2008; Donnelly 2013; Hutchings

2017). Synchronous and asynchronous discussion groups, mediated by written or verbal messages, are organised formally through the institution and informally by researchers seeking like-minded scholars online. For doctoral candidates working at a distance from their supervisors and peers, a structured programme of regular online interactions can provide an important antidote to the isolation and loneliness that come from working alone as 'long-distance researchers' (Andrew 2012; Gannon-Leary, Fontainha & Bent 2011). Importantly, such communities can facilitate peer relationships between candidates (Pilbeam & Denyer 2009; Pyhältö, Stubb & Lonka 2009; Shacham & Od-Cohen 2009), creating opportunities to share knowledge of university systems and the informal curriculum of doctoral studies.

Online supervision communities can accommodate the needs of both team supervision and group or cohort supervision when members are dispersed through numerous locations. For this to be effective, however, supervisors need to be capable online facilitators to ensure participants feel safe to explore ideas openly in the group, rather than be criticised or set in competition against each other (Donnelly 2013; Hutchings 2017). When handled well, online meetings create a sense of trust and belonging for all members of the research group – candidates and supervisors alike.

It is also possible for online forums to promote the concept of PhD candidates as co-creators of knowledge rather than merely consumers of expert knowledge (Lai 2015; Maor & Currie 2017). A connectivist perspective reminds us that in online communication "knowledge is actuated through the process of a learner connecting to and feeding information into a learning community" (Donnelly 2013:359). Consistent with the less hierarchical, more reciprocal relationships between supervisors and candidates mentioned above, the wider reach of online researcher communities can promote independence and confidence in candidates. Tweedie, Clark, Johnson and Kay (2013) note how powerfully sustaining extra-institutional online forums can be for doctoral candidates. One effect, then, of academic mobility might be that doctoral candidates are positioned to develop their independence as researchers more readily than traditional practices of one-on-one, face-to-face supervision tend to do.

Enculturation into the research community and the discipline more broadly has long been a key outcome of doctoral education (see, for example, Gardner 2007; Lee 2008). In the past, this has taken place in person through interactions on campus and at conferences and scholarly meetings. Online forums now facilitate this learning (Maor & Currie 2017; Maor, Ensor & Fraser 2016), so candidates are no longer restricted to finding like-minded researchers in their shared physical space. Wider networks are now readily available to candidates, regardless of their geographic location; interaction with these online communities should be actively encouraged as a core supervision pedagogy. This fits comfortably with a greater focus on the PhD producing a researcher rather than only a thesis (Grant 2003).

Supervision, like other academic and intellectual activity, is increasingly employing digital technologies, for both those who are physically present and those who work (temporarily or more permanently) at a distance. This allows for different kinds of relationships to evolve between PhD candidates and their supervisors, their peers and also others in their discipline. Although this potentially takes pressure off the supervisor, expectations around the intensive working relationship between candidate and supervisor continue to rely on concepts originating in the traditional one-on-one, dyadic mode of supervision (see, for example, Benmore 2016; Jones 2013; Lee & Green 2009). Despite the ability to draw on advice and feedback from multiple sources (from team supervision through to writing groups and language and literacy experts), there appears to be a continuing reliance on 'my supervisor', at least in much of the existing research and publication on the topic of supervision.

## EFFECTS OF PHYSICAL MOBILITY OF ACADEMICS

Alongside the ubiquity of technology lie expectations that academics will move to wherever the work is located. Online accessibility can seem to erase national boundaries, allowing academics to maintain supervision responsibilities across institutions and across countries. However, discussion is emerging (Krockow 2019; Maor & Currie 2017; Moss 2018; Shepherd 2018) that explores how expectations around mobility are taking a toll on academic staff and supervisors: the human cost of this mobility has previously been mostly overlooked, especially in the discourses that advise early career researchers on how to obtain a satisfying academic career with a stable, tenure-track position.

Maor and Currie (2017:10-11) caution that the affordances of digital technologies can have a detrimental effect on supervisors, particularly in relation to their availability to cater to students' needs. Concerns about being present to the PhD candidate must be tempered by maintaining boundaries and managing expectations about response times to queries. This is the case for those on the ground, too, but can become heightened in the face of academic mobility and supervisor 'absence'.

The mental health and general well-being of researchers is increasingly being highlighted and serious attention paid to the unrealistic demands of the academy on its workers (Guthrie, Lichten, Van Belle, Ball, Knack & Hofman 2017; Krockow 2019; Shepherd 2018). These pressures are amplified in the face of expectations around mobility (Krockow 2019). As well as concerns around psychological well-being, personal relationships and family planning come under intense pressure when academics move about repeatedly. Living in new cities or migrating to new countries takes a toll on the ability to maintain friendships and build strong relationships with life partners; attempting to raise children at a distance from existing networks is an added challenge for those who do manage to form partnerships. On top of these emotional costs are the direct financial costs of relocation (moving house, setting up anew) and the lost productivity caused by the disruptions of learning to negotiate new institutions, cities, countries.

The strains of running family life across vast distances and time zones, and the long commutes that are increasingly common in some parts of the world (Moss 2019) are finally being acknowledged as harmful to both individuals and the education they are able to provide. These work habits apply not only to those working in the 'gig economy'; they are also becoming part of the lives of tenured staff who now move around more than previously in the form of 'temporary migration' for various reasons such as promotion or attempts to be closer to family members.

## NEW PRACTICES IN SUPERVISION

The discussion above points to the ways in which academic mobility opens up spaces for support in doctoral studies beyond the traditional supervisor-candidate dyad. Given the physical absence of the supervisor, candidates seek broader support, from peers and also from other professionals in the doctoral space, particularly from researcher developers and writing teachers (Guerin, Aitchison & Carter 2019). These services have been available for some time, both in person and online, within institutions and beyond. As academic mobility continues to move researchers around the world, so too the reliance on supervisors as the sole source of development increasingly moves to incorporate other influences available through digital technologies, facilitating more collaborative pedagogies.

As the motivations for undertaking a PhD and the outcomes of doctoral education continue to change in relation to academic mobility and digital technology, so too supervision practices continue to evolve. The value of providing informal and extended learning opportunities linked to community building is increasingly acknowledged as we see evidence that much of the 'hidden curriculum' of doctoral education is embodied in peers rather than supervisors (Elliot, Baumfield, Reid & Makara 2016). Pressures on academic staff to achieve more and do it faster in the 'accelerated academy' (Carrigan 2017) mean that even geographically present supervisors are less available to PhD candidates than they might have been in the past; temporary or long-term mobility exacerbates this inaccessibility. Fortunately, how and where doctoral candidates learn to become researchers is by no means restricted to only the information provided by supervisors.

Digital technologies are mobilised to build collaborative research cultures online. Rather than leaving this to chance, however, supervisors and candidates are recognising the need to actively create cohorts for mutual learning and support. We have known for some time about the detrimental effects of the loneliness and isolation experienced by many PhD candidates (Gannon-Leary et al. 2011). Research has identified the importance of connection and a sense of belonging to aid social integration of candidates, which in turn leads to persistence and eventually completion (Rockinson-Szapkiw, Spaulding & Spaulding 2016).

## CONCLUSION: DO WE NEED A NEW MODEL OF SUPERVISION?

Even though there is strong evidence that the relationship with supervisors is a key to successful doctoral experience, should we place much greater emphasis on team supervision rather than attaching to 'my supervisor'? The highly personalised approach may be undermining the confidence of candidates who feel dependent on that apprenticeship model. For example, the mobility of supervisors moving between institutions and countries can lead to disruptions in supervision that candidates find distressing. Models of team supervision can readily operate on less hierarchical principles wherein all supervisors are regarded as equally involved in overseeing the project and supporting the candidate (Guerin, Green & Bastalich 2011). Setting up expectations from the outset that a researcher will be raised by a 'village' of researchers, peers, writing specialists, disciplinary experts and knowledge workers may serve both supervisors and candidates much better. These professionals may be located within the university or externally in other institutions or organisations. For those fortunate enough to have efficient, reliable internet access, that village can be found online in today's digital academy.

Just because we are in the habit of thinking that a PhD requires 'supervision' and 'a supervisor' as we know them, does not mean it will always be this way. After all, there is already a range of people who support doctoral candidates, such as researcher developers, academic writing teachers, administrative staff and peers (Guerin, Aitchison & Carter 2019). Perhaps institutional structures could recognise and formally invite these stakeholders to contribute their knowledge and expertise. By shifting the focus in candidature towards the broader research community rather than only the supervisor-candidate relationship, we can prepare novice researchers for resilient, collaborative mindsets that are likely to enhance their success both during and on completion of their research degrees.

As the purpose and motivations to undertake a PhD continue to shift, opportunities to reimagine how supervision and support are provided to educate the next generation of scholars and researchers also begin to appear. The English metaphysical poet John Donne's conceit of the compass with a fixed point is no longer a fit model for the purposes of supervision: "Thy firmness makes my circle just, / And makes me end where I begun". Rather than a single point of reference ('my supervisor'), candidates might be better served by a concept of 'my PhD research community/ network' with themselves as the sole continuity through the research journey. That research community will require careful positioning to ensure that candidates are properly supported by clear institutional structures as they transform into independent researchers.

## REFERENCES

Altbach P, Androushchak G, Kuzminov Y, Yudkevich M & Reisberg L (eds.). 2013. *The global future of higher education and the academic profession: The BRICs and the United States*. Palgrave Macmillan. https://doi.org/10.1057/9780230369795

Andrew M. 2012. Supervising doctorates at a distance: Three trans-Tasman stories. *Quality Assurance in Education*, 20(1):42-53. https://doi.org/10.1108/09684881211198239

Bauder H. 2012. The international mobility of academics: A labour market perspective. *International Migration*, 53(1):83-96. https://doi.org/10.1111/j.1468-2435.2012.00783.x

Benmore A. 2016. Boundary management in doctoral supervision: How supervisors negotiate roles and role transitions throughout the supervisory journey. *Studies in Higher Education*, 41(7):1251-1264. https://doi.org/10.1080/03075079.2014.967203

Bentley P, Coates H, Dobson I, Goedegebuure L & Meek V. 2013. *Job satisfaction around the academic world* (Vol. 7). Dordrecht: Springer Netherlands.

Bilecen B & Van Mol C. 2017. Introduction: International academic mobility and inequalities. *Journal of Ethnic and Migration Studies*, 43(8):1241-1255. https://doi.org/10.1080/1369183X.2017.1300225

Blanden J, Gregg P & Machin S. 2005. *Intergenerational mobility in Europe and North America. Report supported by the Sutton Trust*. Centre for Economic Performance, London: London School of Economics.

Can G & Walker A. 2011. A model for doctoral students' perceptions and attitudes toward written feedback for academic writing. *Research in Higher Education*, 52(5):508-536. https://doi.org/10.1007/s11162-010-9204-1

Carr S, Inkson K & Thorn K. 2005. From global careers to talent flow: Reinterpreting 'brain drain'. *Journal of World Business*, 40(4):386-398. https://doi.org/10.1016/j.jwb.2005.08.006

Carrigan M. 2017. *An introduction to the accelerated academy: by me and @Filvos*. February 10. https://bit.ly/2P9FYXC

Christie H. 2007. Higher education and spatial (im)mobility: Nontraditional students and living at home. *Environment and Planning A: Economy and Space*, 39(10):2445-2463. https://doi.org/10.1068/a38361

Crossouard B. 2008. Developing alternative models of doctoral supervision with online formative assessment. *Studies in Continuing Education*, 30(1):51-67. https://doi.org/10.1080/01580370701841549

De Beer M & Mason RB. 2009. Using a blended approach to facilitate postgraduate supervision. *Innovations in Education and Teaching International*, 46(2):213-226. https://doi.org/10.1080/14703290902843984

De Wit H. 2019. *Intelligent internationalization in higher education: Evolving concepts and trends*. Intelligent Internationalization: Brill Sense. 189-198.

Dekker R, De Grip A & Heijke H. 2002. The effects of training and overeducation on career mobility in a segmented labour market. *International Journal of Manpower*, 23(2):106-125.

Dervin F. 2011. *Analysing the consequences of academic mobility and migration*. Newcastle upon Tyne, UK: Cambridge Scholars Publishing.

Donnelly R. 2013. Enabling connections in postgraduate supervision for an applied eLearning professional development programme. *International Journal for Academic Development*, 18(4):356-370. https://doi.org/10.1080/1360144X.2013.784873

Egron-Polak E. 2017. *Academic mobility in higher education worldwide – Where are we? Where might we go in the future?* Paris: International Association of Universities.

Egron-Polak E & Hudson R. 2014. *Internationalization of higher education: Growing expectations, fundamental values*. IAU 4th Global Survey. Paris: International Association of Universities.

Elliott A & Urry J. 2010. *Mobile lives*. New York & London: Routledge.

Elliot DL, Baumfield V, Reid K & Makara KA. 2016. *Hidden treasure: Successful international doctoral students who found and harnessed the hidden curriculum*. Oxford Review of Education, 42(6):733-748. https://doi.org/10.1080/03054985.2016.1229664

Evans T & Green B. 1995. November. Dancing at a distance? Postgraduate studies, 'supervision', and distance education. In: *Proceedings (electronic) Australian Association for Research in Education Conference*. Hobart, 26-30 November.

Fahey J & Kenway J. 2010. International academic mobility: Problematic and possible paradigms. *Discourse: Studies in the Cultural Politics of Education*, 31(5).

Faist T. 2013. The mobility turn: A new paradigm for the social sciences? *Ethnic and Racial Studies*, 36(11):1637-1646. https://doi.org/10.1080/01419870.2013.812229

Froese F. 2012. Motivation and adjustment of self-initiated expatriates: the case of expatriate academics in South Korea. *The International Journal of Human Resource Management*, 23(6):1095-1112. https://doi.org/10.1080/09585192.2011.561220

Gannon-Leary P, Fontainha E & Bent M. 2011. The loneliness of the long distance researcher. *Library Hi Tech*, 29(3):455-469. https://doi.org/10.1108/07378831111174422

Gardner SK. 2007. "I heard it through the grapevine": Doctoral student socialization in chemistry and history. *Higher Education*, 54(5):723-740. https://doi.org/10.1007/s10734-006-9020-x

Grant B. 2003. Mapping the pleasures and risks of supervision. *Discourse*, 24:175-190. https://doi.org/10.1080/01596300303042

Gray MA & Crosta L. 2018. New perspectives in online doctoral supervision: A systematic literature review. *Studies in Continuing Education*, 41(2):173-190. https://doi.org/10.1080/0158037X.2018.1532405

Guerin C, Aitchison C & Carter S. 2019. Digital and distributed: Learning and teaching doctoral writing through social media. *Teaching in Higher Education*. https://doi.org/10.1080/13562517.2018.1557138

Guerin C, Green I & Bastalich W. 2011. Big love: Managing a team of research supervisors. In: V Kumar & A Lee (eds.), *Doctoral education in international context: Connecting local, regional & global perspectives*. Malaysia: UPM Press. 138-153.

Guthrie S, Lichten CA, Van Belle J, Ball S, Knack A & Hofman J. 2017. *Understanding mental health in the research environment: A rapid evidence assessment*. Santa Monica, CA: RAND Corporation. https://bit.ly/3x4SLM9

Harbon L & England N. 2006. The cultural practice of research higher degree supervision over distance: A case in progress. *University of Sydney Papers in TESOL*, 1:87-107.

Haveman R & Smeeding T. 2006. The role of higher education in social mobility. *The Future of Children*, 16(2)125-150.

Hoffman DM. 2009. Changing academic mobility patterns and international migration: What will academic mobility mean in the 21st century? *Journal of Studies in International Education*, 13(3):347-364. https://doi.org/10.1177/1028315308321374

Hugo G. 2009. Issues and options for enhancing the international mobility of researchers-an Australian perspective. *Omani Journal of Applied Science*, 1(1):9-53.

Hugo G. 2013. What we know about circular migration and enhanced mobility. *Migration Policy Institute*, 7:1-10. https://bit.ly/2P2J0N5

Hutchings M. 2017. Improving doctoral support through group supervision: Analysing face-to-face and technology-mediated strategies for nurturing and sustaining scholarship. *Studies in Higher Education*, 42(3):533-550. https://doi.org/10.1080/03075079.2015.1058352

Jones M. 2013. Issues in doctoral studies – Forty years of journal discussion: Where have we been and where are we going? In: E Cohen & E Boyd (eds.), *Proceedings of the Informing Science and Information Technology Education Conference 2013*. Informing Science Institute. 83-104. https://bit.ly/3tzCVXC

Kim SK. 2016. Western faculty 'flight risk' at a Korean university and the complexities of internationalization in Asian higher education. *Comparative Education*, 52(1):78-90.

Kim T. 2008. Transnational academic mobility in a global knowledge economy. In: D Epstein, R Boden, R Deem, F Rizvi & S Wright (eds.), *The world yearbook of education 2008: Geographies of knowledge and geometries of power: Framing the future of higher education*. London: Routledge. 319-337.

Kim T. 2009. Shifting patterns of transnational academic mobility: A comparative and historical approach. *Comparative Education*, 45:387-403. https://doi.org/10.1080/03050060903184957

Kim T. 2010. Transnational academic mobility, knowledge, and identity capital. *Discourse: Studies in the Cultural Politics of Education*, 31(5):577-591. https//:doi.org/10.1080/01596306.2010.516939

Kim T. 2017. Academic mobility, transnational identity capital, and stratification under conditions of academic capitalism. *Higher Education*, 73(6):981-997. https://doi.org/10.1007/s10734-017-0118-0

Kim T & Brooks R. 2012. *Internationalisation, mobile academics, and knowledge creation in universities: A comparative analysis*. SRHE Research Final Report. https://bit.ly/3gtEEtJ

Krockow E. 2019. *Don't let your academic career determine your every move – Should early career researchers be expected to relocate regularly in order to land a permanent job?* LSE Impact Blog. 21 March. https://bit.ly/3anq7vM

Kuzhabekova A & Lee J. 2018. Relocation decision of international faculty in Kazakhstan. *Journal of Studies in International Education*, 22(5):414-433. https://doi.org/10.1177/1028315318773147

Lai K-W. 2015. Knowledge construction in online learning communities: A case study of a doctoral course. *Studies in Higher Education*, 40(4):561-579. https://doi.org/10.1080/03075079.2013.831402

Lee A. 2008. How are doctoral students supervised? Concepts of doctoral research supervision. *Studies in Higher Education*, 33(3):267-281. https://doi.org/10.1080/03075070802049202

Lee A & Green B. 2009. Supervision as metaphor. *Studies in Higher Education*, 34(6):615-630. https://doi.org/10.1080/03075070802597168

Lee A & Murray R. 2015. Supervising writing: Helping postgraduate students develop as researchers. *Innovations in Education and Teaching International*, 52(5):558-570. https://doi.org/10.1080/14703297.2013.866329

Lee J & Kuzhabekova A. 2018. Reverse flow in academic mobility from core to periphery: Motivations of international faculty working in Kazakhstan. *Higher Education*, 76(2):369-386. https://doi.org/10.1007/s10734-017-0213-2

Maor D & Currie JK. 2017. The use of technology in postgraduate supervision pedagogy in two Australian universities. *International Journal of Educational Technology in Higher Education*, 14(1):1-15. https://doi.org/10.1186/s41239-017-0046-1

Maor D, Ensor JD & Fraser BJ. 2016. Doctoral supervision in virtual spaces: A review of research of web-based tools to develop collaborative supervision. *Higher Education Research & Development*, 35(1):172-188. https://doi.org/10.1080/07294360.2015.1121206

Marginson S. 2016. The worldwide trend to high participation higher education: Dynamics of social stratification in inclusive systems. *Higher Education*, 72(4):413-434. https://doi.org/10.1007/s10734-016-0016-x

McKenna S. 2017. Crossing conceptual thresholds in doctoral communities. *Innovations in Education and Teaching International*, 54(5):458-466. https://doi.org/10.1080/14703297.2016.1155471

Moss R. 2019. Commuting: A life sentence for academics. *Times Higher Education*. 28 February. https://bit.ly/3tzDH6Y

Nunn AE & Price S. 2005. *The 'Brain Drain': Academic and skilled migration to the UK and its impacts on Africa*. Project Report. Report to the AUT and NATFHE. https://bit.ly/3gqkpgG [Accessed 18 May 2020].

Paré A. 2011. Speaking of writing: Supervisory feedback and the dissertation. In: L McAlpine & C Amundsen (eds.), *Doctoral Education: Research-Based Strategies for Doctoral Students, Supervisors and Administrators*. Springer, Dordrecht. https://doi.org/10.1007/978-94-007-0507-4_4

Pietsch T. 2010. Wandering scholars? Academic mobility and the British World, 1850-1940. *Journal of Historical Geography*, 36(4):377-387. https://doi.org/10.1016/j.jhg.2010.03.002

Pilbeam C & Denyer D. 2009. Lone scholar or community member? The role of student networks in doctoral education in a UK management school. *Studies in Higher Education*, 34(3):301-318. https://doi.org/10.1080/03075070802597077

Pyhältö K, Stubb J & Lonka K. 2009. Developing scholarly communities as learning environments for doctoral students. *International Journal for Academic Development*, 14(3):221-232, https://doi.org/10.1080/13601440903106551

Richardson J & McKenna S. 2003. International experience and academic careers. *Personnel Review*, 32(6):774-795. https://doi.org/10.1108/00483480310498710

Robertson S. 2006. Brain drain, brain gain and brain circulation. *Globalisation, Societies and Education*, 4(1):1-5. https://doi.org/10.1080/14767720600554908

Robertson S. 2010. Critical response to special section: International academic mobility. *Discourse: Studies in the Cultural Politics of Education*, 31(5):641-647. https://doi.org/10.1080/01596306.2010.516945

Rockinson-Szapkiw AJ, Spaulding LS & Spaulding MT. 2016. Identifying significant integration and institutional factors that predict online doctoral persistence. *The Internet and Higher Education*, 31:101-112. https://doi.org/10.1016/j.iheduc.2016.07.003

Rumbley LE & De Wit H. 2019. *International faculty mobility: Crucial and understudied*. Intelligent Internationalization: Brill Sense. 33-36.

Saxenian A. 2002. Silicon Valley's new immigrant high-growth entrepreneurs. *Economic Development Quarterly*, 16(1):20-31. https://doi.org/10.1177/0891242402016001003

Saxenian A. 2005. From brain drain to brain circulation: Transnational communities and regional upgrading in India and China. Studies in Comparative International Development, 40(2):35-61. https://doi.org/10.1007/BF02686293

Schreurs B, Verjans S & Van Petegem W. 2006. November. *Towards sustainable virtual mobility in higher education institutions*. EADTU Annual Conference Proceedings. https://bit.ly/3v5hldP

Shacham M & Od-Cohen Y. 2009. Rethinking PhD learning incorporating communities of practice. *Innovations in Education and Teaching International*, 46(3):279-292. https://doi.org/10.1080/14703290903069019

Shepherd A. 2018. *Stressed, depressed, unexpressed*. Linau Nobel Laureate Meetings. 5 June. https://bit.ly/3v7YFKj

Tanner A. 2005. Brain drain and beyond: Returns and remittances of highly skilled migrants. *Global Migration Perspectives*, 24(1):1-13.

Taylor P, Hoyler M & Evans D. 2008. A geohistorical study of 'the rise of modern science': Mapping scientific practice through urban networks, 1500-1900. *Minerva*, 46(4):391.

Teichler U. 2015. Academic mobility and migration: What we know and what we do not know. *European Review*, 23(S1):S6-S37. https://doi.org/10.1017/S1062798714000787

Todaro M. 1985. *Economic development in the Third World*. New York: Longman Publishing Group.

Tweedie MG, Clark S, Johnson RC & Kay DW. 2013. The 'dissertation marathon' in doctoral distance education. *Distance Education*, 34(3):379-390. http://dx.doi.org/10.1080/01587919.2013.835778

Universities Australia. 2019. Higher education: Facts and figures. July. https://bit.ly/3ducoVX [Accessed 18 May 2020].

Varghese N. 2008. *Globalization of higher education and cross-border student mobility*. Paris: UNESCO, International Institute for Educational Planning.

Vertovec S. 2007. *Circular migration: The way forward in global policy?* International Migration Institute, Oxford: IMI. https://bit.ly/3x9eKkO [Accessed 18 May 2020].

Wisker G & Robinson G. 2013. Doctoral 'orphans': Nurturing and supporting the success of postgraduates who have lost their supervisors. *Higher Education Research & Development*, 32(2):300-313. https://doi.org/10.1080/07294360.2012.657160

Yudkevich M, Altbach PG & Rumbley LE (eds.). 2016. *International faculty in higher education: Comparative perspectives on recruitment, integration, and impact*. New York and London: Routledge.

# THE IMPLICATIONS OF DOCTORAL MOBILITY FOR DOCTORAL PROGRAMME DESIGN AND SUPERVISION

Rebekah Smith McGloin

## INTRODUCTION AND OVERVIEW

This chapter explores the trends and flows in academic mobility, the policy imperatives that drive it and the personal experiences of doctoral researchers who undertake it. We use the findings of a 2018 survey of UK doctoral researchers to examine the endogenous and exogenous enablers and constraints to doctoral mobility, and we explore the value of mobility to the respondents in terms of career development and knowledge development. The chapter concludes with some thoughts on how the policy discourse around international mobility and the individual experience thereof intersect and how funders, higher education institutions, graduate schools or doctoral colleges and supervisory teams might mitigate the challenges and risk identified and amplify the positive impacts in order to better support the doctoral community.

Against a backdrop of anti-globalisation in many parts of the world[1] – with ethno-nationalist and anti-immigrant sentiments popular amongst supporters of Trump and Brexit, the rise of polarising and controversial figures in leadership positions in Brazil and Italy, and anti-immigrant policies in Australia, moving to a different country as a doctoral candidate or early-career researcher must be an increasingly daunting prospect. Yet, policy-makers, funders, education researchers and research managers tell us that international collaboration, often manifest as researcher mobility amongst

---

1   The polling company YouGov found that, while respondents in France, the US and the UK were least likely to see globalisation as "a force for good", >70% of respondents in East and Southeast Asia believed that it had been. https://bit.ly/3n08qaT. Both the Chinese president and the Indian prime minister have spoken out in support of globalisation at consecutive Davos meetings in 2017 and 2018.

doctoral candidates and early-career researchers, is vital if we are to find creative solutions to the global challenges that the world faces right now on issues such as global warming, energy and food security.

The Hannover Recommendations 2019[2] are the findings of a group of more than 160 experts from around the world, education researchers together with leaders of doctoral education, early career researchers and funding agency representatives, who met at an international conference in Hannover to discuss the topic 'Forces and forms in doctoral education worldwide'. In a defiant stance against the populist politics of recent years, these recommendations foreground inclusivity in doctoral education and mobility in a variety of forms. The first principle of the recommendations is "the establishment of a joint value system rooted in the universal principles of the United Nations human rights charter, based on respect for the individual, for the equilibrium of knowledges from south, north, east and west – including indigenous knowledges in an "ecology of knowledges". Fundamental to this ecology of knowledges is the ability for researchers at all levels to exchange ideas and to find, share and grow new knowledges. A necessary means of doing this – and a third principle in the recommendations – is a world-wide circulation of scholars to ensure a more balanced distribution of talent around the globe. Particularly at doctoral and early career researcher level it is noted that this community needs to acquire not only traditional academic research competencies and the breadth of professional skills but also the ability (and the opportunity) to work and function in multinational teams and multinational settings.

This reminds us of what Flores and Nerad (2012) refer to as a 'global village', which is needed to support the development of the next generation of researchers. Or, as the Hannover Recommendations (2019:4) put it, these skills and activities are necessary to develop the "original, responsible and ethical thinkers" who can meet the complex challenges our world faces in the 21st century. Researcher mobility is a key activity in realising Flores and Nerad's vision at the start of the decade and the objectives for improved doctoral education and a more inclusive and respectful research environment worldwide that is set out by the Hannover experts at the end.

We note that this particularly positive construct of the value to researchers and to research of a 'circulation of scholars' is distinct from other discourses that focus on the negative consequences of the unidirectional permanent flows of researchers from the Global South to the Global North, first explored as 'brain drain' in the seventies (Bhagwati & Hamada 1974; McCullock & Yellen 1977), following the

---

2  https://bit.ly/3eg1FxJ [Accessed 19 October 2019]

Royal Society report that measured the exodus of British scientists to the United States (USA) and Canada (Royal Society 1963). While the geopolitics of academic capitalism that privileges English and theoretical orientations from North America and Europe unquestionably persist, understandings of mobility have moved on to explore the complexity of types and timings of flow (Bekhradnia & Sastry 2005; Meyer 2001; Universities UK 2007). The picture of academic mobility summarised in the next section describes complex temporary flows of researchers around the globe as they progress through their career and new poles for doctoral training emerging outside of the North Atlantic nexus that has historically trained and retained many researchers from around the world.

## ACADEMIC MOBILITY IN NUMBERS

The numbers of researchers at all career stages who are internationally mobile are well documented. For instance, the Changing Academic Profession (CAP) Survey that was first administered in the early nineties and was followed up in 2007/2008 provided benchmark data from 19 countries[3] around the world. The survey reported from a completed effective sample of 800 at both 'junior' and 'senior' research positions. 38% of senior academic staff and 26% of their junior colleagues had spent at least a year in another country (Teichler, Arimoto & Cummings 2013).

Sugimoto, Robinson-Garcia, Murray, Yegros-Yegros, Costas and Larivière (2017) more recently categorised global flows around the world of researchers across different career stages by analysing bibliometric data based on the records of 14 million papers from nearly 16 million individuals. The study focused on multiple affiliations in different countries by highly published researchers[4] and therefore captured the most productive mobility activity. The authors found that 595 000 researchers (>4%) had at least two different international affiliations in that period.

Sugimoto et al. (2017) also highlighted patterns in mobility over the course of a research career. The authors characterised North America and Northern Europe as producers/cultivators of researchers who attracted many international doctoral and early-career researchers. Western Europe, Oceania, Southern Europe and sub-Saharan Africa were incubators where doctoral graduates from countries such as the USA and the UK moved to for postdoctoral positions; while Asia, Eastern Europe, North Africa and Latin America were recruiters of middle-career and more senior researchers.

---

3 The countries participating in this research were Canada, the USA, Finland, Germany, Italy, the Netherlands, Norway, Portugal, the UK, Australia, Japan, Korea, Hong Kong, Argentina, Brazil, Mexico, South Africa, China and Malaysia.

4 At least eight publications between 2008 and 2015.

At a national level, the effect in the United Kingdom (UK) of what Sugimoto terms global 'brain circulation' is that in the period 1996-2012, out of 266 000 active UK researchers 72% had published articles under a non-UK affiliation (i.e. had worked in that time for another research organisation outside of the UK) (Elsevier 2013, cited in Guthrie, Lichten, Corbett & Wooding 2017).[5] Moreover, the composition of the academic community in the UK continues to internationalise. In 2007/2008, 38 240 academic staff in the UK were non-UK nationals, representing 2% of the total UK academic population (HESA 2009). In 2017/2018 this figure was 66 420, representing 31.3% of UK academic staff (HESA 2019).

South Africa has a much smaller percentage of international academics (Sehoole, Adeyemo, Phatlane & Ojo 2019), resting at 7-10% between 2000 and 2010. While sector-specific data is not currently available for academic migration, Kaplan and Höppli (2017) suggest a steady increase in the outflow of skilled workers from South Africa, predominantly contributing to the South African diaspora in the UK, Australia, New Zealand, Canada and the USA in the latter part of this decade.

However, at doctoral level, South Africa appears to play a regional 'producer/cultivator' role (Sugimoto et al. 2017:31) for the African continent. In 2016, 44% of the 2 916 doctoral graduates in South Africa were international compared to 19.6% of the total from the other SADC countries and 20.2% of the total from other African countries (EUA 2018). This is similar in proportion to the UK, where the international PhD population has more than tripled from 1994/1995 to represent 47% (46 345 doctoral researchers) in 2017/2018.[6]

The comparator data below (Figure 7.1) have been compiled from a variety of national and international sources to provide further context for trends in international doctoral enrolments across a range of countries that produce large numbers of doctoral graduates in global terms. The data are shown within a nine-year window between 2008 and 2017 which accommodates the available data. It should be noted within this period there has also been an overall uplift in numbers of doctorate holders, growing by about 8% across OECD countries. Internationalisation of this growing doctoral community is visible across most countries except for the United States and Germany which show a very small decline.

---

5   For mobility survey findings across a range of countries, see Franzoni, Scellato and Stephan's (2012) review of findings from the 2009 GlobSci survey in the fields of biology, chemistry, materials, and earth and environmental sciences, across the following 16 countries: Australia, Belgium, Brazil, Canada, Denmark, France, Germany, India, Italy, Japan, the Netherlands, Spain, Sweden, Switzerland, the UK and the US.

6   Data referenced in Fernández-Zubieta, Marinelli and Pérez (2013) and updated with HESA (2019).

# CHAPTER 7 • THE IMPLICATIONS OF DOCTORAL MOBILITY FOR DOCTORAL PROGRAMME DESIGN ...

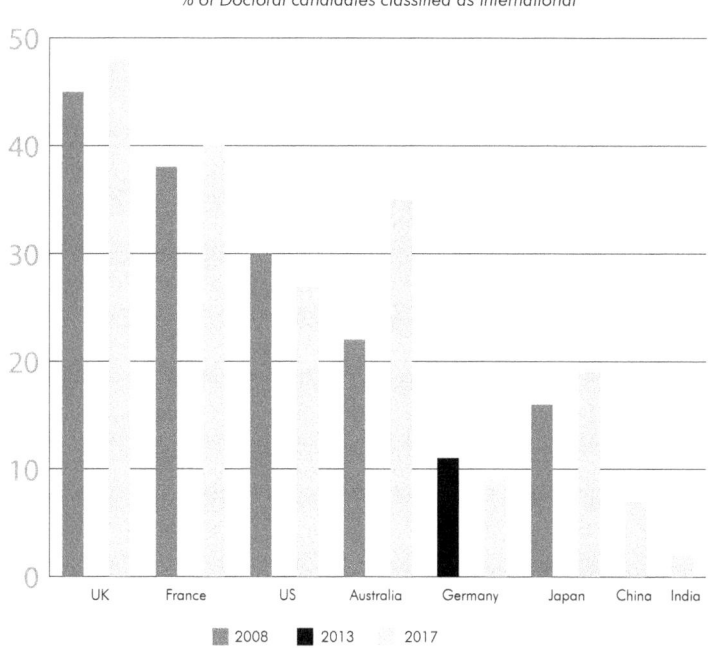

**FIGURE 7.1** Percentage of doctoral candidates classified as international[7]

* 'International' is used here as an umbrella term to represent doctoral candidates termed 'international', 'temporary visa holders', 'foreign', 'non-UK domiciled' or 'Bildungsauslandaender' by the national data-holders.

Despite the contemporary political turmoil and anti-immigrant sentiment of recent years it is clear that academic mobility is a key and growing feature of the global research system. The policy drivers for this will be summarised briefly in the next section.

---

7  Sources and definitions as follows: US – National Science Foundation, 2008 and 2017. 'Doctorates awarded' to 'Temporary visa holder'; France and Japan – Organisation for Economic Co-operation and Development (OECD), 2010 and 2019. 'International or foreign student enrolment as a percentage of total enrolment in tertiary education' at 'doctoral or equivalent'; UK – Higher Education Statistics agency. 'Postgraduate (research) non-UK domiciled'. Enrolled on a postgraduate research degree and measured in academic years 2007/2008 and 2017/2018; Australia - Australian Government Department of Education. 'International students' categorised as 'award course completions' for 'Doctorate by Research'; Germany - German Academic Exchange Service (Deutscher Akademischer Austauschdienst) 'Bildungsauslaender' enrolled on a PhD in the semesters within 2017 (across academic years); India – All India Survey on Higher Education 2017-2018. 'Foreign national students' enrolled on 'PhD and DPhil'; China – Ministry of Education the People's Republic of China. 'International enrolments as doctoral students'. Not including Hong Kong, Macau and Taiwan. Please note while the majority of national data-holders record enrolments, the data for the USA and Australia records awards.

### Policy context and 'imaginaries of mobility'

Within the European Research Area (ERA) mobility is considered a so-called 'fifth freedom' (European Commission 2007). It is one of the European Research Area's five priorities (Borrell-Damián, Morais & Smith 2009), ensuring a circulation of skills and ideas around the world in a so-called global research system in which the best scientists follow the best science and the best resources. Academic mobility is linked in policy to the creation of better, more dynamic networks, improved scientific performance, improved knowledge and technology transfer, enhanced productivity, and ultimately better economic and social welfare.

This policy focus has produced a series of initiatives designed to facilitate doctoral and early-career researcher mobility both within and from outside ERA. In many European countries doctoral candidates are formally employed and consequently the policy interventions have included removing obstacles to cross-border mobility of researchers and movement between public and private research centres; targeting specific actions to support researchers' careers and to encourage transnational, inter-sectoral and interdisciplinary mobility;[8] and creating joint infrastructure such as EURAXESS – a joint initiative of the European Commission and countries participating in the Eurpean Union's (EU) Framework Programme for Research – which manages a network of over 500 service centres in 40 European countries, offering advice and information about the employment and other rights and obligations of researchers and employers in Europe.

Outside of the European Union (EU), there are numerous governmental funding programmes for international doctoral candidates that support doctoral mobility. Examples of these are the United States' prestigious Fulbright postgraduate scholarships programme that operates in more than 160 countries; the UK's Commonwealth, Newton and Saltire scholarships; and China's 'Outstanding Foreign Student Scholarships' that are offered both at both national and regional level.

In addition, there are many developing countries that offer scholarship programmes for academic staff in their universities to undertake a PhD in a more developed research environment, for example the Indonesian government's '5 000 Doktor' programme. The Malaysian government committed in its National Higher Education Strategic Plan Beyond 2020 to accelerating the production of doctorates to produce 100 000 PhD holders by 2020. These have included locally trained, overseas trained, and split-site programmes with universities from outside of the country. The split-site arrangement is gaining popularity in other countries such as the Philippines

---

8 Marie Skłodowska-Curie actions are major research fellowship programmes that have been used by the European Union to support and encourage mobility across European countries.

and Pakistan where a 'two plus three' model is emerging, with two years at the beginning of the doctorate in the home institution followed by three years spent in a developed research environment.

'Distributed' or 'diaspora' knowledge networks (Meyer & Wattiaux 2006; OECD 2010) that have been established through previous doctoral or academic mobility are contributing to the establishment of new joint or dual programmes that usually require the doctoral researcher to spend at least one year in each university.

In South Africa, the Department of Higher Education and Training is working in partnership with other funders to support outgoing mobility for doctoral candidates on the New Generation of Academics Programme (nGAP).

The globalisation discourse, higher education league tables and metrics that privilege international co-authorship and citation numbers also drive policy and practice at an institutional level. Many universities offer fully funded scholarships for the best international candidates based on the perceived value of high-quality doctoral researchers to the research environment and the achievement of key metrics. At the very least, universities are investing funds in temporary placements, exchange programmes, research trips and extended training overseas.

What Dervin and Machart (2015:8) describe as the "imaginaries of mobility" have percolated through all levels of policy and practice without much investigation to date into the human experience of doctoral candidates. The next section moves on to explore exactly this amongst a group of 'mobile' doctoral researchers at three different kinds of UK universities.

## DEFINITIONS AND METHODOLOGY

The research project uses interplay between emerging empirical data with multiple phases of literature review to better understand the experiences of mobile postgraduate researchers and to draw some conclusions about how the challenges they face might be mitigated and the positive impacts amplified. Ethical approval was sought and gained from Coventry University, UK.

Mobility was defined broadly as: (1) undertaking a doctorate outside of the researcher's main country of residence; (2) undertaking a doctorate by international dual or joint award, such as a cotutelle arrangement; and (3) spending more than one month based in a different research institution to the one where the researcher is registered for their doctorate.

The project began with a preliminary review of academic and policy publications with a focus on academic mobility (including but not limited to doctoral candidates). This identified a number of areas for investigation that form the focus of the study. An online questionnaire was chosen as the method of data collection. The survey decision was based on economy, in terms of time and cost to the researcher and the respondents, and reach, in terms of number of institutions and individuals that could be targeted. Importantly it allowed for anonymity in responses.

The limitations of the chosen survey include social desirability response bias (Van de Mortel 2008), lower response rates, the potential for over/under-representation of certain personality types (coverage bias) and the opportunity for respondents to misunderstand the questions posed. Some of these limitations were addressed through a variety of mitigations in the approach, including: a pilot phase where the questionnaire was tested for ease of understanding and subsequently amended; the dissemination of the questionnaire via deans or directors of Graduate Schools or Doctoral Colleges (such that potential respondents would receive the link through a familiar name within their own institution); and the circulation of a number of reminders over a three-month period.

The questionnaire comprised a mixture of open and closed questions – balancing detail with a higher response rate (Fowler 1993:69-93). It contained standardised questions which used a modified Likert-type scale. These responses provided a self-assessment of personal development in two keys areas that related to the mobility activity. The Researcher Development Framework (Vitae 2011) was used as the basis for the self-assessment part of the questionnaire as it is used by the majority of UK universities and therefore offers familiar language and makes common understanding more likely. There were also questions with free text box responses. These provided data for a thematic analysis of narrative tropes relating to the respondents' personal experiences of mobility.

Three UK higher education institutions were chosen to represent a range of types of university and geographical locations:

1. Business-facing, South Coast, small doctoral population.
2. Research-intensive, North, large doctoral population.
3. Business-facing, Midlands, medium doctoral population.

The link to the online questionnaire was circulated by deans or directors using newsletters and direct mail-outs. The questionnaire was initially open from 14 December 2018 until 28 February 2019, with a further extension of one month. A total of 2 290 postgraduate researchers were targeted but only those who had undertaken mobility were invited to respond. There is no available data that show the size of the mobile subset. Altogether 44 responses were received, of which 40 were complete. 38 respondents disclosed their gender: 21 female/f/ 'feminine' and 17 male/m. The respondents came from 31 countries across the Global South and Global North. The majority of respondents were 26-45 years old (65%). 40% described their ethnicity as Black, Asian or Other; 5% declared a disability; 47.5% were single and without children. The breadth of the dataset in terms of ethnicity, gender, those with or without children does not necessarily align with the inequality of engagement in mobility noted in a number of academic papers referenced in the next section. Although the dataset is far too small to draw any conclusions about this, the broad cross-section of respondents did help to ensure that a variety of perspectives were included in the analysis on enablers and constraints.

The interpretation of the questionnaire results was shaped and influenced by further literature-based inquiry on migration, knowledge production and internationalisation of higher education.

## ACADEMIC MOBILITY IN THE LITERATURE

The next section provides a summary of the existing scholarly literature on academic mobility which is largely focused on research staff after completion of their doctorate. This literature has a strong focus on countries and continents where the research infrastructure is most developed. There is a lack of comparative studies between mobility across different disciplines. The considerations of equality of access to mobility opportunities are largely restricted to gender bias and do not extend to other 'protected characteristics', as defined by the UK Equality Act 2010, including disability, sexuality and race.

Like the policy discourse on academic mobility, much of the findings in the literature describe positive outcomes for mobility. The reality that for some, physical mobility provides access to equipment and technology that is not available in the home country or sending institution (Guth 2008) is uncontested. Access to transnational networks that underpin international collaborations is another stated benefit (Woolley, Cañibano & Tesch 2016) although loss of networks and esteem in the home institution is also highlighted (Cruz-Castro & Sanz-Menéndez 2010; Gaughan & Robin 2004; Pezzoni, Sterzi & Lissoni 2012). De Filippo, Casado and Gomez (2009), Jöns (2011) and O'Hara (2009) point to enhanced productivity more generally and greater production of new knowledge specifically during a period of mobility, while Van Heeringen and Dijkwel (1987) suggest – based on empirical data of Dutch scientists – that mobility is a characteristic of productive scientists rather than a means to enhance productivity.

Inequality of engagement between genders (Leemann 2010; Weert 2013) and to some extent personality types (Ackers 2005) is raised as a problem if mobility is linked to promotion opportunities.

More recently, Walakira and Wright (2018) have for the first time set out to capture the personal challenges to mobility in their exploration of feelings of homelessness in PhD fellows who were part of a Marie Curie International Training network in Europe, and the Integrative Graduate Education and Research Training programme in the USA. We might see this, at least to some extent, as part of a shift towards the more human-centred discourse on doctoral education that is embodied by the Hannover Recommendations and away from programme level analyses.

The literature review identified three areas for further investigation through the survey questionnaire. These represent areas where the existing literature was inconclusive or scant. They are: (1) the effect of mobility on career development; (2) the impact of mobility on knowledge development and production; and (3) equality and diversity in uptake of mobility schemes.

## SUMMARY OF SURVEY FINDINGS

This section gives an overview of the preliminary analysis of the survey results, looking in turn at the impact of mobility on the respondents' career development, their cognitive development and their perceptions of the barriers and enablers which, from their perspective, account for the developmental differences. The section concludes with a summary of the narrative tropes found in the questionnaire responses that related either to respondents seeking to pursue their doctoral education outside of their home country or to what prevented them from doing this.

### Confident, clear on values and the burden of starting over

The questions related to career development focused on skills and attributes linked to 'professional and career development' (sub-domain B3 in the Researcher Development Framework). They are perceived awareness of career options, clarity of values, insight into how transition post-PhD might work, confidence to make the most of career opportunities, and the development of networks that might help to secure a job in future. Respondents were asked to rate their progress against what they might consider other doctoral candidates had achieved after a similar period of registration or what their understanding of their supervisor or supervisory team's expectations of them were at the point they completed the questionnaire.

Overall the respondents reported greater than expected development related to a personal understanding of their own values in terms of how these relate to and might influence their future career. They also indicated that their confidence to engage in other opportunities related to their career, including further international travel, had developed more quickly.

On the other hand, perceptions of networking skills were more mixed. Here between 15 and 25% of respondents reported experiencing slower than expected progress in the development of professional networks inside and outside the university, and the ability to use these networks to support next steps in their career, while between 12 and 23% of respondents conversely reported that they were more effective networkers in terms of scale and use, as a result of their international mobility.

Their explanations of the developmental differences suggest that when programmes encourage networking activities and respondents have the confidence to exploit these opportunities, the sheer volume of new people that mobile postgraduate researchers can meet can mean that their networks rapidly expand. However, needing to "start from the ground up with a new institute" for some "stunts progress" and for others it can be very difficult to build networks outside of the main supervisory relationship.

### Creative ideation, language barriers and cultural accommodations

Looking specifically at cognitive function and knowledge acquisition, the respondents were asked to consider how mobility had impacted their subject knowledge, critical thinking, research methods, and their ability to synthesise large amounts of information. Overall, respondents suggested a lag in research methods and information synthesis, where between 10 and 28.5% reported delayed development. However, 17.5 to 29.6% of respondents reported their development in these areas was faster than anticipated.

There was a general sense of faster development across the range of other knowledge and attribute areas with the most significant developmental advantage reported in the ability to contribute novel ideas and the confidence to take intellectual risk. For instance, 46.2% of respondents reported that confidence had developed quicker or significantly quicker than expected.

Respondents' explanations of the developmental differences include ideas of working harder in a new environment. They also valued having access to researchers from all over the world with whom they could meet and share ideas. However, language barriers – specifically "the gap between understanding of (the) subject and articulating it" – were perceived to have caused delays in development, along with a sense of exhaustion from negotiating cultural differences that meant there was less energy to spend on the research. One respondent commented as follows:

> The energy lost in dealing with cultural translations [in] understanding my supervisor, the way in which immigrants are treated by immigration and institutions in general, and also in my personal life while making new friends took a toll on my physical and emotional health. For instance, the fact that I had to go through most of my research without being sure about what my supervisors meant, stunt the development of my critical thinking and academic writing skills taking a lot longer to develop than they could have taken.

Overall, the responses point to language proficiency and cross-cultural competencies (and the support to achieve that) as being key to enabling mobile postgraduates to maximise the benefits to cognitive development of a rich research environment with access to 'experts' and new thoughts and ideas.

### Enablers and barriers to mobility

Beyond the focus on developmental differences respondents were also asked to render free text responses to what they had found to be the key endogenous and exogenous enablers and constraints to doctoral mobility.

When considering their own personal character traits, respondents frequently used the narrative tropes of 'rising to the challenge' and thriving outside of their 'comfort zones'. Curiosity, courage and interest in meeting new people, seeing new places and interacting with 'experts' were strong personal enablers. Funding incentives such as government or university scholarships, or other types of financial support, including university fee waivers, employer funding, loans or gifts from the wider family were seen as external enablers. Emotional support from family, manager, 'advisor' or supervisor was seen as key along with practical support such as universities making mobility requirements flexible, additional funds for childcare and the need for a partner to 'do more'.

Barriers and constraints to mobility were related to the ability (or otherwise) to navigate 'bureaucracies' both external and internal to the university, such as banking, accommodation, visas and insurance, and negotiating ethics, getting access to library and a workspace. Overcoming time zones and communication lags both across supervisory teams such as in co-tutelle arrangements and with family and friends at home was noted as barrier to accessing timely support.

Difficulties in cross-cultural supervision were also noted by a number of respondents as aptly summarised by the following quotation:

> Cultural shock in general and, in special, difficulty of understanding the feedback from my British supervisors. In Brazil, supervisors are more clear and assertive about their feedbacks, whereas UK supervisors tend to be more polite but also share less and give less support when giving feedback.

Finally, loneliness is reported as a major barrier to mobility with respondents expressing the challenges posed by the loss of social networks and the burden of 'building up everything from scratch'. 'Being an outsider' was also a strong motif with one respondent reporting a feeling of "prejudice with abroad people [...] even inside the University". A number of respondents described being left out due to language difficulties.

## CONCLUSION

As academic mobility increases across all levels of seniority there is special responsibility to consider carefully its impact within the doctoral community. This is because doctoral candidates are the next generation of researchers. They are often newcomers in their own research communities of practice. Their major interactions with the host university can often be mediated mainly through a single supervisor or supervisory team and peer interaction and support might be infrequent. For many, the regulatory environment will focus on progression, rather than support, and their financial security through scholarships or loans depends on rapid development to meet pressing deadlines. Some, moving from Global South to Global North, feel they are under a lot of pressure to succeed on a prestigious scholarship programme. Others, undertaking North-South mobility, keenly feel the need to engage fully and equally with new colleagues in very different research environments in order to ensure mutual benefit and to acknowledge and show respect for their colleagues' expertise.

Mobility at a doctoral level has clear advantages which are spelt out in policy and in parts of the academic literature. These advantages are also apparent from the conducted survey questionnaire responses. For instance, 84.6% of the respondents held that mobility had been beneficial to them. The findings highlighted increase in confidence, access to expertise, enhanced knowledge and understanding of self and others and development of problem-solving skills as positive outcomes. However, respondents also indicated the real personal, financial and systemic barriers that they face when undertaking mobility, which can create energy-sapping feelings of being an outsider.

To create the inclusive doctoral community set out in the Hannover Recommendations, we – the global village of supervisors, doctoral colleges or graduate schools and universities – perhaps need to rethink the imaginaries of mobility and to consider the needs of mobile postgraduate researchers. This will require us to look again at issues such as the timing of progression milestones and how flexibility might be built into the early phase of a doctorate, before upgrade, in programmes where candidates register in the first instance for an MPhil. Additional support and time to achieve early milestones would acknowledge the lag felt by some survey respondents in their ability to synthesise information while making cultural adaptations to their new context. The careful addition and balanced front-loading of additional taught elements across doctoral programmes could also offer easier opportunities for international candidates to build networks across the wider academic and professional services communities. Taught classes could also provide a stable, regular framework of formal and informal support in a familiar format for new doctoral researchers who are transitioning from a more structured master's programme. Further exploration of the benefits of pre-doctoral programmes could also be helpful. These programmes, which are currently piloted only by a small number of universities in the UK, might be delivered either remotely as pre-departure support in the candidates' home country or in the first few weeks of residence in the destination country. Such programmes might provide language support tailored for research purposes in the new context alongside an early opportunity to build peer-support networks which could ameliorate subsequent feelings of isolation and loneliness. Buddying programmes between cohorts and nationalities could also be explored as a way to provide informal emotional support, as well as practical help in navigating bureaucracies related to banking, accommodation, visas and access to buildings alongside more formal university services.

Supervisors may benefit from peer-learning opportunities related to their own experiences of mobility or of working with international candidates. Focused training on intercultural supervision with time for open discussion and guided self-reflection may be helpful in supporting supervisors to share their challenges and to work together on ways to better support their doctoral researchers. Considerations of diversity when forming supervisory teams could assist with cross-cultural understanding and awareness in supervisory relationships. Peer observation, where appropriate, could afford supervisors the opportunity to broaden their own intercultural experiences and to observe and reflect on their own practice and of others.

Many of these measures to provide flexibility, to enhance support, and to improve networking and integration would be valuable for the entire doctoral community who – although perhaps not geographically mobile – may well be experiencing a period of transition, or of social or cultural mobility on their personal doctoral journey.

The voices of doctoral researchers from 30 countries – Global North and Global South – have provided fresh insights into how we might enable doctoral candidates to capitalise on their own mobility and encourage our respective institutions to maximise the benefits thereof for the rest of the academic community.

## REFERENCES

Ackers L. 2005. Moving people and knowledge: Scientific mobility in the European Union. *International Migration*, 43:99-131. https://doi.org/10.1111/j.1468-2435.2005.00343.x

Australian Government Department of Education, Skills and Employment. 2020. *Higher Education Statistics* [uCube multi-dimensional data structure]. https://bit.ly/32wyyAO [Accessed 15 May 2020].

Bekhradnia B & Sastry T. 2005. *Brain drain: Migration of academic staff to and from the UK*. Oxford: Higher Education Policy Institute.

Bhagwati JN & Hamada K. 1974. The brain drain, international integration of markets for professionals and unemployment: A theoretical analysis. *Journal of Development Economics*, 1(1):19-42. https://doi.org/10.1016/0304-3878(74)90020-0

Borrell-Damián L, Morais R & Smith J. 2009. *Collaborative doctoral education: University-industry partnerships for enhancing knowledge exchange*. Brussels: European Universities Association.

Cruz-Castro L & Sanz-Menéndez L. 2010. Mobility versus job stability: Assessing tenure and productivity. *Research Policy*, 39(1):27-38. https://doi.org/10.1016/j.respol.2009.11.008

De Filippo D, Casado E & Gómez I. 2009. Quantitative and qualitative approaches to the study of mobility and scientific performance: A case study of a Spanish university. *Research Evaluation*, 18(3):191-200. https://doi.org/10.3152/095820209X451032

Dervin F & Machart R. 2015. Introduction: Global academic mobility and migration – Between reality and fantasy. In: F Dervin & R Machart (eds.), *The new politics of global academic mobility and migration*. Frankfurt: Peter Lang. 7-18. https://doi.org/10.3726/978-3-653-04652-6

Deutscher Akademischer Austauschdienst. 2019. *Wissenschaft Weltoffen 2019: Daten und Fakten zur Internationalität von Studium und Forschung in Deutschland*. Bonn: Deutscher Akademischer Austauschdienst. https://bit.ly/3sF37Pq [Accessed 15 May 2020].

EUA (European Universities Association). 2018. *Doctoral education in South Africa: Ambitions and challenges*. Brussels: European Universities Association.

European Commission. 2007. *Strategic report on the renewed Lisbon strategy for growth and jobs: Launching the new cycle (2008-2010) – Keeping up the pace of change*. Brussels: European Commission.

Fernández-Zubieta A, Marinelli E & Pérez S. 2013. What drives researchers´ careers? The role of international mobility, gender and family. *Sociología Y tecnociencia/Sociology and Technoscience*, 3(3):8-30.

Flores E & Nerad M. 2012. Peers in doctoral education: Unrecognized partners. *New Directions for Higher Education*, 157(Spring):73-83. https://doi.org/10.1002/he.20007

Fowler Jr F. 2013. *Survey research methods*. Thousand Oaks: Sage.

Franzoni C, Scellato G & Stephan P. 2012. *Foreign born scientists: Mobility patterns for sixteen countries*. Cambridge MA: National Bureau of Economic Research. https://doi.org/10.3386/w18067

Gaughan M & Robin S. 2004. National science training policy and early scientific careers in France and the United States. *Research Policy*, 33(4): 569-581. https://doi.org/10.1016/j.respol.2004.01.005

Government of India, Ministry of Human Resource Development. 2018. *All India Survey on Higher Education 2017-2018*. New Delhi: Ministry of Human Resource Development.

Guth J. 2008. The opening of borders and scientific mobility: The impact of EU enlargement on the movement of early career scientists. *Higher Education in Europe*, 33(4):395-410. https://doi.org/10.1080/03797720802522601

Guthrie S, Lichten C, Corbett J & Wooding S. 2017. *International mobility of researchers A review of the literature*. London: RAND. https://doi.org/10.7249/RR1991

HESA. See Higher Education Statistics Agency.

Higher Education Statistics Agency. 2009. *Higher education statistics 2007-2008*. Cheltenham: HESA.

Higher Education Statistics Agency. 2011. *Higher education statistics 2009-2010*. Cheltenham: HESA.

Higher Education Statistics Agency. 2019. *Higher education statistics 2017-2018*. Cheltenham: HESA.

Jöns H. 2011. Transnational academic mobility and gender. *Globalisation, societies and education*, 9(2):183-209. https://doi.org/10.1080/14767724.2011.577199

Kaplan D & Höppli T. 2017. The South African brain drain: An empirical assessment. *Development Southern Africa*, 34(5):497-514. https://doi.org/10.1080/0376835X.2017.1351870

Leemann R. 2010. Gender inequalities in transnational academic mobility and the ideal type of academic entrepreneur. *Discourse: Studies in the Cultural Politics of Education*, 31(5):605-625. https://doi.org/10.1080/01596306.2010.516942

McCullock R & Yellen JT. 1977. Factor mobility, regional development and the distribution of income. *Journal of Political Economy*, 85(1):79-96. https://doi.org/10.1086/260546

Meyer JB. 2001. Network approach versus brain drain: Lessons from the diaspora. *International Migration*, 39(5):91-110. https://doi.org/10.1111/1468-2435.00173

Meyer J & Wattiaux J. 2006. Diaspora knowledge networks: Vanishing doubts and increasing evidence. *International Journal on Multicultural Societies*, (1):4-24.

Ministry of Education, The People's Republic of China. 2019. *Statistical report on international students in China for 2018*. Beijing: Ministry of Education. https://bit.ly/3ewnTf5 [Accessed 15 May 2020].

National Science Foundation. 2008. *Survey of Earned Doctorates*. Alexandria: NSF.

National Science Foundation. 2017. *Survey of Earned Doctorates*. Alexandria: NSF.

O'Hara S. 2009. Internationalizing the academy: The impact of scholar mobility: Higher education on the move. *New developments in Global Mobility*, 3:29-47.

OECD. See Organisation for Economic Co-operation and Development.

Organisation for Economic Co-operation and Development. 2010a. *Education at a glance 2008*. Paris: OECD.

Organisation for Economic Co-operation and Development. 2010b. *Measuring innovation: A new perspective*. Paris: OECD.

Organisation for Economic Co-operation and Development (OECD). 2019. *Education at a glance 2017*. Paris: OECD.

Pezzoni M, Sterzi V & Lissoni F. 2012. Career progress in centralized academic systems: Social capital and institutions in France and Italy. *Research Policy*, 41(4):704-719. https://doi.org/10.1016/j.respol.2011.12.009

Royal Society. 1963. *The emigration of scientists*. London: Royal Society.

Sehoole C, Adeyemo K, Phatlane R & Ojo E. 2019. Academic mobility and the experiences of foreign staff at South African higher education institutions. *South African Journal of Higher Education*, 33(2):212-229. https://doi.org/10.20853/33-2-2788

Sugimoto C, Robinson-Garcia N, Murray D, Yegros-Yegros A, Costas R & Larivière V. 2017. Scientists have most impact when they're free to move. *Nature*:29-31. https://doi.org/10.1038/550029a

Teichler U, Arimoto A & Cummings W. 2013. *The changing academic profession*. Dordrecht: Springer. https://doi.org/10.1007/978-94-007-6155-1

Universities UK. 2007. Talent wars: The international market for academic staff. Policy Briefing, July.

Van de Mortel T. 2008. Faking it: Social desirability response bias in self-report research. *Australian Journal of Advanced Nursing*, 25(4):40-48.

Van Heeringen A & Dijkwel P. 1987. The relationships between age, mobility and scientific productivity. Part I: Effect of mobility on productivity. *Scientometrics*, 11(5-6):267-280. https://doi.org/10.1007/BF02279349

Vitae. 2011. *Researcher development framework*. Cambridge: Vitae.

Walakira L & Wright S. 2018. 'I'm like a snail carrying my entire house with me': Doctoral fellows' experiences of a mobile life. *Learning and Teaching*, 11(2):51-68. https://doi.org/10.3167/latiss.2018.110204

Weert E. 2013. *Support for continued data collection and analysis concerning mobility patterns and career paths of researchers*. Brussels: European Commission.

Woolley R, Cañibano C & Tesch J. 2016. *A Functional Review of Literature on Research Careers*. Brussels: European Commission.

# QUALITY DOCTORAL EDUCATION IN AFRICA

A QUESTION OF SETTING THE RIGHT STANDARDS?

Jan Botha, Mike Kuria, Murat Özgören and Marc Wilde

## INTRODUCTION

Much of the teaching at universities in Africa is done by academic staff members who do not have doctoral degrees. In South Africa, for example (in 2017), only 46% of the academic staff of the public universities held a doctoral degree (DHET 2019:48). This has implications for the quality of teaching and research and the capacity to deliver more doctoral graduates. In other African countries, the situation is not different. According to a study of eight "flagship" African universities by Cloete, Bunting and Van Schalkwyk (2018:50), the situation (in 2015) at these universities was as follows: at the University of Botswana 57% of academic staff appointed in permanent posts held doctoral degrees, University of Cape Town (South Africa) 65%, University of Dar es Salaam (Tanzania) 52%, Eduardo Modlane University (Mozambique) 21%, University of Ghana 42%, Makerere University (Uganda) 43%, University of Mauritius 50% and University of Nairobi (Kenya) 24%. Some countries, for example Nigeria (Fatunde 2011) and Kenya (Commission for University Education 2014), adopted policies that all academic staff members employed by universities must obtain a doctoral degree within set timelines or risk losing their jobs. Consequently, many lecturers embarked on doctoral studies, adding to the ever increasing number of doctoral enrolments. A great need for doctoral education exists on the continent and the rapid increase in enrolments puts institutions under pressure to ensure the quality of the degrees. This makes the quality of doctoral provision in Africa an urgent topic for further investigation.

PART TWO • CURRENTS AND CURRENCIES

At a seminar in Nairobi, Kenya, in September 2016, organised by the German Academic Exchange Service (DAAD), the Inter-University Council for East Africa (IUCEA) and Kenya's Commission for University Education (CUE), the most pressing needs to improve doctoral education in Africa were analysed and recommendations for further action were formulated (Kuria & Ndivo 2016). The seminar participants identified two priority areas, namely the provision of professional development opportunities for doctoral supervisors affiliated to African universities, and the development of quality benchmarks for the offering of doctoral degrees at African universities. The DAAD, in the framework of its Dialogue on Innovative Higher Education Strategies (DIES) programme, and the IUCEA joined forces to attend to these priority areas. As a result, the DIES/CREST training course for doctoral supervisors at African universities was launched in 2018, offered by the Centre for Research on Evaluation, Science and Technology (CREST) in collaboration with the Centre for Higher and Adult Education (CHAE) at Stellenbosch University and the Centre for Higher Education Research, Teaching and Learning (CHERTL) at Rhodes University (cf. Botha, Vilyte & De Klerk 2019; Makoni 2019). Responding to the second priority identified at the Nairobi Seminar, the IUCEA coordinated a process of drafting standards and guidelines for doctoral education in East Africa as a test case for other African regions (IUCEA 2018). Independent of the process in East Africa, South Africa adopted a National Doctoral Qualification Standard in 2018, to be followed by a national review process during 2020-2021 in terms of which all higher education institutions offering doctoral degrees have to evaluate their qualifications against this standard (CHE 2019).

In this chapter we describe the development of doctoral standards and guidelines for doctoral education in three different parts of the world, namely Europe, East Africa and South Africa. In each case we consider the current state of the development of doctoral standards and guidelines and the rationale for developing them and then we comment on the potential difficulties and benefits of setting and implementing such standards and guidelines.

The overarching concern that prompted this chapter is the issue of doctoral standards. The questions that arose are: (a) is the setting of formal doctoral standards the panacea that will ameliorate the widely held concerns about the quality of doctoral education in Africa? and (b) given the differences in history, social and economic context and needs and priorities, is the setting and implementation (and enforcing) of standards necessarily the best or only way forward? The dilemma with setting standards and expecting everyone to meet them is well illustrated by this cartoon.[1]

---

1   Original cartoon: Chancengleichheit ('egial chances') by German cartoonist Hans Traxler, 1975.

CHAPTER 8 • **QUALITY DOCTORAL EDUCATION IN AFRICA**

So, does it make sense to think along the line of setting the 'right' standards for Africa? What would that mean?

Terms such as 'standards', 'principles', 'guidelines (for good practice)', 'benchmarks' (or 'quality benchmarks'), and 'criteria' and 'regulations' are used throughout the chapter, in accordance with the use of particular term(s) in each context. As shorthand for the multifaceted phenomenon under discussion, we use the term 'standards and guidelines'.

## CURRENT CHALLENGES FOR DOCTORAL EDUCATION IN AFRICA

Expansion, relevance, innovation and competition are among the most pertinent challenges affecting doctoral education in Africa. These challenges are by no means limited to African higher education only. They are part of the 'global revolution' in higher education described by Altbach, Reisberg and Rumley (2010). Yet, in Africa, where most countries are lower- or medium-income countries and where many universities are not always adequately resourced, these challenges manifest in unique and perhaps even more serious ways than elsewhere.

Mohamedbhai (2014) recorded the drastic increases in student enrolments at many African universities in recent years. The expansion was not restricted to undergraduate level. Also at master's and doctoral levels, many African universities have enrolled many more students, in many cases beyond their capacity (Cloete et al. 2018 ; IAU 2010). In some countries (e.g. Ethiopia, Kenya and Uganda) many new higher education institutions were established over a fairly short period, and new providers (in particular, private institutions) entered the higher education system. These expansions necessitated the further development of quality assurance mechanisms in institutions and national and regional quality assurance bodies.

Due to this expansion new concerns arose about the relevance of higher education. It is generally believed that there is an increase in graduate unemployment (although there are no studies available of graduate employment in sub-Saharan Africa) (Mohamedbhai 2014:73). One of the reasons for this is the misalignment between higher education curricula and the needs of the labour market. So, it is important to strengthen university-business cooperation and to promote applied research in order to enhance the employability of graduates.

Mouton (2018) argues that innovation and competitiveness must remain high on the agenda if Africa wants to increase its participation in the knowledge economy. However, currently there is insufficient capacity for graduate education and research at many African universities and there is also a great need for more investment in research. In particular, Africa needs tens of thousands more doctoral candidates to drive scientific output and innovation (McGreggor 2013). In order to deliver more graduates, many more well-prepared supervisors are needed.

## BUILDING PHD CAPACITY IN SUB-SAHARAN AFRICA AND THE ROLE OF INTERNATIONAL AGENCIES AND PARTNERSHIPS

The British Council (BC) and the DAAD conceived and supported a study to investigate the nature of research and doctoral training across sub-Saharan Africa. The study was commissioned to the African Network for Internationalisation of Education (ANIE) and its network of researchers across sub-Saharan Africa. The report, *Building PhD capacity in Sub-Saharan Africa*, published in 2018 consists of six country reports (Ethiopia, Ghana, Kenya, Nigeria, Senegal and South Africa) and a synthesis report presenting the study's main findings and recommendations (ANIE 2018).

The aim of the ANIE study was to provide evidence in support of decision-making at policy and institutional levels. This was motivated by the observation of the BC and the DAAD that doctoral education was not a priority for national policy-making in many African countries given the general idea that it was more important to focus first on the undergraduate level. However, the report emphasises the interdependence between these levels, arguing that "[a]dequate staffing for the undergraduate level, and a thriving and innovative research environment, to a large extent depend on the possibilities of high quality *doctoral* study" (ANIE 2018:4).

The findings on PhD provision in the six African countries were reported in terms of the following themes: student characteristics; the structure and format of PhD degrees; the disciplinary spread of PhD provision; factors driving its expansion; the institutions that are providing doctoral education; funding of PhD provision; the quality of PhD provision from the perspective of alumni; and post-PhD trajectories (ANIE 2018:15-22). The findings can be summarised as follows:

- A minority of academic staff in these countries have doctorates (ranging from 8% in Ethiopia to 43% in Nigeria and South Africa) but governments tend to tighten up laws that regulate lecturers' qualifications.
- Most PhD students are mature students studying part-time (for example, the mean age in South Africa is between 35 and 45 years); female representation is low.
- The duration of programmes varies from three to six years and drop-out rates and the prolonged time to completion are major challenges.
- There is usually a focus on science, technology, engineering and mathematics (STEM) in PhD provision and there is often a disconnect between PhD research topics and the broader institutional or national research agendas.
- Supervision is not adequate due to the lack of suitable supervisors with relevant expertise and missing regulations (e.g. handbooks on supervisory ethics).
- The proportion of university budgets allocated to research and PhD provision is low.
- The majority of PhD graduates work in higher education (or expect to get academic positions) with little absorption into industry or the private sector.

The report includes various recommendations (ANIE 2018:23-24), including the following:

- African countries need to expand their pool significantly and increase their rate of production of PhD graduates to ensure the quality of HE provision at undergraduate level and to create a vibrant research environment at institutional level.
- There must be a substantial increase of investments in doctoral education to ensure timely and successful completion of studies and to promote equal access.
- The quality of the doctoral programmes must be strengthened in terms of research infrastructure, qualified PhD supervisors (e.g. via training and international partnerships) and robust processes of quality assurance.
- Higher education systems need to seek a balance between the concentration of doctoral studies in a few institutions or to diffuse these programmes across new public institutions, as well as private higher education institutions, and to ensure a broad disciplinary spread in doctoral programmes.

- Stronger linkages must be developed between universities, communities, industry and government to ensure that research addresses relevant development needs of society.
- More extensive and reliable data must be collected from institutions to inform policymaking around PhD provision.
- International partnerships should play a crucial role in strengthening PhD provision, provided they are aimed at supporting capacities within the African continent rather than attracting talents for the Global North.

Preceded by but also validated by the findings and recommendations of this report, the DAAD's Africa strategy (DAAD 2014) has for many years been to focus on the upgrading of the qualifications of university lecturers and to build capacity for graduate education and research through their scholarship programme. Examples of how the DAAD gives effect to this strategy include the DAAD's In Country/In-Region-Programme (providing master's and PhD scholarships at selected universities across the continent, supporting high quality research at master's and PhD level and strengthening internationalisation via intra-Africa mobility), the Centres of African Excellence initiative promoting 10 specialised university centres in eight sub-Saharan African countries to establish centres for the training of future leaders in African universities, and a variety of partnership schemes that facilitate cooperation with German higher education institutions, for example, to jointly develop curricula for degree programmes that are relevant to the current and future labour markets in Africa. Further, in the frame of the DIES programme, the DAAD has established itself – in collaboration with the German Rectors' Conference (HRK) – as an active provider of training opportunities to enhance university management, quality assurance, the acquisition of third-party funding and the quality of doctoral education.

From early on in the DIES projects located in Africa, a close partnership with relevant regional university associations has been part of the DAAD's implementation strategy. In the East African region, the IUCEA played a crucial role, particularly in a joint project (2006-2015) to develop capacities and regional structures in the field of quality assurance, followed by the initiative (launched in 2016) to support the IUCEA with the development of standards and guidelines for doctoral education in Eastern Africa.

However, before we discuss the doctoral standards and guidelines that were developed in the East African region and in South Africa, we will first consider developments in Europe. This is done because, as we will demonstrate, Europe made significant strides in this regard before the processes in East and South African countries commenced, and the African regions and countries were in a position to learn from the results of the European process. However, this does not mean that the European standards and guidelines served as the blueprint for the standards that were developed in Africa. We will return to the issue of global standards and the contextualisation of doctoral standards in the discussion at the end of the chapter.

## DOCTORAL STANDARDS, REGULATIONS AND GUIDELINES IN EUROPE

Various role players in Europe were involved in the development and implementation of doctoral standards, guidelines for good practices in doctoral education and regulations for the provision of doctoral qualifications and programmes, including, at a regional level (e.g. the European Commission (EC), the European University Association (EUA) and disciplinary associations), national level (government departments and other agencies) and institutional level (higher education institutions).

The EUA, one of the prominent regional bodies that contributed to the creation of European doctoral standards, was established in 2001. It is a non-governmental membership organisation with a membership of more than 800 universities across 48 countries, including 34 national Rectors' Conferences. Its main purposes are to provide a forum for information exchange and collaboration for its members, improve European university performance via peer learning, influence public policy, and stand as a representative on behalf of European universities in regional and global forums (EUA 2019a). The EUA also organises events and provides services to its members via the EUA Council for Doctoral Education (EUA-CDE), EUA Solutions and the Institutional Evaluation Programme (IEP). Through its activities and services, the EUA brings together a community of academic leaders and professionals in higher education. One of the EUA's focus areas, led by the EUA-CDE, is doctoral education policies and good practices in the provision of doctoral education. To advance its work in this focus area, the EUA-CDE organises conferences, workshops, focus group discussions and webinars (EUA 2019b).

Working through its members, the EUA follows a participatory process to develop guiding principles to reform doctoral education in Europe, resulting from a general realisation of the need to adapt policies and practices given the changing conditions of doctoral education not only in Europe but also globally. The EUA has played a role in the Bologna Process, a series of meetings and agreements between 48 European countries for the purpose of ensuring the quality and comparability of standards in higher education in Europe (EUA 2019c). The Bologna Process established the European Higher Education Area in 2010 and strives to establish a European Education Area by 2025, which would allow "all young people to benefit from the best education and training, and to find employment across Europe" (EC 2005). In light of the increased importance being placed on doctoral education in Europe as highlighted through the Bologna Process, three important documents were produced by the EUA (EUA 2005; EUA-CDE 2010; EUA-CDE 2016) related to doctoral standards. Furthermore, the EC itself published important documents stemming from the Bologna Process, such as the Bergen Communique and Seven Principles for Innovative Doctoral Education. We first discuss the three EUA documents, followed by two EC documents.

In 2003 the EUA started a project, 'Doctoral programmes for the European knowledge society' (EUA 2005). Those discussions resulted in consensus among the participating institutions on 10 common principles for doctoral education reform, known as the Salzburg Principles which were adopted in 2005 at the EUA seminar on the theme, 'Doctoral Program for the European Knowledge Society', held in Salzburg (EUA 2005). These principles cover topics such as the advancement of knowledge through original research; the status of doctoral candidates as early career researchers; the need to ensure that there is a diversity of doctoral programmes across Europe and that a critical mass must be reached in each programme; the crucial role of supervision and assessment; the duration of the doctorate between three and four years; and the promotion of innovative structures and mobility. Hasgall, Saenen and Borrel-Diamian (2019:6) highlight three implications of the adoption of the Salzburg Principles, namely that doctoral candidates were considered as early career researchers who are able to undertake different career paths both in and outside academia, that it was the responsibility of higher education institutions to ensure a fair, transparent and healthy environment for their doctoral candidates, and that the diversity of doctoral programmes in Europe was recognised and identified as a strength of doctoral education in Europe.

In 2010 the Salzburg II Recommendations were released by the EUA, drawing on the lessons learnt from the doctoral reforms since 2005 and in particular, drawing on the initiatives to give effect to the Salzburg Principles (EUA-CDE 2010). Hasgall et al. (2019:7) identified three key messages from the Salzburg Recommendations, namely that doctoral education was recognised as the third cycle in the qualifications structure of the European Higher Education Area (EHEA) (as distinct from the first two cycles, the bachelor's and master's); that, since doctoral education is highly individual and based on original research, it was recognised that doctoral candidates must be allowed independence and flexibility to grow and develop; and that doctoral education must be developed by autonomous and accountable institutions taking responsibility to cultivate a research mindset, to adopt flexible regulations, and to create special structures and instruments to advance European doctoral education.

In 2016 the EUA-CDE published a new set of recommendations, *Taking Salzburg Forward – Implementation and New Challenges* (EUA-CDE 2016). This document reiterated the key aspects of the Salzburg Principles and Recommendations, but it also included three new topics, namely research ethics and research integrity, the increased importance of digitalisation and all its implications for the doctorate, and the implications of the globalisation of research.

Informed by the Salzburg Principles (among many other initiatives and processes in higher education), a number of EU documents on doctoral education were developed, such as the Bergen Declaration (European Ministers Responsible for Higher Education 2005). In this Declaration, the Ministers Conference confirmed the guiding principle that the advancement of knowledge through original research is the core component of doctoral training. It also confirmed the duration of doctoral studies in Europe as three to four years of full-time study and it urged member states and universities to avoid over-regulation. In 2011, with the "Report of mapping exercise on doctoral training in Europe – Towards a common approach", seven "Principles of innovative doctoral training" were identified (very similar to the Salzburg principles), namely research excellence, an attractive institutional environment, interdisciplinary research options, exposure to industry and other relevant employment sectors, international networking, transferable skills training, and quality assurance.

Along with these processes at regional level in the context of the EU, some European countries have introduced national regulations, standards and guidelines. Not all European countries have these kinds of national regulations and in some countries processes to develop such regulations are currently under way. Examples of countries that have adopted extensive national regulations on doctoral education are Spain in 2011,[2] Italy in 2013,[3] Ireland in 2015[4] and France in 2016.[5]

---

2   Royal Decree 99/2011, of January 28, which regulates the official doctoral studies. *Real Decreto 99/2011, de 28 de enero, por el que se regulan las ensenanzas officiales de doctorado*, (Ministerio de Educacíon 2011).

3   Regulations containing Accreditation Procedures for Doctoral Courses and Criteria for the Establishment of Doctoral Courses by Accredited Bodies. *Regolamento recante modalità di accreditamento delle sedi e dei corsi di dottorato e criteri per la istituzione dei corsi di dottorato da parte degli enti accreditati*, (Ministero dell'Istruzione, dell'Università e della Ricerca 2013).

4   *National Framework for doctoral education*, (Higher Education Authority 2015).

5   Order of May 25, 2016 setting the National Training Framework and the Procedures leading to the Assurance of the National Doctorate Diploma. *Arrêté du 25 mai 2016 fixant le cadre national de la formation et les modalités conduisant à la délivrance du diplôme national de doctorat,* (République Francais 2016).

In addition to the regional and national bodies discussed thus far, a number of disciplinary associations in Europe have also developed guidelines or codes on doctoral education, for example, the Standards for PhD Education in Biomedicine and Health Sciences in Europe, developed jointly by the Organisation of PhD Education in Biomedicine and Health Sciences in the European System (ORPHEUS), the Association for Medical Schools in Europe (AMSE) and the World Federation for Medical Education (WFME) (ORPHEUS/AMSE/WFMW Task Force, 2012) and the European Code of Practice for Doctoral Studies in Management and Business developed by the European Institute for Advanced Studies in Management (EAISM) in collaboration with the European Doctoral programmes Association in Management and Business Administration (EDAMBA) (EISSM/EDAMBA Joint Task Force 2014).

Finally, higher education institutions have developed their internal institutional guidelines for the organisation of doctoral education. The extent to which higher education institutions have adopted and are implementing institutional guidelines on doctoral supervision was the focus of a study by Hasgall et al. (2019), and their findings illustrate that the institutionalisation of best practices in doctoral supervision is still a work in progress in many Europe universities (see Figure 8.1).

While much progress with doctoral reforms has been made in Europe along the lines of the Salzburg Principles, in particular also with regard to the development and implementation of doctoral standards and guidelines, it is an ongoing process and much remains to be done as new challenges emerge and as contexts change. The EUA-CDE has identified nine key priorities for their immediate and future activities (see Hasgall et al. 2019; O'Malley 2019), namely to develop an ethos of research integrity, to respond to and engage with the digital challenge (in particular the Open Science movement), to embrace the globalisation of research (e.g. collaboration and attracting doctoral candidates), to engage with and contribute to the knowledge society, to take care of the mental health and mental well-being of doctoral candidates, to develop and track the careers of doctoral graduates, to provide postdoctoral opportunities and to enhance their working conditions, to focus much more on research assessment, and, lastly, to contribute to the UN's sustainable development goals.

CHAPTER 8 • **QUALITY DOCTORAL EDUCATION IN AFRICA**

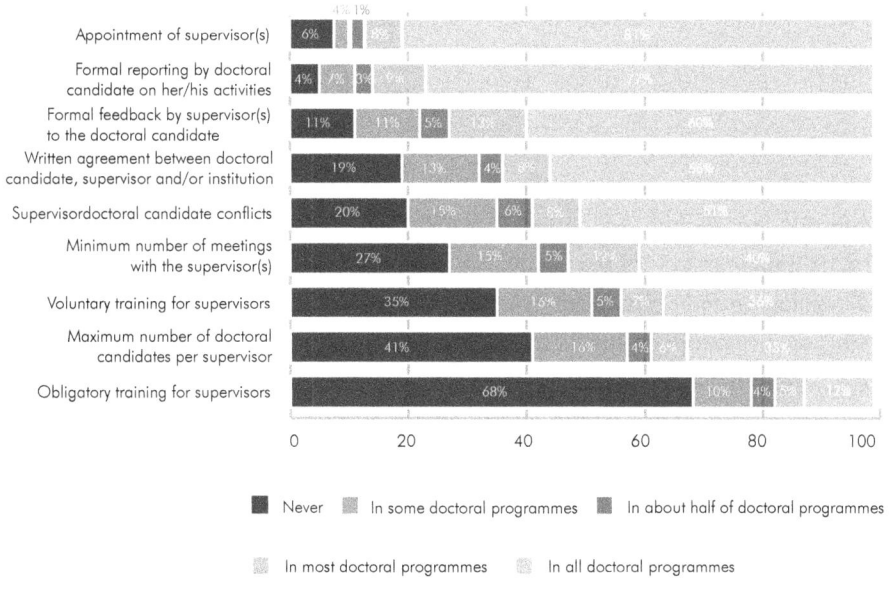

**FIGURE 8.1**   Rules and guidelines on supervision (Source: Hasgall *et al.* 2019:23)

As mentioned above, we did not discuss the doctoral standards and guidelines in Europe first because we consider that to be the blueprint or the global standard. However, given the pioneering work in Europe and the UK, African regions, countries and institutions had the opportunity to learn from the European experience. It remains important remember that the European and African contexts differ and the European standards and guidelines could not simply be copied in Africa. In the next two sections, we attend to the situations in East Africa and South Africa.

## THE DEVELOPMENT AND IMPLEMENTATION OF DOCTORAL STANDARDS AND GUIDELINES IN EAST AFRICA

The IUCEA is one of the institutions responsible for higher education in the EAC, which consists of six states, namely Burundi, Rwanda, Uganda, South Sudan, Kenya and Tanzania. The IUCEA came into being through the Protocol on the Establishment of the Inter-University Council for East Africa of 2002 (Republic of Uganda 2002) and the East African Community Supplement Act of the IUCEA Act adopted by the East African Legislative Assembly (Republic of Uganda 2009). Its mandate is (a) to enhance networking between universities in the region (for example on new methods of teaching and learning, information dissemination, linkage between universities, and with research partners), (b) to promote collaborative research and development and (c) to enhance the quality of higher education. The IUCEA does not have any accreditation powers. That remains the prerogative of each of the member states through their respective national councils and commissions.

The IUCEA played a key role in the development of a comprehensive regional quality assurance framework, including the development of the East African Qualifications Framework for Higher Education (EAQF). The EAQF, which was adopted in 2015, is implemented by the respective national commissions and councils. The EAQF builds on the national qualifications frameworks of the partner states, such as the Kenya National Qualifications Framework (KNQF) adopted in 2015, the Rwanda National Qualifications Framework (adopted in 2007), the Ugandan Vocational Qualifications Framework adopted in 2008, and the Tanzania National Qualifications Framework (proposed in 2008, while Burundi and South Sudan are currently engaged in the development of an NQF. The NQFs are developed by national qualifications authorities established by Acts of Parliament. The mandate of these bodies includes regulation, accreditation, comparison and validation of qualifications while IUCEA's mandate is regional coordination and harmonisation. On the basis of the regional quality assurances tools and instruments developed by IUCEA, the EAC heads of state declared East Africa a common higher education area (in May 2017). The IUCEA is charged with the responsibility of implementing this common higher education area through the harmonising of higher education practice in the EAC partner states. This is the context in which IUCEA embarked on development of postgraduate standards and guidelines since 2017.

Included in their (comprehensive) NQFs, the EAC member states have (short) statements on the characteristics and formal requirements for doctoral qualifications. These statements are currently their formal doctoral standards. Furthermore, universities have standards and guidelines for postgraduate studies as part of their own internal curriculum standards and guidelines.

While the regional EAQF also includes the high-level descriptions of postgraduate qualifications, there was a need for more detailed and harmonised principles and guidelines for postgraduate studies, as identified during the IUCEA/DAAD Nairobi Seminar in 2016 (Kuria & Ndivo 2016). The process to develop a guiding document commenced in 2016. It was facilitated by a team of experts drawn from the EAC partner states and included experts from Germany and Austria, supported by the DAAD. In 2018 the IUCEA published the *Standard and Guidelines for Postgraduate Studies in East Africa* which was subsequently circulated in the region to all stakeholders in the member states of the EAC, to be formally adopted after the consultation process (IUCEA 2018).

The IUCEA Standards and Guidelines document consists of 13 sections (or themes) broadly following the life-cycle of the provision of postgraduate studies. In each section the principles, the standard and the guidelines relevant to that particular thematic aspect of postgraduate studies are described. The 13 sections are (1) student admission into postgraduate studies, (2) duration of postgraduate programmes, (3) researcher development and skills training, (4) research findings dissemination and thesis/dissertation depository, (5) policies governing the conduct and management of postgraduate studies, (6) internationalisation, (7) supervision, (8) intellectual property rights, research ethics and integrity, (9) quality assurance and quality enhancement, (10) institutional capacity building, (11) complaints and appeals, (12) assessment and postgraduate degree awards and (13) withholding or revocation of a degree (IUCEA 2018).

There were a number of drivers for the development of the NQF document and later also the more comprehensive Standards and Guidelines. These divers include the need for quality promotion and enhancement, the need for the regulation of the many new providers of higher education who entered the region, the promotion of the mutual recognition of qualifications (at regional, national, and institutional levels), the promotion of the regional integration of labour, the mobility of students, and the development and implementation of the idea of an East African Common Higher Education Area (IUCEA 2015).

It is expected that the implementation of the NQFs and the Standards and Guidelines will result in improvement in quality and increased public confidence in the qualifications awarded by universities in the region. Furthermore, it is expected that regional, continental and international recognition of qualifications that are comparable and compatible will lead to freer mobility of labour and students and that it will support the implementation of the EAC Common Market Protocol. Free movement of labour is a focus of the EAC and it is seen as one of the key pillars of regional integration (IUCEA 2015).

The most pertinent difficulty with implementation of the regional East African Qualifications Framework for Higher Education (EAQFHE) – and possibly also with the new Standards and Guidelines – is the diversity of practices and legal frameworks in the six partner states. There are sometimes opposing forces associated with national priorities (and even nationalism) versus regional integration. The fact that the IUCEA does not have accreditation or regulatory powers inhibits the mainstreaming of the EAQFHE and standards at institutional level in the different member states. Furthermore, in some countries there are more than one national bodies with shared roles and overlapping mandates (such as KNQF and CUE in Kenya) and conflicts between these authorities may also inhibit or delay the effective implementation of the newly developed Standards and Guidelines.

## THE DEVELOPMENT AND IMPLEMENTATION OF A DOCTORAL QUALIFICATION STANDARD IN SOUTH AFRICA

The comprehensive South African National Qualifications Framework (NQF) was developed in terms of the provisions of the South African Qualifications Authority Act, No. 58 of 1995. Within that broader framework, the Higher Education Qualifications Framework (HEQF) was adopted in 2007 to establish a single qualifications framework for higher education (DoE 2007). However, in 2008 the amended NQF Act, No. 67 of 2008 led to the adoption of the more detailed Higher Education Qualifications Sub-framework (HEQSF) in 2009 (revised in 2013) (DHET 2013).

Three national authorities are involved in the oversight and management of the implementation of the HEQSF. The Department of Higher Education and Training is responsible for the approval of the "programme and qualification mix" of public institutions. The Higher Education Quality Committee (HEQC) of the Council on Higher Education (CHE) has the mandate to accredit all higher education qualifications and programmes. SAQA is responsible to register qualifications on the NQF. The South African CHE is an independent statutory body established in 2001 in terms of the Higher Education Act, No. 101 of 1997 as amended). The CHE advises the Minister of Higher Education and Training on higher education and is responsible for quality assurance and promotion through its HEQC. In the process of exercising its accreditation mandate, the CHE/HEQC developed the HEQSF (in consultation with higher education institutions, professional councils and all the relevant national authorities), as well as a number of national policy frameworks, such as the national Framework for Programme Accreditation (HEQC 2004a) and its accompanying Criteria for Programme Accreditation (HEQC 2004b), and more recently, the Framework for Qualification Standards in Higher Education (HEQC 2013).

In the South African Higher Education Qualifications Sub-framework (HEQSF), qualification descriptions and regulations are provided for all the different types of higher education qualifications, including two types of doctoral qualifications, the (general) doctoral degree and the professional doctoral degree (DHET 2013). While the (general) doctoral degree consists of only a full doctoral dissertation, the professional doctoral degree includes a coursework component (accounting for one third of the total credits) in addition to a dissertation of a more limited scope (accounting for two thirds of the total credits). For each of the two doctoral qualification types, the HEQSF stipulates the formal requirements for matters such as the minimum admission requirements, the duration of study, the NQF level, the credit load and the thesis. The HEQSF also includes stipulations (stated very briefly) on the purpose, the defining characteristics and information on doctoral graduate attributes. Starting with the original NQF (adopted in 1995) culminating after various revisions in the revised HEQSF (adopted in 2013), much thinking and conceptualising around the purpose, nature and characteristics of the doctoral qualification have been done in South Africa.

However, these brief qualification description statements in the HEQSF did not amount to a full doctoral standard. Along with the development of the HEQSF, the CHE/HEQC also developed the Framework for Qualification Standards in Higher Education (adopted in 2013) in which the notion of a qualification standard was spelled out in much more detail (HEQC 2013:6), based on this definition: "A qualification standard is [...] a generic statement of the learning domains, the level of achievement and the graduate attributes that characterise and are required for the award of the qualification." The framework document (2013:9-12) also stipulates what can be expected from a qualification standard (e.g. it can be used to guide the accreditation, to recognise a learning programme and to establish benchmarks for the international comparability of qualifications), and what cannot be expected from a qualification standard (e.g. to provide a resolution to all issues surrounding the academic quality or to guarantee the recognition of learning credits for students).

In January 2017, in collaboration with the National Research Foundation, the CHE/HEQC commenced a process to develop a fully-fledged South African Doctoral Qualification Standard to meet the requirements of the Framework for Qualification Standards. Based on extensive research on international doctoral standards and a consideration of the local South African conditions for doctoral education, the CHE/HEQC technical team produced a draft National Doctoral Qualification Standard document and after a broad consultative process it was approved by the CHE in November 2018 (CHE 2018).

The Qualification Standard consists of five sections: (1) Preamble and rationale, (2) Purpose, (3) NQF level and credits, (4) Graduate attributes, (5) Context and conditions for the supervision and assessment of the doctoral qualification.

The rationale for the adoption of the Qualification Standard is indicated as "to help ensure that the HEIs in South Africa not only maintain the standing of their doctoral programmes and graduates, but seek, through innovation and enhancement, to develop their procedures and quality assurance" (CHE 2018:8) and "to set benchmarks for acceptable quality across the national higher education system on a par with global standards" (CHE 2018:10). Much effort was put into the preamble and rationale to contextualise the standard so that it is relevant and appropriate for the specific conditions of doctoral provision in South Africa without compromising alignment with global standards. Reference is made to the relevance and importance of doctoral education against the background of key policy documents such as South Africa's *Ten Year Innovation Plan 2008-2018* which states that South Africa needed to increase its growth rate of doctoral graduates "by a factor of 5 over the next 10-20 years" (DST 2008:29) and the *National Development Plan* which recognises the importance of the PhD for the development of innovation in the country, for transformation of the graduate cohort, for the mission of universities in a high skills economy, and which sets the ambitious target that the country should produce 5 000 doctoral graduates per year (in 2010 it was 1 420) (National Planning Commission 2012). The Qualification Standard specifically refers to the fact that the growth in doctoral enrolments and the diversity of doctoral candidates at South African universities led to concerns about quality and a greater burden on the supervisory corps who are supervising more students and increasingly also outside their areas of expertise (CHE 2018:10).

The statement of the purpose of the doctoral qualification comprises items generally included in standards across the world reflecting the recognition of the importance of setting the standard on par with global standards (including, for example, the key characteristic of the doctorate to develop "the highest level of holistic and systematic understanding of scholarship in, and stewardship of, a field of study through an original contribution that advances the frontiers of knowledge" and "the ability to engage independently in an extended course of research, showing thematic and conceptual coherence") (CHE 2018:11).

The statements on the doctoral graduate attributes (the knowledge and skills expected to be acquired by each doctoral graduate) form the heart of the Qualification Standard. Five knowledge attributes are listed (specialised knowledge of a discipline; specialised knowledge of a specific area of research; insight into the interconnectedness of the topic of research with other cognate fields; ethical awareness in research and professional conduct; and an original contribution to the field of study) and four high-levels skills are listed (research skills; reflection and autonomy; communication skills; and critical and analytical thinking for problem-solving). Achieving all these graduate attributes is the minimum threshold that each doctoral graduate must meet (HEQC 2018:13-14). However, to provide convincing evidence that each graduate has achieved all the attributes is perhaps the most challenging dimension of a quality review of doctoral provision.

In the last part the Qualification Standard sets out the context and conditions for supervision and for the assessment of a doctoral qualification, including the institutional conditions for doctoral provision (namely recruitment, selection and enrolment; supervision; appointment of supervisors; roles and responsibilities), the institutional mechanisms to monitor progression, the process, form and substance of the submission of the thesis, and the conditions for final assessment (selection of examiners; coordination and approval of examiners' reports; viva; joint, dual and co-badged degrees; appeals).

In 2019 the CHE embarked on a national review of the doctoral qualification. The Qualification Standard forms the basis for the assessment of all doctoral degrees offered and awarded by each higher education institution (public and private) in South Africa that has accredited doctoral programmes. Although this is a review and not a (re)accreditation, the consequences can be quite severe if a specific institution does not meet the standards. The HEQC may decide on a set of requirements to be addressed by the institution, together with timelines for improvement plans and progress reports. The process of reporting to the HEQC would continue until such time that the HEQC is satisfied that all requirements pertaining to the standards have been met (CHE 2019:6).

## DISCUSSION AND CONCLUSION

It would take us beyond the scope of this chapter to do a detailed comparison of the three contexts discussed above: Europe, East Africa and South Africa. We conclude, therefore, with a brief reflection on four issues: (1) meeting 'global standards' while provision is made for regional and national needs; (2) emerging commonalities in doctoral standards with regard to quality assurance arrangements; (3) moving beyond participatory (bottom-up) development processes to effective implementation; and (4) our guiding question: Can the setting and implementation of doctoral standards (or the 'right' doctoral standards) adequately address the quality concerns with doctoral education in Africa?

Firstly, notwithstanding the diverse research contexts in the three regions, the guiding principle of all the doctoral standards is the common goal of research excellence. For this book with its overarching focus on the global scholar, this is a key finding to be emphasised: the doctoral qualification is a global qualification, perhaps more so than other qualifications and demonstrating research excellence is the sine qua non of doctorateness everywhere in the world. The global nature and significance of the doctoral degree is probably one of the reasons for the keen interest and support of international funders (such as the British Council and the DAAD) in doctoral education in Africa.

However, in doctoral standards, global, regional and national (and even institutional) contexts and needs have to be balanced. Doctoral reforms in Europe, as we have illustrated, are informed and guided by the exchange of good practices, aiming to find common principles as articulated in the various documents discussed (e.g. the Salzburg documents). In Europe there is a widely held expectation that these principles can lead to a common understanding of quality in doctoral education. This does not mean, however, that it will no longer be necessary to take the specificities of the different subjects, institutional structures and strategies into account. There is a recurring question in debates on standards whether over-standardisation would not stifle creativity and innovation; that is, when "standards are conceived as a form of technology that travels unaffected by social influences" and result in all programmes everywhere looking more and more the same (isomorphism) and being implemented in the same way (isopraxism) (Stensaker, Harvey, Huisman, Langfeldt & Westerhuijden 2010). On the other hand, we maintain that, given current quality gaps between doctoral education in Africa and in other parts of the world (see the findings of the study on building PhD capacity in Africa reviewed above (ANIE 2018)), the potential benefits of the introduction of doctoral standards outweigh this potential pitfall, at least in the short to medium term.

Secondly, to unpack the issue of the contextualisation of standards a bit more, let us look at some of the commonalities and differences that can be identified in the area of quality assurance arrangements at doctoral level. There is emerging consensus in Europe that the assurance of the quality of doctoral education (across all fields and all institutions), requires, among other things, appropriate and effective QA arrangements in the areas listed in Table 8.1. From our overview of the recently developed doctoral standards in East Africa and South Africa, it is clear that most of these areas are covered – albeit in more or less detail and adapted to the conditions of Africa. Notably, support for international mobility is not included in the standard for South Africa, even although in practice the mobility of sub-Saharan African students (the number of students from a given region enrolled abroad expressed as a percentage of total tertiary enrolment) is among the highest in the world (UNESCO 2015:76).

**TABLE 8.1** Areas requiring effective QA arrangements: A comparison across regions

| Areas requiring effective QA arrangements | Europe | East Africa | South Africa |
|---|---|---|---|
| Professional development opportunities for supervisors | Salzburg I Principle 5 | Cluster 7 | Par 5.1 |
| Formal agreements between the doctoral candidate, supervisor and institution | Salzburg II par 2.7; Salzburg III | Clusters 5 and 9 | Par 5.1 |
| Standards of the process of thesis defence | Salzburg I Principle 5 | Cluster 12 | Par 5.3 and 5.4 |
| Procedures to enhance and ensure compliance with the requirements of research integrity and research ethics | Salzburg III | Cluster 8 | Par 2 |
| Procedures for the monitoring of the progress | Salzburg II Par 2.7 | Cluster 5 | Par 5.2 |
| Opportunities for flexible and optional transferable skills development | Salzburg II Par 2.8 | Cluster 3 | Par 4 |
| Support for internationalisation and mobility | Salzburg I Principle 9, Salzburg III | Cluster 10 | |
| Up-to-date information on monitoring indicators such as time to degree, completion rates, and graduate employment | Salzburg III | Cluster 5 and 9 | Par 5.2 |

Thirdly, it is clear that a participatory bottom-up approach has been followed in the development of doctoral standards in all three contexts. Irrespective of whether the initiative to develop standards came from an independent advocacy body (such as the EUA), or from a coordinating body with official recognition by the participating member states (such as the IUCEA), or from a statutory body (such as the CHE/HEQC), an iterative process of deep consultation with a range of stakeholders was followed in all cases, involving higher education institutions themselves as the providers of doctoral education, as well as a range of other stakeholders. However, even though the standards that were eventually accepted were the result of such bottom-up processes, the implementation of the standards (or, to ensure or enforce compliance with the standards), presents a different challenge. Various role players with different mandates are involved in complex processes. Even in the comparably more favourable circumstances of the European Higher Education Area and with the much longer period of concerted attention to doctoral reform, the recent survey of Hasgall et al. (2018) (see Figure 8.1 above), showed that much remains to be done in Europe and many institutions are not yet meeting all the standards. Learning from this experience, African countries can also expect to grapple with the implementation challenges in the years to come. It is one thing to have formally adopted regional and national standards. It is another thing to actually meet the standards. Bureaucratic regulations may also pose the risk of complicating collaborations in a manner that it is not feasible. It is crucial that successful doctoral education must take into account the current and future challenges confronting doctoral candidates.

Finally, is it only a matter of setting (and ensuring alignment with) the 'right' standards to address the concerns over the quality of doctoral provision in Africa? It is important to distinguish between the formal and the substantial dimensions of doctoral standards: the quality assurance arrangements (such as policies, procedures and monitoring) in distinction from the substantial aspects such as the purpose, nature and rationale of doctoral qualifications and the achievement of appropriate doctoral graduate attributes. Received wisdom often repeated in debates on quality assurance in South Africa is that effective quality assurance arrangements are necessary but not a sufficient condition for quality. Undoubtedly, the doctoral standards developed in recent years in different regions and countries in Africa are of great significance and represent a major step ahead, particularly if alignment with the formal dimensions of the doctoral standards can be ensured through effective implementation processes. Success in that regard can be an important proxy for the achievement (or not) of the substantial dimensions of doctoral standards, which is the real challenge awaiting African universities.

## REFERENCES

Altbach P, Reisberg L & Rumbley LE. 2010. Tracking a global academic revolution. *Change*, 42(2):30-39.

ANIE (African Network for Internationalisation of Education). 2018. *Building PhD capacity in Sub-Saharan Africa (ANIE)*. https://bit.ly/3sF1elH [Accessed 8 June 2020]. https://doi.org/10.1080/00091381003590845

Botha J, Vilyte G & De Klerk M. 2019. Digital training can help supervisors lift PhD output. *The Conversation*, 14 November. https://bit.ly/3n8xWL7 [Accessed 7 January 2020].

CHE (Council on Higher Education). 2018. *Qualification Standard for Doctoral Degrees*. Pretoria: Council on Higher Education

CHE (Council on Higher Education). 2019. *National Review Manual: Doctoral Qualifications*. Pretoria: Council on Higher Education.

Cloete N, Bunting I & Van Schalkwyk F. 2018. *Research universities in Africa*. Somerset West: African Minds. https://doi.org/10.47622/9781928331872

Commission for University Education. 2014. *Harmonized criteria and guidelines for appointment and promotion of academic staff in universities in Kenya*. Nairobi: Commission for University Education.

DAAD (Deutscher Akademischer Austauschdienst). 2014. *DAAD Strategies for countries and regions: Academic collaboration with the countries of Sub-Saharan Africa*. Bonn: DAAD.

DHET (Department of Higher Education and Training). 2013. *The Higher Education Qualifications Sub-Framework (HEQSF)*. Pretoria: Department of Higher Education and Training.

DHET (Department of Higher Education and Training). 2019. *Report on the evaluation of the 2017 universities' research output*. Pretoria: Department of Higher Education and Training.

DoE (Department of Education). 2007. *Higher Education Qualifications Framework (HEQF)*. Government Gazette, 30353.

DST (Department of Science and Technology). 2008. *Innovation Towards a Knowledge-Based Economy. Ten-Year Innovation Plan 2008-2018*. Pretoria: Department of Science and Technology.

EC (European Commission). 2005. *Towards a European Education Area*. https://bit.ly/3ekgn6N [Accessed 30 January 2020].

EIASM/EDAMBA Joint Task Force. 2014. *A European Code of Practice for Doctoral Studies in Management and Business drafted by an EIASM/EDAMBA Joint Task Force*. https://bit.ly/3auGHKl [Accessed 21 January 2020].

EUA (European University Association). 2005a. *Doctoral Programmes for the European Knowledge Society*. https://bit.ly/3dDt6Cs [Accessed 11 February 2020].

EUA (European University Association). 2005b. *Salzburg II Recommendations: European universities*. Geneva: European Universities Association.

EUA (European University Association). 2019a. *European University Association: The voice of Europe's universities*. https://bit.ly/2Qlg6bC [Accessed 11 February 2020].

EUA (European University Association). 2019b. *Council for Doctoral Education. Who we are*. https://bit.ly/3gtRkkk [Accessed 30 January 2020].

EUA (European University Association). 2019c. *Bologna Process*. https://bit.ly/3aNpoo7 [Accessed 30 January 2020].

EUA-CDE (European University Association Council on Doctoral Education). 2010. *Salzburg II Recommendations*. https://bit.ly/3dDsFI8 [Accessed 11 February 2020].

EUA-CDE (European University Association Council on Doctoral Education). 2016. Doctoral Education – Taking Salzburg forward. Implementation and new challenges. https://bit.ly/3xelsox [Accessed 11 February 2020].

European Ministers Responsible for Higher Education. 2005. *The European Higher Education Area – Achieving the Goals*. Bergen. https://bit.ly/3xel2OZ [Accessed 4 February 2020].

Fatunde T. 2011. NIGERIA: Urgent need for more academics with PhDs. *University World News*, 11 December. https://bit.ly/3nhQ19G [Accessed 7 January 2020].

Hasgall A, Saenen B & Borrel-Diamian L. 2019. *Doctoral education in Europe today: approaches and institutional structures.* https://bit.ly/32BC0dh [Accessed 28 October 2019].

Higher Education Authority (HEA). 2015. *National Framework for Doctoral Education.* Dublin: Higher Education Authority.

HEQC (Higher Education Quality Committee). 2004a. *Framework for Programme Accreditation.* Pretoria: Council on Higher Education.

HEQC (Higher Education Quality Committee). 2004b. *Criteria for programme accreditation, Council on Higher Education.* https://bit.ly/2RTy1H0 [Accessed 8 June 2020].

HEQC (Higher Education Quality Committee. 2013. *Framework for Qualification Standards in Higher Education.* https://bit.ly/2QKaEz8 [Accessed 8 June 2020].

IAU (International Association of Universities). 2010. *Changing Nature of Doctoral Studies in sub-Saharan Africa.* https://bit.ly/3guiwPX [Accessed 8 June 2020].

IUCEA (Inter-University Council for East Africa). 2015. *East African Qualifications Framework for Higher Education.* Kampala: IUCEA.

IUCEA (Inter-University Council for East Africa. 2018. *Standards and Guidelines for Postgraduate Studies in East Africa.* Kampala: IUCEA.

Kuria M & Ndivo L. 2016. *Rapporteur's Comprehensive Report of DIES Seminar: Quality Doctoral Education – A prerequisite for strong universities in Africa.* Nairobi: DAAD.

Makoni M. 2019. New online course helps to plug doctoral supervision gap. *University World News*, 21 March. https://bit.ly/3dFpPT17 [Accessed 7 January 2020].

McGreggor K. 2013. Where to from here for the African PhD? *University World News*, 2 November. https://bit.ly/3naXdUR [Accessed 4 February 2020].

Ministerio de Educacíon. 2011. *Real Decreto 99/2011, de 28 de enero, por el que se regulan las enseñanzas oficiales de doctorado.* https://bit.ly/3sD6iH7 [Accessed 8 June 2020].

Mohamedbhai G. 2014. Massification in higher education institutions in Africa: Causes, consequences, and responses. *International Journal of African Higher Education*, 1(1):60-83. https://doi.org/10.6017/ijahe.v1i1.5644

Mouton J. 2018. African science: A legacy of neglect. In: C Beaudry, J Mouton & H Prozesky (eds.), *The next generation of scientists in Africa.* Somerset West: African Minds. 3-12.

National Planning Commission. 2012. *National Development Plan 2013. Our future – make it work.* Pretoria: National Planning Commission, Department of the Presidency.

O'Malley B. 2019. Research ethics now a strategic priority for doctoral schools. *University World News*, 18 January. https://bit.ly/2QQgf6l [Accessed 4 February 2020].

ORPHEUS/AMSE/WFME Task Force. 2012. *Standards for PhD Education in Biomedicine and Health Sciences in Europe.* https://bit.ly/3vbl6yi [Accessed 8 June 2020].

Republic of Uganda. 2002. *Protocol on the establishment of the Inter-University Council for East Africa.* Arusha.

Republic of Uganda. 2009. *East African Community Act Supplement. The Inter-University Council for East Africa Act.* Entebbe: Uganda Printing and Publishing Corporation.

République Francais. 2016. *Arrêté du 25 mai 2016 fixant le cadre national de la formation et les modalités conduisant à la délivrance du diplôme national de doctorat.* https://bit.ly/32BO0LT [Accessed 20 January 2020].

Stensaker B, Harvey I, Huisman J, Langfeldt L & Westerhuijden DF. 2010. The impact of the European Standards and Guidelines in agency evaluations. *European Journal of Education*, 45(4):577-587. https://doi.org/10.1111/j.1465-3435.2010.01450.x

UNESCO. 2015. *UNESCO Science Report: Towards 2030.* Paris. https://bit.ly/3n9HaGU [Accessed 5 February 2020].

# PART THREE

## TRAJECTORIES

# THE INTERDISCIPLINARY PHD

## PROCESSES, OUTCOMES AND CHALLENGES

Karri A. Holley

## INTRODUCTION

Increasing concern exists in supporting the interests of PhD students who seek to study and work in interdisciplinary areas. This interest is evident across national contexts, particularly in ways that federal governments seek to motivate interdisciplinary outcomes for graduate-level training. For decades, the National Science Foundation in the USA has prioritised interdisciplinary research and the role of graduate students in such research, with specific programme solicitations and funding support for these efforts (Holley 2018). In the UK, the Engineering and Physical Sciences Research Council (EPSRC) has funded over 50 000 doctoral students in the last 25 years in pursuit of innovative (typically interdisciplinary) learning programmes (Owen 2014). Similar approaches are evident in the work of the South African National Research Foundation, which supports graduate students in pursuit of new and innovative forms of knowledge production (NRF 2014).

These programmes are widespread, and the investment made in interdisciplinary doctoral education by multiple federal bodies and higher education institutions is significant. Such realities make understanding the process and outcomes of these efforts important, especially questions of how interdisciplinary doctoral programmes influence their graduates and the career trajectories of these scholars after degree completion. Interdisciplinary work is presumed to hold potential to produce original and innovative knowledge in part because of the integration of different disciplinary bodies of knowledge (Holley 2009). The persistence and expansion of wicked global problems, such as climate change, public health, poverty, and sustainability illustrate the limitations of relying on knowledge produced from traditional disciplinary confines, and suggest that interdisciplinary efforts at a doctoral level will only continue to grow.

## PART THREE • TRAJECTORIES

While the need exists for interdisciplinary programmes of study, so does recognition that such programmes provoke cultural, social, and organisational tension within higher education institutions (Holley 2019; Lyall 2019). Indeed, the development of most academic institutions focused the disciplines as a central component of organisational structure. Reflections of the disciplinary foundation of higher education permeate nearly every aspect of institutional life, ranging from financial allocations to campus buildings. Beyond the disciplinary structure of higher education are questions about job placement and professional outcomes (Begg, Bennett, Cicutto, Gadlin, Moss, Tentler & Schoenbaum 2015; McAlpine & Norton 2006). Two of these questions are: what are PhD students being trained for and how might training in interdisciplinary areas influence a graduate's experience in the job market?

How doctoral supervisors might effectively engage in and manage the experience of interdisciplinary PhD students is of particular relevance, given the competing demands on academic staff; the challenging nature of doctoral supervision; and the need to quickly adapt doctoral education to 21st century realities. Doctoral supervisors may not be trained in interdisciplinary areas themselves or may work in academic institutions without formal guidelines for interdisciplinary endeavours. These complications raise more questions about the interdisciplinary PhD experience.

This chapter provides a snapshot of interdisciplinary doctoral education through theoretical and empirical lenses with a specific focus on different national efforts and literature from different national contexts. The chapter is structured in three parts. The first is a literature review, including definitions of interdisciplinarity; the various forces driving interests in and funding for the interdisciplinary PhD; and different theoretical frameworks that have been used to understand the issue. Then, a review of national contexts and literature related to the interdisciplinary PhD is presented, where data are available. The chapter concludes with questions for policy makers and researchers for future work in this area.

## LITERATURE REVIEW

One challenge of understanding the interdisciplinary PhD student experience is that of defining interdisciplinarity. Various definitions of the term emphasise the idea of integrating knowledge from two or more disciplines (Holley 2018). Effective interdisciplinary learning requires "interaction of knowledge from different disciplines; integration of knowledge from different disciplines; and an overarching topic, theme, or problem that shapes the learning experience" (Holley 2017, abstract). Knowledge can be broadly defined, and can include research methodologies, and field-specific content areas, among other aspects. Structural and cultural efforts are common in achieving interdisciplinary outcomes, including jointly appointed academic staff, cross-departmental or cross-institutional programming, core curriculum that crosses departmental boundaries, and a funding source outside of a single college or department. But the definition of interdisciplinarity is not limited to institutional efforts. Rather, the term is one that requires social interaction and engagement among individuals. It is through the interaction of scholars from different disciplines that interdisciplinary outcomes result.

A related challenge is defining the "interdisciplinary PhD" (Callard & Fitzgerald 2015; Lyall 2019). Consider the various ways in which interdisciplinary work might manifest under such a label. Perhaps the student enrols in a degree programme that spans two or more academic departments; the student might be required to have co-supervisors (one from each of the constituent disciplines) or conduct research as part of an interdisciplinary laboratory. Another option might be if the student enrols in a traditional, single-discipline programme, but works as part of an interdisciplinary research team. Even a doctoral student enrolled in a traditional programme conducting independent research that crosses disciplinary boundaries might identify with the concept of interdisciplinarity. The student might receive funding from an interdisciplinary research initiative or construct a master's and doctoral programme of study in a way that allows for an interdisciplinary focus. Acknowledging the innumerable ways in which the interdisciplinary PhD might be experienced, and for the sake of consistency, this chapter defines the interdisciplinary PhD as a programme where students work with academic staff, curricula, or research topics in ways that include more than one academic field, within a single department or across multiple departments.

Not all interdisciplinary PhD degree programmes are connected to federal initiatives or funding. Defining the role of external forces in shaping the interdisciplinary experience can be difficult. Those programmes with explicit connections are easiest to classify, such as programmes where students and/or academic staff receive direct financial support from the federal government or other external stakeholder. Other programmes exist without this external support. Academic institutions might see interdisciplinary PhD programmes as potential "signature areas", or efforts to capitalise on academic staff interests and expertise while also signalling institutional innovation (Stone, Bollard & Harbor 2009). Programmes might also be stepping-stones towards later external grant funding, or a response to a local need or demand. Interdisciplinary PhD programming could develop in response to a market opportunity and the need for specialised training that does not exist elsewhere.

## PART THREE • TRAJECTORIES

While much of the extant research on the interdisciplinary PhD focuses on STEM (science, technology, engineering, and mathematics)-related fields, interdisciplinary experiences are found in a range of areas, including those broadly defined as humanities, social sciences, and professional areas of study. Persistent global problems that span across not only institutional boundaries, but also across national contexts, are one force driving interdisciplinary work. These problems are those without a straightforward planning response (Sun & Yang 2016); in other words, traditional approaches are unlikely to be effective. More recently, scholars and policymakers have considered those wicked global problems such as climate change that have an accelerating timeline, a short window in order to act, and little to no central authority to define and administer a solution. Interdisciplinary scholars focused on climate change might have training in (as a few examples) ecology, environmental studies, sociology, hydrology, or public policy – an endless list of potentially relevant disciplines, each with a unique contribution to understanding the causes of climate change and the actions required to combat it.

The topic of climate change represents not only the potential of interdisciplinary work, but also the messiness of the process (Hein, Ten Hoeve, Gopalakrishnan, Livneh, Adams, Marino & Weiler 2018). The growing body of research on climate change and interdisciplinary programming suggests attention to all levels of the academic progress. In an evaluation of an interdisciplinary climate change programme, Pharo, Davison, Warr, Nursey-Bray, Beswick, Wapstra and Jones (2012:497) conclude, "[There is a] need for recognition of the benefits of interdisciplinary learning to be matched by recognition of the need for financial and other resources to support collaborative teaching initiatives." Regardless of the interdisciplinary topic, academic institutions face the need for change in all aspects of their work: how students are trained; how curricula are designed; how academic staff are allocated; how admissions are conducted; how research programmes are funded; and how students are prepared for careers after graduation. For interdisciplinary PhD graduates, the last issue is especially relevant, considering the dearth of traditional academic staff jobs, as well as an uncertain global job market. The question of how interdisciplinary doctoral students should experience their curriculum is inevitably intertwined with questions of how they might engage in their career, after degree completion. How might graduates employ their newly acquired skills (skills that could be labelled as 'interdisciplinary') in the job market? Answers to this question remind that such graduates may work inside academia, but they might also work in multiple settings outside of academia, such as industry, policy, or government contexts. Recognising the need to change the doctoral curriculum to support interdisciplinary work is ideally accompanied with considerations of a student's professional trajectory after degree completion.

It is important not only to engage in research that defines the interdisciplinary PhD and understands the multiple forces shaping this experience, but also to consider what theoretical and methodological tools can be used to engage in this research. Scholars have employed different theoretical frameworks to understand the PhD student experience, most commonly the frameworks of socialisation and identity development. While each proves useful in understanding aspects of enrolment, they also have limitations when applied to the study of doctoral education. For example, the frameworks do not always serve well when thinking about student experiences after degree completion or the experiences of minority or underrepresented students. Further, these frameworks give insight into student enrolment in traditional disciplinary-based programmes, and their utility for highlighting aspects of innovative interdisciplinary curricula is unclear. Definitions of socialisation emphasise the acquisition of knowledge, skills and values relevant for a specific community (Weidman, Twale & Stein 2001). Concepts of identity development also suggest that doctoral students participate in a community. McAlpine and Norton (2006) define these communities as departmental/disciplinary, institutional, and societal/international, recognising that student experiences occur not only within the academic institution, but also outside of it. These multiple experiences (formal and informal) contribute to students not only conceiving of their own identity as an academic, but also performing and being recognised as one.

Frameworks of socialisation and identity development allow for insight into how enrolment changes an individual's identity and sense of belonging, but questions remain. One set of questions concerns how these forces operate within an interdisciplinary setting, perhaps one that includes multiple disciplines with overlapping or conflicting norms. Interdisciplinary students may find themselves as perpetual 'outsiders' in multiple disciplinary communities. Another lingering question is how external funding, such as that provided by federal governments or other non-academic agencies, might influence the interdisciplinary PhD. Yet another set of questions concerns how immersion in an interdisciplinary community shapes student outcomes, especially related to choices graduates make upon degree completion in addition to their advancement in their chosen careers.

Using these frameworks complemented by those with a focus on career development or progression illuminates the totality of the interdisciplinary PhD experience. One example is Laudel and Glaser (2008); their analysis of the 'apprentice to colleague' development of early career researchers emphasises (a) the cognitive career, (b) the organisational career, and (c) the community career. These various aspects focus on an individual's maturation as a researcher (such as continuity in research projects, or the ways in which findings might build upon each other, or how the scholar might construct an interdisciplinary community as research matures). The approach recognises that doctoral graduates move through different organisational types (some being higher education institutions, and some not) while receiving different organisational labels (e.g. assistant director). Ultimately, the communities that graduates build while enrolled in an interdisciplinary PhD programme expand in unique ways specific to the individual. Other theoretical approaches under the social cognitive career label (Lent, Brown & Hackett 2002) illustrate that interdisciplinary PhD graduates are indeed subject to the influences shaping the global job market, but also make individual choices that contribute to individual career outcomes – meaning that there is no single outcome for interdisciplinary training.

The various elements necessary for understanding the interdisciplinary PhD student experience exist. These programmes are prevalent, and multiple forces are involved in shaping programme structure, funding, and mission. Researchers also have various theoretical tools to use in their study of the interdisciplinary PhD. Being able to ground this research in contemporary efforts that reflect the variety of approaches internationally requires documenting the empirical evidence of national initiatives and other related literature. This reality is tempered by the availability of data. The following section offers snapshots of different national contexts to illustrate the processes and outcomes inherent to the interdisciplinary PhD experience.

## NATIONAL PERSPECTIVES ON THE INTERDISCIPLINARY PHD

An analysis of different national perspectives related to the interdisciplinary PhD experience allows for insight into similarities and differences, as well as questions related to institutional structure, support, and funding. Andres, Bengtsen, Castaño, Crossouard, Keefer and Pyhältö (2015:15) concluded that "[u]nderstandings of global and local levels of doctoral education are deeply linked, as global drivers saturate local doctoral education and supervision practice". Among these drivers are the massification and professionalisation of doctoral education, as well as the development of quality assurance systems. The number of awarded doctorates continues to grow at the same time as the perception of the degree as necessary for a range of careers, not simply those within academia. Given the social and economic benefits presumed inherent in the degree, federal governments are motivated to monitor postgraduate investments and outcomes. The interdisciplinary PhD is one example of this investment; ironically, despite this motivation, there exists a sparse amount of available data and published research documenting processes and outcomes for interdisciplinary programming at the doctoral level.

### The United States of America as a case study

Much of the extant research related to the interdisciplinary PhD in the USA focuses on STEM-related fields of study. Nearly 300 interdisciplinary doctoral programmes in STEM-related fields exist in American higher education, including degrees in materials science, neuroscience, environmental studies, bioinformatics, and marine science (Association for Interdisciplinary Studies 2020). One focus of research has been on those programmes identified as Integrated Graduate Education and Research Traineeship (IGERT) programmes, the flagship interdisciplinary initiative funded by the National Science Foundation. An evaluative study (Carney, Martinez, Dreier, Neishi & Parsad 2011) concluded that the majority of IGERT participants were already interested in interdisciplinary work before enrolling in an affiliated programme, meaning their undergraduate degrees or other professional experiences likely shaped their perception of interdisciplinarity. Further, nearly all the IGERT graduates surveyed described using more than one discipline in their professional positions; they were able to make use of the knowledge and skills gained in their programme after graduation. In addition, half of the graduates indicated they were required to engage with new disciplines or bodies of knowledge in their place of employment (and were comfortable doing so). Carney et al. (2011) found that the majority of IGERT graduates held positions at academic institutions in either research or teaching positions, similar to PhD graduates from traditional disciplinary programmes, although other research (Kniffin & Hanks 2017) documented that interdisciplinary PhD graduates earned a higher salary working outside the academic sector, raising questions about the attractiveness of an academic career.

The skills gained as part of the interdisciplinary PhD experience are crucial for understanding student learning and outcomes. Begg et al. (2015), in a summary review of multiple interdisciplinary PhD programmes, found that while the skills vary based on the topic of interest, common areas of emphasis included leadership, teamwork, and communication. These areas were especially important for scholars to be able to do work across disciplinary boundaries – lead a team of diverse disciplinary researchers, for example, or communicate key ideas to a diverse disciplinary audience. Rather than a depth of knowledge within a single discipline, interdisciplinary scholars might hold a breadth of knowledge across a range of disciplines and possess the integrative skills necessary to bring the disciplinary range together.

A longitudinal qualitative study of interdisciplinary PhD graduates (Holley 2018) found that such graduates faced the same challenges as those from traditional disciplinary-based programmes. A weak academic job market and an elusive balance between professional and personal demands exacerbated the challenge of developing an interdisciplinary career. Concerns over the job market and uncertainty regarding career pathways frequently overshadowed conversations about being able to engage in interdisciplinary work – graduates were more likely to worry over getting a job close to family, or in a location where their partner might also find work, than they were with working in an interdisciplinary setting. The graduates did express confidence in engaging across disciplinary boundaries, and with individuals from other fields of study, but expressed concern over being able to define and promote their professional identities in the job market (Holley 2018). The interdisciplinary label of the degree did not always match the job description or title. In sum, the effectiveness of the interdisciplinary PhD cannot be divorced from the job market that its graduates enter.

These graduates gain exposure to novel forms of research in addition to different disciplinary bodies of knowledge. One result is a professional network that may not reflect the network of a traditional disciplinary PhD graduate. Little if any research has examined what role this professional network might play in the job-seeking behaviours of interdisciplinary PhD graduates or how this network might evolve once graduates are in the workforce.

### Other relevant factors across national contexts

Although whether or not doctoral students undertake coursework as part of their degree programme varies widely by country, the question of how doctoral students learn to engage in interdisciplinary activities remains significant. In a review of interdisciplinary programmes in Canadian universities, Gillis, Nelson, Driscoll, Hodgins, Fraser and Jacobs (2017) found evidence of widespread interdisciplinary efforts across both undergraduate and graduate levels, but also noted a lack of emphasis on integrative mechanisms, or helping students understand ways in which different disciplinary bodies of knowledge can be brought together. They concluded that the most common effort was "a trickle-down approach that does not disrupt the traditional academic framework" (Gillis et al. 2017:214). This challenge is also seen in the research laboratory. The concept of integration is essential to interdisciplinary outcomes, although consensus does not exist on how students might master the concept or be able to employ it consistently in their interdisciplinary efforts.

A related component of the PhD across national contexts is that of supervision, which is widely considered to be at the core of a successful PhD experience. Supervision of doctoral students enrolled in an interdisciplinary PhD programme is likely especially challenging for academic staff, many of whom were themselves trained in a traditional disciplinary-based programme. Research from Australia illustrates the challenges of supervision at all stages of the interdisciplinary PhD. Adkins (2009) showed how supervisors themselves experience methodological challenges related to the interdisciplinary doctorate. Commenting on the need for deeper reflection about the underlying foundation of dissertation research, Adkins (2009:10) suggests that "[t]he integration at stake potentially needs to occur not only at the substantive level but also in the logics and rationales of inquiry itself". Interdisciplinary PhD students with co-supervisors, joint supervision, or other alternative forms of supervision than the traditional single model may encounter personal, professional, or institutional tensions. Kiley (2009) documented how the selection of an examiner for the dissertation can be especially fraught with respect to students in interdisciplinary PhD programmes, namely the selection of a scholar with content-area expertise who is open to the methodology and focus of the study while also able to assess the topic as an integrative whole.

Related to questions of curriculum and supervision, how interdisciplinary PhD programmes can best manage their relationships with government, industry, and other stakeholders is a point of consideration. Writing about the growth of Cooperative Research Centres in Australia, Harman (2008) maintained that such training enhanced the marketability of graduates while at the same time promoted professional development skills and opportunities necessary for the graduates' career. Additional research on these centres suggests that the role of the supervisor may be less influential in an interdisciplinary programme with industry partners (Strengers 2014). A related study on Italian doctoral supervisors (Maguire, Prodi & Gibbs 2018) revealed how doctoral supervision might be enhanced by interdisciplinary partnerships, with academic supervisors able to upgrade their skills and knowledge by engaging with workplace professionals.

## FUTURE WORK ON THE INTERDISCIPLINARY PHD

After examining extant knowledge related to the interdisciplinary PhD, this section offers questions for policymakers and researchers for future work in this area. The need for more work on the process of the interdisciplinary PhD is evident from the lack of empirical evidence and literature on the topic. Areas of concern include not only programme structure and student support, but also such issues as doctoral supervision, curriculum design, peer engagement, external partnerships (e.g. with government and industry), and programme longevity. Should such programmes eventually become more stable, traditional departments in the model of the academic discipline? What value if any might be gained from supporting such programmes outside of this traditional model?

Even less knowledge exists about the outcomes of the interdisciplinary PhD, not only for students, but also for academic staff, institutions, and society. One obvious approach would be for more attention to externally funded programmes; this approach would illustrate the 'return on investment' for funding agencies to help shape future funding priorities. But other approaches should closely examine the student experience and the ways in which the completion of an interdisciplinary PhD shapes professional outcomes, particularly in relation to peers who complete more traditional disciplinary-based programmes. It is assumed that interdisciplinary programmes offer a 'value-added' experience, but this assumption is not always supported by empirical evidence.

These questions could consider how interdisciplinary PhD graduates navigate the job market and what choices they make relative to their professional personal goals. Other questions might consider how these graduates actually employ the knowledge and skills gained in their programmes and in what ways the curriculum proved advantageous or lacking. This sort of data would be valuable for academic staff and institutions as they consider ways to strengthen not just the interdisciplinary PhD, but also the experiences of all PhD students, regardless of the disciplinary basis of their programme.

A related focus on outcomes should be whether and how these graduates might contribute to the interdisciplinary base of knowledge considered so crucial for the resolution of the global issues that plague contemporary society. After degree completion, how do graduates put their newfound skills and knowledge to use? In what settings, and to what end? Recognising that the PhD exhibits unique characteristics based on the institution and the national context, an international examination of these questions is necessary to inform the behaviours and beliefs of higher education.

## CONCLUSION

The desire to train doctoral students in an interdisciplinary curriculum and produce scholars capable of crossing disciplinary boundaries is an important characteristic of global higher education in the 21st century. As this chapter documents, however, more attention is needed to understand not just the process of how interdisciplinary doctoral education might operate, but also the outcomes at an individual, institutional, and social level. On the one hand, interdisciplinary programmes allow for the kind of innovative knowledge production expected of higher education institutions. Investments at the doctoral level provide for cohorts of scholars with skills and knowledge inherent in the integrative process. Yet on the other hand, such programmes run counter to both the norms of doctoral education and the conventional institution; these tensions do not disappear simply because external stakeholders offer funding for interdisciplinary work. The previous century brought specialisation of knowledge, resulting in the departmental structure common today. How doctoral programmes might most effectively cope with the evolution of knowledge in this century and especially the epistemological challenge of interdisciplinary integration is a topic that demands the attention of academic staff, institutions, and external stakeholders alike.

## REFERENCES

Adkins B. 2009. PhD pedagogy and the changing knowledge landscapes of universities. *Higher Education Research & Development*, 28(2):165-177. https://doi.org/10.1080/07294360902725041

Andres L, Bengtsen SS, Castaño LG, Crossouard B, Keefer JM & Pyhältö K. 2015. Drivers and interpretations of doctoral education today: National comparisons. *Frontline Learning Research*, 3(3):5-22. https://doi.org/10.14786/flr.v3i3.177

Association for Interdisciplinary Studies. 2020. Directory of IDS doctoral programs. https://bit.ly/3nd0i76 [Accessed 1 January 2020].

Begg MD, Bennett LM, Cicutto L, Gadlin H, Moss M, Tentler J & Schoenbaum E. 2015. Graduate education for the future: New models and methods for the clinical and translational workforce. *Clinical and Translational Science*, 8(6):787-792. https://doi.org/10.1111/cts.12359

Callard F & Fitzgerald D. 2015. *Rethinking Interdisciplinarity across the Social Sciences and Neurosciences*. London: Palgrave Macmillan. https://doi.org/10.1057/9781137407962

Carney J, Martinez A, Dreier J, Neishi K & Parsad A. 2011. *Evaluation of the National Science Foundation's Integrative Graduate Education and Research Traineeship Program (IGERT): Follow-up Study of IGERT Graduates*. Arlington, VA: National Science Foundation.

Gillis D, Nelson J, Driscoll B, Hodgins K, Fraser E & Jacobs S. 2017. Interdisciplinary and transdisciplinary research and education in Canada: A review and suggested framework. *Collected Essays on Learning and Teaching*, 10:203-222. https://doi.org/10.22329/celt.v10i0.4745

Harman KM. 2008. Challenging traditional research training culture: Industry-oriented doctoral programs in Australian cooperative research centres. In: J Valimaa & O Ylijoki (eds.), *Cultural Perspectives on Higher Education*. Dordrecht: Springer. 179-195. https://doi.org/10.1007/978-1-4020-6604-7_12

Hein CJ, Ten Hoeve JE, Gopalakrishnan S, Livneh B, Adams HD, Marino EK & Weiler C. 2018. Overcoming early career barriers to interdisciplinary climate change research. *Wiley Interdisciplinary Reviews: Climate Change*, 9(5):e530. https://doi.org/10.1002/wcc.530

Holley KA. 2009. *Understanding Interdisciplinary Challenges and Opportunities in Higher Education* (ASHE Higher Education Report Series). San Francisco, CA: Jossey-Bass. 32-35.

Holley KA. 2017. Interdisciplinary curriculum in higher education. In: G Noblit (ed.), *Oxford Research Encyclopedia of Education*. https://bit.ly/2RXBJ2j [Accessed 1 January 2020]. https://doi.org/10.1093/acrefore/9780190264093.013.138

Holley KA. 2018. The longitudinal career experiences of interdisciplinary neuroscience PhD recipients. *The Journal of Higher Education*, 89(1):106-127. https://doi.org/10.1080/00221546.2017.1341755

Holley KA. 2019. Learning from Klein: Examining current interdisciplinary practices within U.S. higher education. *Issues in Integrative Studies*, 37(2):17-32.

Kiley M. 2009. 'You don't want a smart Alec': Selecting examiners to assess doctoral dissertations. *Studies in Higher Education*, 34(8):889-903. https://doi.org/10.1080/03075070802713112

Kniffin K & Hanks A. 2017. Antecedents and near-term consequences for interdisciplinary dissertators. *Scientometrics*, 111, 1225. https://doi.org/10.1007/s11192-017-2317-y

Laudel G & Gläser J. 2008. From apprentice to colleague: The metamorphosis of early career researchers. *Higher Education*, 55(3):387-406. https://doi.org/10.1007/s10734-007-9063-7

Lent RW, Brown SD & Hackett G 2002. Social cognitive career theory. In: D Brown (ed.), *Career Choice and Development*. San Francisco: Wiley. 255-311.

Lyall C. 2019. *Being an Interdisciplinary Academic: How Institutions Shape University Careers*. London: Palgrave Macmillan. https://doi.org/10.1007/978-3-030-18659-3

Maguire K, Prodi E & Gibbs P. 2018. Minding the gap in doctoral supervision for a contemporary world: A case from Italy. *Studies in Higher Education*, 43(5):867-877. https://doi.org/10.1080/03075079.2018.1438114

McAlpine L & Norton J. 2006. Reframing our approach to doctoral programs: An integrative framework for action and research. *Higher Education Research & Development*, 25(1):3-17. https://doi.org/10.1080/07294360500453012

NRF (National Research Foundation). 2014. *National Research Foundation Strategy 2020*. Pretoria, South Africa: National Research Foundation.

Owen R. 2014. The UK Engineering and Physical Sciences Research Council's commitment to a framework for responsible innovation. *Journal of Responsible Innovation*, 1(1):113-117. https://doi.org/10.1080/23299460.2014.882065

Pharo EJ, Davison A, Warr K, Nursey-Bray M, Beswick K, Wapstra E & Jones C. 2012. Can teacher collaboration overcome barriers to interdisciplinary learning in a disciplinary university? A case study using climate change. *Teaching in Higher Education*, 17(5):497-507. https://doi.org/10.1080/13562517.2012.658560

Stone T, Bollard K & Harbor JM. 2009. Launching interdisciplinary programs as college signature areas: An example. *Innovative Higher Education*, 34(5):321. https://doi.org/10.1007/s10755-009-9119-y

Strengers YA. 2014. Interdisciplinarity and industry collaboration in doctoral candidature: Tensions within and between discourses. *Studies in Higher Education*, 39(4):546-559. https://doi.org/10.1080/03075079.2012.709498

Sun J & Yang K. 2016. The wicked problem of climate change: A new approach based on social mess and fragmentation. *Sustainability*, 8(12):1312. https://doi.org/10.3390/su8121312

Weidman JC, Twale DJ & Stein EL. 2001. *Socialization of graduate and professional students in higher education: A perilous passage?* (ASHE-ERIC Higher Education Report). San Francisco, CA: Jossey-Bass. 28.

# FINDING ACADEMIC JOBS IN STRATIFIED COUNTRIES

THE EFFECTS OF SOCIAL CLASS OF ORIGIN IN THE DEVELOPMENT OF ACADEMIC NETWORKS FOR CHILEAN PHDS

Roxana Chiappa

## INTRODUCTION

In the same way that the South African government seeks to participate actively in the Fourth Industrial Revolution, Chile has sought to increase its scientific and technological capacity to participate in the so-called knowledge economy since the middle of 2000 (CNIC 2006, 2007, 2008). To achieve this goal, one of the strategies of the Chilean government was to increase the number of postgraduate fellowships exponentially. Within the period of 2008-2018, the government awarded 10 000 doctoral fellowships to fund doctoral degrees in Chilean and foreign universities (CONICYT 2018). This fellowship programme largely explains the rapid increase to an estimated 714 new doctorates in 2016 – twice the number of graduates in 2007 (RYCIT 2018.). It is estimated that more than a third of the scholarships were awarded to individuals who completed doctoral degrees in foreign universities, primarily in England, USA, Spain and Australia (CONICYT 2018; Perez Mejias, Chiappa & Guzmán-Valenzuela 2018).

The increasing access to doctoral credentials poses the classical question about the equalising power of education to close gaps among individuals who grew up in different social class groups in highly stratified societies (see Arum, Gamoran & Shavit 2007; Bastedo 2014; Collins 1979). Chile, like South Africa, has a high level of income inequality, which is manifested in all aspects of the people's social life, including higher education (PNUD 2017). Yet, there are few studies in Chile and elsewhere that have empirically evaluated to what extent social class of origin influences labour outcomes – chances of being hired, income level, and promotion – after completing a doctorate (Chiappa & Perez Mejias 2019; González-Canché 2017; Oldfield & Conant 2001; Jungbauer-Gans & Gross 2013; Hartmann 2010; Torche 2018).

Social class of origin refers to the socio-economic background of one's family (Bourdieu 1987), commonly indicated by occupation and education of parents (Hout 2008; Torche 2018). Different to gender and race, social class of origin is expected to be an imperceptible attribute of individuals with doctorates, since this group of professionals possesses advanced skills that position them as an elite in the workforce of their respective countries. In Chile, 80% of doctoral graduates are working in higher education institutions (MINECON 2015a) and it is estimated that those with doctoral degrees have a less than 1% chance of unemployment (INE 2019).

Some of the few studies that have considered the effect of social class of origin on the career of doctorate holders in different countries suggest the already well-known dynamic of 'accumulative advantage' reproduced through unequal access to prestigious higher education institutions (for Chile, see Chiappa & Perez Mejias 2019; for the USA, see González-Canché 2017; Torche 2018; for Germany, see Jungbauer-Gans & Gross 2013; Hartmann 2010). In the specific case of Chile, doctorate holders working as academics who come from upper social class families went to more reputable undergraduate universities and consequently gained access to more prestigious PhD-granting universities as compared with their peers from lower social class groups. The level of prestige of PhD-granting university is one of the main predictors of income (Chiappa & Perez Mejias 2019).

Likewise, other empirical research on academic job placement shows a direct relationship between the level of prestige of a prestigious PhD-granting university attended and the prestige of the current employing university (Burris 2004; Clauset, Arbesman & Larremore 2015; Cowan & Rosello 2018, Hadani, Coombes, Das & Jalajas 2012; Headworth & Freese 2015). For instance, in an analysis of academic job placement between 1970 and 2004 in South Africa, Rowen and Collen (2018) found that the five most prestigious universities had produced between 48 and 58% of all PhD graduates working as academics in South African universities. These five universities tend to hire PhD holders who graduated from this elite group.

Based on such evidence, one may assume that social class of origin intervenes in the chances of securing academic jobs at prestigious universities, but to my best knowledge, there is no study that has looked at the connection between social class of origin and *how* people with doctorates go about securing faculty jobs.

## CHAPTER 10 • FINDING ACADEMIC JOBS IN STRATIFIED COUNTRIES

In this chapter, I contribute to filling this knowledge gap through discussing a study in which I undertook a qualitative analysis of how early-career doctorate holders (hereafter ECDs) in engineering found academic jobs at universities in Chile. The sample comprised 10 cases of ECDs who grew up in different social class groups and found a tenure-track academic position at Chilean universities with different levels of institutional prestige within two years after PhD completion. I pay special attention to how social class of origin intervened in the ways that ECDs used and developed academic networks to find their current jobs. I focused on ECDs in engineering because Chilean scientific and technological government agencies had set engineering as one of the key disciplinary fields advancing a knowledge economy (CNIC 2007, 2008). Two research questions guided the project: (1) How do ECDs in engineering from different social classes of origin find academics jobs? (2) To what extent did social class of origin of doctorate holders influence the ways in which doctorate holders relied on their academic networks to find their current jobs?

The evidence presented in this chapter links to the central theme of this book in two ways. First, it addresses a fundamental question on the equalising power of (doctoral) education in countries with emerging economies, which have recently expanded their doctoral enrolment to participate in the knowledge economy. Second, the evidence presented in this chapter ratifies the relevance of having access to international networks to secure academic positions.

## CHILEAN INCOME INEQUALITY REPRODUCED IN THE HIGHER EDUCATION SYSTEM

Until October 2019, Chile was considered an exception in terms of economic and political stability in the Latin American region. The social protests that stopped the normal functioning of the country during the last weeks of 2019 until the writing of this chapter indicate that Chile's exceptionality in Latin America relied on pillars of profound income and social inequality. Indeed, Chile has the highest income per capita (USD 25,168 PPP) (OECD n.d.), the lowest level of poverty (4% of the population live on less than 5.5 USD per day) (World Bank n.d.a) and the highest coverage of higher education enrolment in the Latin American region (40% of the enrolment of the population between 19 and 24 years old) (OECD 2020a). However, Chile has a GINI index of income inequality of 44.4 (World Bank n.d.b), equivalent to countries like Zimbabwe (44.3) whose level of poverty is 20 times greater than the Chilean one (World Bank n.d.a). Latest statistics show that 20% of the richest Chilean population earns 10 times more than the 20% poorest (OECD 2020b).

The reproduction of income inequality in higher education stems from the relationship between socioeconomic status, the capacity of families to pay for high school (Mizala & Torche 2012), and the score obtained in the national college admission test (PSU), which finally determines the possibility of accessing universities of varying academic standards (Canales 2016; Perez Mejias 2012) and institutional prestige (Revista Qué Pasa 2017; Revista América Economía 2017).

The Chilean Ministry of Education's 2017 enrolment statistics show that students from public (completely state-funded) and subsidised high schools (partially funded by families) accounted for approximately 32% and 52% of the undergraduate enrolment in Chile respectively, but they were over-represented in open-access universities with low accreditation and vocational colleges that do not require minimum PSU test scores. On the other hand, students from private high schools (fully paid by families) accounted for only 16% of undergraduate enrolment, albeit concentrated in a few highly selective, accredited universities with high research capacity (MINEDUC 2018). This degree of social stratification gives rise to a university system differentiated not only by its institutional characteristics and accreditation status, but also by the socioeconomic profile of its students (Canales 2016).

There are no comprehensive data on the socio-demographic profile of academics in Chile, but available data on the careers of doctorate holders living in Chile in 2015 suggest that Chilean universities with the highest research capacity tend to hire their undergraduate alumni, which indicates that social class of origin may have an indirect effect on the possibility of being hired by top prestigious universities (MINECON 2015b).

## USE OF ACADEMIC NETWORKS TO SECURE ACADEMIC JOBS: EVIDENCE FROM OTHER COUNTRIES

Networks are crucial assets to secure a job in most economic sectors throughout the world (Granovetter 1995), including academia (e.g. Brink & Benschop 2013; Burris 2004; Clauset et al. 2015; Hadani et al. 2012; Nielsen 2015). Therefore, social networks matter in applying for academic positions because information about job openings and requirements are not made completely public in some countries (for Denmark, see Nielsen 2015; for Finland, see Husu 2000; for the Netherlands, see Brink & Benschop 2013).

Further studies show that academic networks matter in the process of applying for a tenure-track academic position because faculty members involved in hiring committees want to reduce the uncertainty of whether 'new' appointees will actually fit with the needs and culture of academic departments, particularly because tenure-track academic positions are long-lasting (Musselin 2009). It is expected that candidates who are known by professors within the academic network will not engage in actions that could affect the already existing ties (Cole & Cole 1973). As such, academics involved in decisions on hiring may prefer candidates who are directly connected to their academic network or recommended by their close colleagues, both because they have more information about these candidates and because there are mechanisms of social control that rely on mutual trust with the candidates or with those who recommend them.

Similarly, it appears that academics prefer the 'known candidates', not only because they have a greater degree of information about them and have less uncertainty about the process of hiring staff, but also because academics are social beings, and are naturally prone to socialising with people who look similar to them (homophilic). Candidates for academic positions who are known by their peers or recommended by department ties are more likely to share similar characteristics, as they are part of the same network, as compared with candidates who do not belong to their network (Granovetter 1995).

Now, the chances to participate in academic networks are not exempt from the unequal social structure. For instance, studies have shown that female and male academic applicants participate in network development differently (Brink & Benschop 2013; Husu 2000; Nielsen 2015). In a comprehensive study about processes of academic recruitment in medical science departments in the Netherlands, Brink and Benschop (2013) found that male academics in hiring committees tend to recruit a larger proportion of male candidates than females. In contrast, some male and female academics at the same institutions, being aware of the low representation of female academics, purposely seek female candidates in the process of recruitment. Likewise, in a study of the process of hiring and promotion of academics at a Danish university, Nielsen (2016) found that female academics applied in lower proportion to non-publicly-announced academic job calls as compared with men, which indirectly reflects that women may not have the same chances of accessing the academic ties that control job information as men.

As indicated earlier, a vast body of empirical research suggests the existence of academic hiring networks associated with the level of prestige of universities (Burris 2004; Clauset et al. 2015; Cowan & Rosello 2018, Hadani et al. 2012; Headworth & Freese 2015). In a comparative analysis of academic job placement in Chile and South Korea, Celis and Kim (2018) found that industrial engineering academic departments at research-intensive universities in both countries are preferentially recruiting doctorate holders who graduated from top-ranked foreign universities. Celis and Kim's findings suggest that hiring PhDs with doctoral credentials granted by prestigious universities is used as a strategy to expand international research networks.

## CONCEPTUAL FRAMEWORK

I incorporated three theoretical perspectives, namely social and cultural reproduction (Bourdieu 1983, 1987, 1988; Bourdieu & Passeron 1977), human capital (Becker 1967; Mincer 1984; Schultz 1970), and network theory (Burt 2000; Granovetter 1973; Lin 2001) to analyse how doctorate holders from different social class groups found academic jobs and how they used their networks to find such jobs.

Social and cultural reproduction theory posits that education is one of the main systems through which power and symbolic relations among social groups are reproduced (Bourdieu & Passeron 1977). The social class positioning of individuals depends not only on their economic wealth, but also on the amount and exclusivity of cultural and social capital that individuals accumulate (Bourdieu 1983, 1987).

Within the context of the expansion of doctoral education, doctorate holders are increasingly differentiated according to the prestige of PhD-granting universities (Pázstor & Wakeling 2018), their networks (social capital) with reputed academics, and their scientific productivity, typically measured in publications and grants (Pinto 2016). From this perspective, the close connection and interdependence between different types of capitals trigger socialisation processes and group closure that end up reproducing social class disparities among individuals, even after achieving the doctorate.

In contrast, human capital scholars (Becker 1967; Mincer 1984; Schultz 1970) stress the role of education as an enabler that allows individuals from all social class groups to achieve the skills, knowledge and networks to compete successfully in the labour market. According to this conceptual framework, doctorate holders in this study represent a selective minority, since they invested at least 20 years in education and successfully completed several intellectual milestones. They acquired the knowledge and skills of the disciplinary field, as well as the norms and values of the academic culture, regardless of their social class of origin.

It is worth noting that human capital theorists (Becker 1967; Mincer 1984; Schultz 1970) do not neglect the class-stratified higher education system or the relevance of networks for accessing valuable information regarding job opportunities. Yet, promoters of the theory of human capital would expect that the chances of finding a job are less associated with a person's social class of origin than their individual productivity. With respect to the prestige of PhD-granting universities, human capital representatives would accept the assumption that the prestige of a PhD-granting university matters only when it signals the academic quality of the institution.

Network theorists (Burt 2000; Granovetter 1973, 1995, Lin 2001) posit that greater success in the job market and in life is not necessarily due to the investment of individuals in education, but rather stems from their social relationships. Similar to what the tenets of social and cultural reproduction propose, network theorists recognise that the power and resources that individuals access are strongly associated with the social status they have in society; however, the total value of the network is not only measured by the accumulated resources of network members, but also in the diversity of resources that they bring and the strong or weak ties that connect these networks.

From this framework, doctorate holders who develop the largest number of strong ties with faculty members occupying strategic positions in academic staff hiring processes are expected to be better off during the job search, compared to their colleagues who lack these connections. The depth of a network tie is reflected by the degree of intensity, frequency of intimacy, reciprocity, and acknowledged obligation (Granovetter 1973).

## METHODOLOGY

The inquiry involved a qualitative case study (Merriam 2009; Yin 1981) on how 10 ECDs in engineering went about finding their current academic jobs, taking into account their social class of origin. Sample design was purposive (Patton 2002) and included two steps. First, a group of universities with research capacity was selected based on a set of institutional characteristics and geographic location. Second, ECDs in engineering who graduated within the period 2010-2015 and were listed as academics in the industrial engineering department of the selected universities were invited to participate. To secure complete anonymity of participants and their respective institutional affiliations, all original names of employing universities and ECDs were replaced with pseudonyms.

The sample included male academics only. This selection was not intentional, but rather confirms the lack of representation of women in the engineering field in Chile (Berríos 2007).

Data were generated via semi-structured personal interviews conducted between January and April 2017, the curriculum vitae (CV) of each participant, and memos written after each interview. During the interviews, participants were asked to narrate their entire educational experience from the moment they left high school up through the strategies they used to find their current academic jobs. CVs and memos were used to complement and contrast the information generated through interviews.

## ANALYTICAL TECHNIQUES

One of the research aims was to identify what role social class of origin plays in the way academics find their academic jobs and how this influences the development of their academic networks. Yet, participants were not asked about their social class of origin nor whether the social class of their family had shaped their academic trajectory because these types of questions could have predisposed candidates to talk about their social class of origin. The first task was thus to identify the social class of origin of participants, relying on the data provided during interviews. So, I first coded line by line the interviews with each of the participants, paying special attention to participant's family's status before starting their undergraduate degrees. A validation question was included at the end of each interview protocol that indirectly asked about parental level of education (see Appendix 1).

Relying on the definition of social class of origin discussed above (Bourdieu 1987) and the class attributes identified in another study (Chiappa & Perez Mejias 2019), at least three data points were used to capture participants' social class: (1) capacity of parents to pay for private high school (economic capital), (2) foreign second-language acquisition at an early stage of life (cultural capital), and (3) level of education and/or occupation of the parents (social and cultural capital). Speaking a foreign second language in Chile is associated with having attended a private high school (MINEDUC 2015) and greater access to international travelling. Table 10.1 summarises a description of the participants' social classes of origin.

**TABLE 10.1**   Characterisation of participants in the sample

| Participant's names | Social class of origin assigned | Variables of social class | | |
|---|---|---|---|---|
| | | High school type | Education and/or occupation of parents, as described during the interview | Spoke a foreign language |
| Alan | Upper | Private | Both parents with college degree | Yes |
| Gonzalo | Upper | Private | Mom has a college degree in the area of heath science, dad owns a small business | Yes |
| Mario | Upper | Private | Mom and dad completed a college degree | Yes |

**TABLE 10.1**  Characterisation of participants in the sample [continue]

| Participant's names | Social class of origin assigned | Variables of social class | | |
|---|---|---|---|---|
| | | High school type | Education and/or occupation of parents, as described during the interview | Spoke a foreign language |
| Antonio | Upper | Private | Dad has a PhD degree and is a faculty professor, grandfather was part of the regional economic elite | Yes |
| Gino | Upper | Private | Dad has a college degree; mom is a housewife | Yes |
| Carlos | Middle | Not identified | Mom has a technical degree; dad is the owner of a small public transportation company | No |
| Francisco | Middle | Public | Dad owns a small business, attended a highly selective public high school | Yes |
| Omar | Low | Public | Mom did not complete high school; he does not refer to his dad | No |
| David | Low | Public | First-generation college student, self-reported | No |
| Gabriel | Low | Public | Participant did not refer explicitly to parental level of education, but he had limited economic resources to study in another city | No |

## FINDINGS

Table 10.2 provides a summary of how ECDs in engineering from different social classes of origin found their academic jobs. Participants faced three different job search scenarios six months before completing their doctorates. Some participants had already secured an academic tenure-track position (Omar, David, Carlos, Mario); others had some type of temporary academic position (Gabriel, Francisco); and the last group were actively engaged in applying for a tenure-track academic position (Alan, Antonio, Gino, Gonzalo). The process of academic job searching varies for early-career doctorate holders, depending on the type of links with senior academics in charge of hiring processes and their decision of studying towards a doctoral degree in Chile or elsewhere. Social class of origin was a salient factor to determine both, namely the links with senior academic networks and the decision of studying towards a doctoral degree abroad.

PART THREE • TRAJECTORIES

### Social class and the structural role of the undergraduate university in the configuration of academic networks

Due to the close association between social class of origin and chances of entering selective research universities in the Chilean higher education context, social class of origin gets reproduced via unequal access to information and resources during the undergraduate degree to select the PhD programme. The following stories of Gonzalo (upper), Gabriel (low) and Omar (low) eloquently show how social class of origin and resources leveraged during undergraduate university affect the decision to study for a doctorate and the choice of the PhD-granting university.

Gonzalo (upper) grew up in Santiago with parents who had completed college degrees and had attended a highly selective private high school. He obtained a perfect score in the national college admission test, so he picked the university that had the greatest research capacity and offered him the best package of fellowship options. During his undergraduate programme, he rapidly became aware of the possibility of pursuing a doctorate, since several other students of his undergraduate programme had attended foreign universities for a graduate education. He also met an acquaintance at a conference who had just returned to Chile after earning a doctorate, and who helped him to find out which university to attend. He applied to only top-ranked universities in the USA, according to the international ranking Shanghai Jiao Tong (also known as ARWU ranking). He finally chose one of the top three doctoral programmes in his area of expertise. Six months before completing his doctorate, he applied for academic jobs in different parts of the world but decided to return to Chile for the sake of his family and being connected with his old professors who were working at the top-research intensive universities in the country.

In contrast, Gabriel (low) grew up in a small town in the south of Chile, with parents who had not completed high school. After he graduated from high school, he selected the closest university to home, even though he had been admitted to a university with greater research capacity located in another city, because his family could not afford for him to live elsewhere. While he was completing his undergraduate degree, Gabriel started to work with a young professor of his undergraduate programme who was finishing his doctorate at a Chilean university. This professor became Gabriel's undergraduate thesis supervisor, and according to Gabriel, was the person who most encouraged him to pursue a doctorate.

Gabriel revealed: "There was very little information about doctoral fellowships at my undergraduate university […] Nobody was talking about the foreign postgraduate fellowship programme. In my case, it was my supervisor who told me about the idea of doing a doctorate degree, and who knew about the fellowship [to study towards a doctorate in Chile]." Asked about the possibility of studying at a foreign university, Gabriel explained that he had initially considered studying abroad, but he needed to support his family financially. He completed his PhD in a highly reputed doctoral programme in Chile that has the highest research capacity. Yet, the decision to study in Chile restricts chances of working as an academic in those universities with research capacity in the country, since these institutions do not to hire their own PhD alumni.

On a different path, Omar (low) who self-identifies as a person from a low social class, explains that he only applied to one well-ranked university in France, primarily because he had been able to visit France as part of a research project during his undergraduate studies, and because he negotiated a pre-hire agreement with his former undergraduate university. Omar's undergraduate university has faced difficulties recruiting academics with PhDs in engineering, so it created a special programme to recruit alumni with foreign fellowships to study abroad.

Through this programme, Omar was hired as an instructor at his former university, which allowed him to contribute to his family income. He explains: "I come from a low social class […] so I sought to get hired by this university [before starting the PhD] in order to leave an income for my family [while completing the doctorate]. [My undergraduate thesis supervisor] encouraged me to apply to a programme in the School of Engineering that pre-hired students who had obtained one of the foreign doctoral fellowships."

The barriers that Omar faced due to his social class of origin –responsibility to contribute financially to family income and lack of international experience – were partially compensated by the resources that he found at his undergraduate university.

**PART THREE • TRAJECTORIES**

**TABLE 10.2** The process of securing an academic job

| Name | Social Class / Main source of funding during PhD | Ranking* of universities, geographical location | Main academic ties during job application | Months actively seeking academic jobs | Number of formal job applications to faculty tenure-track positions | Employment situation six months before completing PhD | Process of looking for a job |
|---|---|---|---|---|---|---|---|
| Alan | Upper / Chilean Gov Fellow + PhD university funding | UG: Top 500, Met area, Chile / PhD: Top 50, USA | PhD adviser & professors of the PhD academic department. Colleagues met in the doctorate programme. Professors from his UG degree programme. | 4 | Chile: 3 faculty tenure-track positions; but held informal conversations with academics at second-tier research universities who were interested in hiring him. | Actively seeking a faculty tenure-track job. | Applied to three or four job calls at different Chilean universities within the last 10 months before PhD completion. Visited Chile one year before ending the doctorate programme and offered to give talks at different universities. |
| Gonzalo | Upper / Chilean Gov Fellow + PhD university funding | UG: Top 500, Met area, Chile / PhD: Top 50, USA | PhD adviser. Colleague met in the doctorate programme. Professors from his UG degree programme. Professor working at his former employer. | 6 | USA: 6 tenure-track positions; Chile: 1 tenure-track university; had 1 European postdoc. | Actively seeking a faculty tenure-track job. | Applied to all job calls at different Chilean and USA universities within the last 10 months before PhD completion. He collaborated with a Chilean colleague who was completing the doctorate programme at the same time to keep track of all job openings in different countries worldwide. |

**CHAPTER 10 • FINDING ACADEMIC JOBS IN STRATIFIED COUNTRIES**

**TABLE 10.2** The process of securing an academic job [continue]

| Name | Social Class / Main source of funding during PhD | Ranking* of universities, geographical location | Main academic ties during job application | Months actively seeking academic jobs | Number of formal job applications to faculty tenure-track positions | Employment situation six months before completing PhD | Process of looking for a job |
|---|---|---|---|---|---|---|---|
| Mario | Upper / Chilean Gov Fellow + PhD university funding | UG: Top 500, Met area, Chile / PhD: Top 50, USA | UG thesis supervisor, PhD adviser. | 0 | Chile: 1 faculty tenure-track position (application during second year of the doctorate). | Hired in a faculty tenure-track position. | In the second year of his PhD, he saw a job opening at his former UG university. Contacted his undergraduate professors asking whether he had any chance to get the position. |
| Gino | Upper / Chilean Gov Fellow + PhD university projects | UG: Non-ranked, south area, Chile / PhD: Top 500, Met area, Chile | PhD supervisor. Colleagues from doctorate programme. Professors from his UG degree programme. | 6 | Chile: 3 faculty tenure-track positions; but hold informal conversations with another university. | Actively seeking a faculty tenure-track job. | Made sure to meet minimum requirements of publications before finishing his PhD. Applied to open positions as suggested by his PhD supervisor and the colleagues he had met during the doctorate programme. |

PART THREE • TRAJECTORIES

TABLE 10.2 The process of securing an academic job [continue]

| Name | Social Class / Main source of funding during PhD | Ranking* of universities, geographical location | Main academic ties during job application | Months actively seeking academic jobs | Number of formal job applications to faculty tenure-track positions | Employment situation six months before completing PhD | Process of looking for a job |
|---|---|---|---|---|---|---|---|
| Antonio | Upper / Own funding first year, second year university funding | UG: Non-ranked, Central Region, Chile / PhD: Non-ranked, Germany | PhD supervisor Close UG friend working as an academic. Family friends and acquaintances in academic positions. | 24 | Chile: 10 faculty tenure-track positions; had multiple informal interviews at Chilean university and one with a private firm that hired him. | Actively seeking a faculty tenure-track job. | Applied to around 10 open job calls. Contacted peers who were already working in academia, asking them to tell their colleagues that he was looking for a job. |
| David | Low / Chilean Gov Fellow + Faculty salary | UG: Non-ranked, Met area, Chile / PhD: Non-ranked, France | Pre-hiring agreement. UG thesis supervisor. | 0 | No need to apply for jobs. | Hired in a faculty tenure-track position. | Pre-hire agreement with his former UG academic department during the second year of his PhD. |
| Omar | Low / Chilean Gov Fellow + Faculty salary | UG: Non-ranked, Met area, Chile / PhD: Top 50, France | UG thesis supervisor. PhD supervisor and colleagues. | 0 | No need to apply for jobs. | Hired in a faculty tenure-track position. | Pre-hire agreement with his former UG academic department before starting the PhD. |
| Gabriel | Low Chilean Gov Fellow + Additional part-time teaching jobs | UG: Non-ranked, South area, Chile / PhD: Top 500, Met area, Chile | PhD supervisor Colleagues from doctorate programme. | 3 | Chile: 1 faculty tenure-track position (after he was already working as a part-time instructor). | Working as an instructor in a temporary position. | Found a lecturing job through his PhD classmates during his doctorate. University opened a tenure-track vacancy and he formally applied. |

CHAPTER 10 • **FINDING ACADEMIC JOBS IN STRATIFIED COUNTRIES**

TABLE 10.2  The process of securing an academic job [continue]

| Name | Social Class / Main source of funding during PhD | Ranking* of universities, geographical location | Main academic ties during job application | Months actively seeking academic jobs | Number of formal job applications to faculty tenure-track positions | Employment situation six months before completing PhD | Process of looking for a job |
|---|---|---|---|---|---|---|---|
| Name | Social Class Main source of funding during PhD | Ranking* of universities, geographical location | Main academic ties during job application. | Months actively seeking academic jobs | Number of formal job applications to faculty tenure-track positions. | Employment situation six months before completing PhD. | Process of looking for a job |
| Carlos | Middle/ Chilean Gov Fellow + Additional part-time teaching jobs | UG: Non-ranked, Central area, Chile  PhD: Non-ranked, Met area, Chile | PhD supervisor Colleagues from doctorate programme. | 0 | Chile: 1 application Was contacted by his supervisor who told him about the vacancy. Had an interview; sent his formal documents afterward. | Hired in a faculty tenure-track position. | PhD supervisor notified him of a position available at the university where his supervisor had recently been hired. |
| Francisco | Middle  University fellowship from the first year | UG: Non-ranked, Central area, Chile  PhD: Non-ranked, Spain | PhD supervisor. Colleagues from doctorate programme. Professors from his UG degree programme. | 4 | No need to apply. Europe: 3 post-doc positions; China: 1 postdoc; Chile: 1 postdoc position; faculty position was found. | Working as a postdoctoral fellow in his former PhD-academic department. | Applied to a competitive post-doc grant funded by the Chilean government while he was finishing his first post-doc in Europe. This allowed him to negotiate a faculty tenure-track position with his Chilean postdoc institution. |

UG: Undergraduate University

Met area: Metropolitan area

*I used the international ranking Shanghai Jiao Tong, also known as ARWU, to inform the university positioning.

### Strong ties with professors working in Chile to secure faculty jobs: Different experience for doctorate holders from different social class of origin

The study findings show that those participants who were from low- and middle-class backgrounds developed strong connections with their former professors and relied on these professors to secure their current positions. These former professors had access to privileged information about faculty hiring processes or directly participated in faculty hiring, which provided participants from low- and middle-class groups advantageous access during the hiring processes. As Table 10.2 shows, all participants in this sample from low and middle social classes had already secured an academic position six months before completing their doctorates.

Participants from the upper social class also developed strong connections with former undergraduate and doctorate professors working in Chile, but they relied on their former professors to a lesser extent in comparison to their peers from lower social classes. Because of the inherent advantages from their family backgrounds, participants from upper social class backgrounds were exposed to more opportunities for developing ties with acquaintances beyond their formal undergraduate and doctorate programmes.

For instance, Antonio (upper), who studied his undergraduate degree at a regional university, is the only participant who openly said that he comes from a rich family and whose father was a university professor. Contrary to the other participants in the sample, he commented that he did not have a good relationship with his undergraduate thesis supervisor. He made the decision to study for a doctorate because one of his best friends from his undergraduate programme encouraged him to enter a PhD programme in Europe.

According to Antonio, he could study for his doctorate in Germany without the support of his undergraduate supervisor, which curtailed his chances of applying for a government fellowship. This was primarily because he had ample economic resources, as well as other colleagues and acquaintances beyond his academic supervisor who guided him during the process. He recalled: "It is very unfair. I could [study towards a doctorate abroad] because my grandfather was a millionaire. I did not have any debt from my undergraduate university, so I could save money and visualise the possibility of studying abroad without a fellowship, even without any support from my undergraduate thesis supervisor."

After completing his doctorate in Germany, Antonio spent two years seeking a faculty job. At the end of the first year, he decided to talk to one of his father's former colleagues, who at that time was the head of the research laboratory of an important private firm in Chile. This family friend hired him. He comments: "To be honest,

I think he only hired me because he knew my dad." Eventually, one of Antonio's colleagues advised him to apply for his current faculty position. He was despondent at the time, due to his several failed attempts at securing a faculty job, but this friend helped him by talking to the dean about him. Antonio recalled:

> I got this job thanks to my neighbour, who is next to me [pointing to the neighbouring office]. I had applied here twice before [using open calls], and for the third one [my friend] said, "You know […] I think you have an opportunity now, because the dean now is [name of the dean], and he is much more objective in the hiring process. He will pay more attention to the CV rather than to anything else." But my neighbour helped me by talking to the dean about me.

Antonio's experience reflects the importance of having strong ties with professors who are already working in academic departments, and the extra advantages that upper social class academics may have by initiating ties with actors who could have influential positions in the processes of hiring academic staff.

By contrast, Carlos (middle class) went to the same undergraduate university as Antonio, and is currently working in the same academic department, but Carlos did not have to seek jobs because his doctorate supervisor, ex-undergraduate adviser, informed him about a job opening that fitted his profile, long before Carlos completed his doctorate in Chile and entered the job market. He said, "I did not know about this job opportunity, but I did what my adviser suggested," Carlos explains, "I went to an interview, I sent my papers and CV afterwards, and a few weeks later, they notified me that I had been selected […] Why did they pick me? I think I matched the profile they were looking for […] and I also think the reference of my former supervisor influenced the decision to hire me." Carlos's doctorate supervisor had been recently appointed to an important position at the University of the West and had known Carlos since his undergraduate days.

### Strong ties, PhD in foreign countries, and competitive research grants

The participants in the study who earned their doctorates in Chile – Gino (upper), Carlos (middle), Gabriel (low) – inevitably developed strong ties with professors and colleagues working at the most reputable engineering departments in Chile, who had been their supervisors and colleagues, regardless of their social class of origin. Nonetheless, their chances of securing faculty jobs were restricted to fewer institutions of lower research capacity than their former PhD alma mater. Academic departments at research-intensive universities do not hire their PhD alumni, but rather PhD holders who studied at prestigious foreign universities.

On the other hand, those participants who studied abroad and did not secure a faculty job before finishing their doctorates, all of whom were upper class, had lost contact with their networks. With the exception of Antonio (upper), they purposely sought to reconnect with their undergraduate supervisors. As Alan explained, one year before finishing his doctorate: "I came to Chile and volunteered to give talks at several Chilean universities where I had contacts." He knew "how competitive the process was, so [he] needed to reconnect with [his] past networks". Alan applied for around five faculty positions only in Chile, partially because his romantic partner wanted him to come back to Chile, and partially because he had obtained a government fellowship which required him to come back.

Francisco (middle) represents a distinct experience in seeking a faculty job, one in which professional ties with the academics in a given academic department are not as important as the capacity to earn competitive research grants. He went to an undergraduate university that had the lowest level of accreditation within the sample, but he was able to connect with a professor there who had recently finished his doctorate in Spain. As with most of the participants in this study, this supervisor helped Francisco connect with reputable Spanish universities. Francisco was admitted to a master's degree programme, and while there, he decided to pursue a doctorate. After completing his PhD in Spain, he stayed at this academic department as a postdoctoral fellow for a couple of years, funded by a grant from the European Union. When this postdoctoral position neared its end, he applied to a highly competitive grant funded by Chilean institutions that enabled him to fund his own research agenda. After receiving this grant, Francisco received several job offers enabling him to negotiate a contract in a tenure-track position. He picked the university with the greatest research capacity and prestige in his area of expertise.

Francisco is the only person in the sample who was able to get hired at a more prestigious university than his undergraduate university. He acknowledges that without his postdoctoral grant and a credential from a foreign university, he would probably not have secured the job he has today. Francisco commented: "The structure of the university is fixed, and the number of people that get hired is less, as compared to the number of people who are arriving from their doctorate degrees and applying for jobs. Hence, what matters are the details that differentiate the profiles of candidates. A PhD from a foreign university, some publications at good journal and if you know the right people, that can make a difference …"

## DISCUSSION

This study sought to gain a deeper understanding of how early career doctorate holders developed and used their networks to obtain their current jobs, considering their social class of origin. It is worthwhile to mention that the sample design provides evidence exclusively for those doctorate holders who were able to secure tenure-track faculty positions at universities with research capacities and which are located in the regions -metropolitan and central area- that concentrate the largest number of higher education institutions in the country. As such, the experience of academics in this chapter represent an already selective, biased group among early career doctorate holders in Chile.

The findings show that social class affected the ways in which ECDs in engineering found their current academic jobs. First, social class of origin of doctorate holders indirectly influenced the chances of finding academic jobs in highly reputable Chilean universities, primarily because academic departments in engineering at research-intensive universities tend to hire candidates who graduated from foreign highly prestigious universities (Celis & Kim 2018). In line with the social and cultural reproduction theory (Bourdieu & Passeron 1977) and other studies (Canales 2016; Perez Mejias et al. 2018), the economic, social, and cultural assets inherited from one's family translate first into unequal access to selective and research-intensive universities at the undergraduate level. Likewise, social class of origin informed the EDCs' choice to study towards a doctorate in a foreign country, even when access to doctoral funding could have been available through government fellowships. Participants who come from low social class conditioned their decision of studying towards a doctorate in a foreign country, depending on their ability to secure an income for their families while completing their doctoral studies (the case of Omar and Gabriel). One upper social class participant, on the other hand, did not have to contribute to family income, but could even rely on his family wealth to fund his doctoral studies at a foreign university (Antonio).

Second, participants' stories also reveal that undergraduate thesis supervisors and colleagues met during the undergraduate degree were key connections to find out about academic job announcements. In line with what network theorists (Granovetter 1973; Lin 2001) and social and cultural reproduction tenets argue (Bourdieu & Passeron 1977), social class of origin relates to the level of prestige of educational institution attended, and consequently, the academic networks ECDs could access during their career.

Moreover, social class of origin also influenced the extent to which doctorate holders relied on their academic colleagues during the process of job search. Participants from low and middle social classes, because of their lack of economic and informational resources, seem to have developed strong ties with their professors and colleagues met during their undergraduate and doctoral studies, which facilitated their process of finding academic jobs. All participants from low and middle social class took less time in seeking academic jobs as compared with their peers from upper social class. This finding raises the questions whether ECDs from low social class would have obtained the same academic positions without having connections with senior academics working at research intensive universities.

Granovetter (1973) observed earlier that the depth of ties is defined by relationships of mutual reciprocity, trust and the duration of connections between participants and the members of their networks. This does not mean that participants from the upper social class in this study did not develop strong ties with former professors and colleagues, but because of their family social class status they had a greater number of connections and opportunities linked to academia on which they could rely, beyond their former doctoral advisors and colleagues. For some participants, this additional capital allowed them to apply to a greater number of positions and select the best potential hiring option (Allan, Gonzalo). For another participant (Antonio) the advantages inherited from his class allowed him to connect with a family friend who helped him to secure a job in the private industry, but his social class advantages did not guarantee a position in the Chilean academia without having the connections to the employing universities.

It is worth mentioning that the strategic role of academic networks to secure academic jobs in Chile does not entirely negate the principles of human capital theory (Becker 1967; Mincer 1984; Schultz 1970). As recognised by all of the participants and aligned with what human capital theorists argue (Becker 1967; Mincer 1984; Schultz 1970), they would not have obtained their current jobs if they had not completed their doctorates and demonstrated their research productivity. Likewise, the participant (Francisco) who secured a competitive grant after having studied and worked outside of Chile for longest was the one who could negotiate his hiring process at a university that is significantly more prestigious than his former undergraduate university, albeit still not among the top research-intensive universities in Chile.

Overall, the evidence collected in this study raises important questions about the formal and informal mechanisms through which labour opportunities in academia are distributed among early-career doctorate holders who come from historically underrepresented social groups. This inquiry is worth replicating, especially in countries that have intentionally aimed to increase their research productivity through the production of a greater number of PhDs in a short period of time, such as South Africa, Mexico, and Brazil. Further research in Chile and elsewhere could explore the process of seeking faculty jobs for doctorate holders who applied but could not secure a tenure-track academic position. A detailed analysis of the sociodemographic characteristics of these persons, their disciplinary fields, and educational and professional trajectories would benefit the endeavour of understanding the possibilities and limitations of the promise of human capital in highly stratified higher education systems.

## ACKNOWLEDGEMENTS

The elaboration of this article was sponsored by the Chilean Centre for Social Conflict and Cohesion Studies (www.coes.cl), ANID/FONDAP/15130009

## REFERENCES

Arum R, Gamoran A & Shavit Y. 2007. More inclusion than diversion: Expansion, differentiation, and market structure in higher education. In: Y Savit (ed.), *Stratification in higher education: A comparative study*. Stanford, CA: Stanford University Press. 1-37.

ARWU. 2018. Academic ranking of world class universities 2018. https://bit.ly/3slwqAk [Accessed 10 January 2020].

Bastedo MN. 2014. Institutional stratification and the postcollege labor market: Comparing job satisfaction and prestige across generations. *The Journal of Higher Education*, 85(6):761-791. https://doi.org/10.1353/jhe.2014.0037

Becker GS. 1967. *Human capital and the personal distribution of income: An analytical approach*. Ann Arbor: Ann Arbor Institute of Public Administration.

Berríos P. 2007. El sistema de prestigio en las universidades y el rol que ocupan las mujeres en el mundo académico. *Calidad en la Educación*, 23:349-361. https://doi.org/10.31619/caledu.n23.301

Bourdieu P. 1983. The field of cultural production, or the economic world reversed. *Poetics*, 12:4-5, 311-356. https://doi.org/10.1016/0304-422X(83)90012-8

Bourdieu P. 1987. What makes a social class? On the theoretical and practical existence of groups. *Berkeley Journal of Sociology*, 32:1-17.

Bourdieu P. 1988. *Homo Academicus*. Cambridge: Polity Press in association with Basil Blackwell.

Bourdieu P & Passeron JC. 1977. *Reproduction in education, society and culture*. London/Beverly Hills: Sage Publications.

Brink M & Benschop Y. 2013. Gender in academic networking: The role of gatekeepers in professorial recruitment. *Journal of Management Studies*, 51(3):460-492. https://doi.org/10.1111/joms.12060

Burris V. 2004. The academic caste system: Prestige hierarchies in PhD exchange networks. *American Sociological Review*, 69(2):239-264. https://doi.org/10.1177/000312240406900205

Burt RS. 2000. The network structure of social capital. *Research in Organizational Behavior*, 22(C):345-423. https://doi.org/10.1016/S0191-3085(00)22009-1

Canales A. 2016. Socioeconomic differences in the application to Chilean universities: The role of academic and non-academic factors. *Revista Calidad en la Educación*, 44:129-157. https://doi.org/10.4067/S0718-45652016000100006

Celis S & Kim J. 2018. The making of homophilic networks in international research collaborations: A global perspective from Chilean and Korean engineering. *Research Policy*, 47(3):573-582. https://doi.org/10.1016/j.respol.2018.01.001

Chiappa R & Perez Mejias P. 2019. Unfolding the direct and indirect effects of social class of origin on faculty income. *Higher Education*, 78:529-555. https://doi.org/10.1007/s10734-019-0356-4

Clauset A, Arbesman S, & Larremore DB. 2015. Systematic inequality and hierarchy in faculty hiring networks. *Science Advances*, 1(1):6. https://doi.org/10.1126/sciadv.1400005

CNIC. 2006. *Final Report: National Council of Innovation for Competitiveness*. Advisor to the President of the Republic. CNIC: Santiago.

CNIC. 2007. *Towards a National Innovation Strategy for Competitiveness*, Vol I. CNIC: Santiago.

CNIC. 2008. *Towards a National Innovation Strategy for Competitiveness*, Vol II. CNIC: Santiago.

Cole J & Cole S. 1973. *Social stratification in science*. Chicago: University of Chicago Press.

Collins R. 1979. *The credential society: An historical sociology of education and stratification*. New York: Academic Press.

CONICYT. 2018. Fellows of the advanced human capital program. https://bit.ly/32Flo4y [Accessed 2 January 2020].

Cowan R & Rossello G. 2018. Emergent structures in faculty hiring networks, and the effects of mobility on academic performance. *An International Journal for all Quantitative Aspects of the Science of Science, Communication in Science and Science Policy*, 117(1):527-562. https://doi.org/10.1007/s11192-018-2858-8

González-Canché MS. 2017. Community college scientists and salary gap: Navigating socioeconomic and academic stratification in the US higher education system. *The Journal of Higher Education*, 88(1):1-32. https://doi.org/10.1080/00221546.2016.1243933

Granovetter MS. 1973. The strength of weak ties. *American Journal of Sociology*, 78(6):1360-1380. https://doi.org/10.1086/225469

Granovetter M. 1995. *Getting a job. A study of contacts and careers*. Chicago: Chicago University Press. https://doi.org/10.7208/chicago/9780226518404.001.0001

Hadani M, Coombes S, Das D & Jalajas D. 2012. Finding a good job: Academic network centrality and early occupational outcomes in management academia. *Journal of Organizational Behavior*, 33(5):723-739. https://doi.org/10.1002/job.788

Hartmann M. 2010. Achievement or origin: Social background and ascent to top management. *Talent Development and Excellence*, 2(1):105-117.

Headworth S & Freese J. 2015. Credential privilege or cumulative advantage? Prestige, productivity, and placement in the academic sociology job market. *Social Forces*, 94(3):1257-1282. https://doi.org/10.1093/sf/sov102

Hout M. 2008. How class works: Objective and subjective aspects of class since the 1970s. In: A Laureu & D Conley (eds.), *Social class: How does it work?* New York: Russell Sage Foundation. 25-64.

Husu L. 2000. Gender discrimination in the promised land of gender equality. *Higher Education in Europe*, 25:221-228. https://doi.org/10.1080/713669257

INE. 2019. *National survey of employment 2019 – Table unemployed by term and educational level*. https://bit.ly/3tHFNBN [Accessed 10 January 2020].

Jungbauer-Gans M & Gross C. 2013. Determinants of success in university careers: Findings from the German academic labour market. *Zeitschrift für Soziologie*, 42(1):74-92. https://doi.org/10.1515/zfsoz-2013-0106

Lin N. 2001. *Social capital. A theory of social structure and action*. Cambridge: Cambridge University Press. https://doi.org/10.1017/CBO9780511815447

Merriam S. 2009. *Qualitative Research. A guide to design and implementation*. San Francisco: Jossey-Bass.

Mincer J. 1984. Human capital and economic growth. *Economics of Education Review*, 3(3):195-205. https://doi.org/10.1016/0272-7757(84)90032-3

MINECON. 2015a. Career of doctorate holders survey Version 2014 – CDH. Unpublished data set.

MINECON. 2015b. *Main Results of the CDH Project, reference year 2011*. Santiago: MINECON. https://bit.ly/3vaRTUb [Accessed 10 January 2020].

MINEDUC. 2015. *High School Assessment 2014, English*. Santiago: MINEDUC. https://bit.ly/3sGpKTv [Accessed 10 January 2020].

MINEDUC. 2018. *Historic Enrolment Dataset 2007-2018*. https://bit.ly/3tUG6tf [Accessed 10 January 2020].

Mizala A & Torche F. 2012. Bringing the schools back in: The stratification of educational achievement in the Chilean voucher system. *International Journal of Educational Development*, 32:132-144. https://doi.org/10.1016/j.ijedudev.2010.09.004

Musselin C. 2009. *The market for academics*. New York: Routledge. https://doi.org/10.4324/9780203863060

Nielsen MW. 2015. Limits to meritocracy? Gender in academic recruitment and promotion processes. *Science and Public Policy*, 43(3):386-399. https://doi.org/10.1093/scipol/scv052

Oldfield K & Conant RF. 2001. Professors, social class, and affirmative action: A pilot study. *Journal of Public Affairs Education*, 7(3):171-185. https://doi.org/10.1080/15236803.2001.12023512

OECD. n.d. *Gross domestic product (GDP): GDP per capita, USD, current prices and PPPs.* https://stats.oecd.org/index.aspx?queryid=61433 [Accessed 10 January 2020].

OECD. 2020a. *Enrolment rate in secondary and tertiary education (indicator).* https://doi.org/10.1787/1d7e7216-en

OECD. 2020b. *Income inequality (indicator).* https://doi.org/10.1787/459aa7f1-en

Ostrove JM, Stewart AJ & Curtin NL. 2011. Social class and belonging: Implications for graduate students' career aspirations. *The Journal of Higher Education*, 82(6):748-774. https://doi.org/10.1080/00221546.2011.11777226

Patton M. 2002. *Qualitative research and evaluation methods.* Thousand Oaks, CA: Sage Publications.

Pásztor A & Wakeling P. 2018. All PhDs are equal but … Institutional and social stratification in access to the doctorate. *British Journal of Sociology of Education*, 39(7):982-997. https://doi.org/10.1080/01425692.2018.1434407

Pérez Mejías P. 2012. *School and individual factors that contribute to the achievement gap in college admissions tests in Chile.* University of Maryland, College Park, Maryland. https://bit.ly/3xkxQ7S [Accessed 10 January 2020].

Pérez Mejías P, Chiappa R & Guzmán-Valenzuela C. 2018. Privileging the privileged: The effects of international university rankings on a Chilean fellowship program for graduate studies abroad. *Social Sciences*, 7(12):243. https://doi.org/10.3390/socsci7120243

Pinto C. 2016. Reflexiones sobre la inserción laboral de doctores en universidades Chilenas. *FRONTERAS – Revista de Ciencias Sociales y Humanidades*, 3(1):109-124.

PNUD. 2017. *Inequality. Origins, changes and challenges of the socio-economic gap in Chile.* Santiago: PNUD. https://bit.ly/3n9NcaF [Accessed 10 January].

Revista América Economía. 2010. *The map of Chilean universities.* https://bit.ly/3xl3Ad5 [Accessed 10 January 2020].

Revista Qué Pasa. 2017. *Ranking of Chilean Universities 2017.* https://bit.ly/3tO7kRW [Accessed 10 January 2020].

RICYT. 2018. *Doctorates.* https://bit.ly/32FA6s0 [Accessed 10 January 2020].

Schultz TW. 1970. *Investment in human capital: The role of education and of research.* New York: Free Press.

Torche F. 2018. Intergenerational mobility at the top of the educational distribution. *Sociology of Education*, 91(4):266-289. https://doi.org/10.1177/0038040718801812

World Bank. n.d.a. *Poverty headcount ratio at $5.50 a day (2011 PPP) (% of population).* https://bit.ly/3vp1cAj [Accessed 10 May 2020].

World Bank. n.d.b. *GINI index (World Bank estimate).* https://bit.ly/3aws5Kw [Accessed 10 May 2020].

Yin RK. 1981. The case study as a serious research strategy. *Science Communication*, 3(1):97-114. https://doi.org/10.1177/107554708100300106

## CHAPTER 10 • FINDING ACADEMIC JOBS IN STRATIFIED COUNTRIES

## APPENDIX 1

Questionnaire: Protocol for early-career academics in engineering departments

1. Why did you decide to pursue a doctorate?

   Potential follow-up questions: Who helped you to decide whether or not to pursue a doctorate? When you were completing your bachelor's degree, how aware were you of the option of studying for a doctorate?

2. And now, think about your undergraduate university choice. How did you select this undergraduate university versus others? What factors made you to select the university you picked?

3. To what extent, if it all, did your undergraduate experience influence your decision of studying towards a doctorate?

4. Please walk me through the process of how you decided which university to apply to for your PhD. Which considerations and factors did you consider?

5. What was your family situation when you started your PhD? Were you in a relationship? Did you have kids?

6. What was the process of looking for a job? Please walk me through to the moment when you started looking for a job.

7. When did you start looking for a job? Which type of sources did you use to find this job? Who helped you? How many months were you looking? How many jobs did you apply for? How long?

8. From the open calls that you saw, what were the most attractive job positions? What made them so attractive? Were they all faculty positions?

9. Which positions did you apply for, and why?

10. What was the hiring process for your current position? Walk me through the different steps of the application process. How did you prepare your CV? What information did you include for this position, and why?

11. What characteristics of your profile as a candidate do you think were relevant to this job? Which do you think were the most important ones? What do you think helped you to get this job?

12. Taking into account your experience applying for faculty jobs and now being hired as a faculty member, what recommendations would you give to students interested in getting a job in academia? What information would you recommend them to include in their CVs?

13. In the USA it is very common for faculty members to follow the academic path, because their parents or a close relative was working at the university as a professor. Does this statistic resonate with your interest in your academic career?

14. Are there any questions or comments that you would like to add about your experience in the process of faculty hiring that I have not asked?

# TOWARDS A THEORETICAL FRAMEWORK FOR EXPLORING EMOTION IN DOCTORAL EDUCATION

## CRITICALLY EXPLORING FAMILIAR NARRATIVES IN STUDENT EXPERIENCES

Sherran Clarence

## INTRODUCTION

For many students in different university and disciplinary contexts, doing a doctorate can be a lonely, isolated, frustrating, uncertain, difficult business. Many different research studies, published papers and books, as well as tweets and Facebook posts convey this. There is a sense that many doctoral students are not overflowing with excitement, happiness, and constructive confusion as they work their way steadily towards a completed thesis with a super-supportive supervision team and friends and family cheering them on. Rather, the sense is that many students are struggling, feeling mostly frustrated, paralysed or stuck in response to feedback, uncertain, like a fraud, with small bursts of triumph and excitement that cut through the struggle every now and then. Levels of support, especially from supervisors, seem uneven across the field of doctoral studies and in most, if not all, higher education contexts given the wide-ranging published research, Twitter posts and blogs online.

I completed my own doctorate in 2014 after a somewhat bumpy start in 2010 that led to a temporary suspension of registration in 2011 and a complete change of project. I did not find doing my doctorate easy, and parts of the research and writing process were deeply frustrating and challenging. But, looking back now and even at the time, my overall experience – my narrative – was one of constructive engagement with my study, supervisor and peers, and pleasure, even enjoyment, in the mental and emotional challenges the process engendered. However, when I shared this with fellow PhD travellers at the time, I was struck by two things: that my narrative was not a very familiar one, and that in enjoying, and dare I say, loving the experience of doing my doctorate, I was an odd bird.

This has bothered me for a long time. I now work with postgraduate students as both a writing mentor and a research supervisor and I interact with many doctoral students especially through my professional role in my university, through my social media profile on Twitter, and through my blog, which is written for postgraduate student researchers and research supervisors. Over and over, I see a different narrative than my own being reinforced, so much so that this has become *the* narrative of doctoral study. This is the narrative of isolation, frustration, struggle and suffering, and it is a familiar one for anyone conversant with both research and practice in doctoral education the world over (see, for example, Aitchison & Mowbray 2013; Carter, Blumenstein & Cook 2013; Mewburn 2011; Trafford & Leshem 2009).

This narrative seems to cut across national and regional higher education boundaries, and across race, class, gender, sexuality and able-bodiedness. Several studies have looked particularly at how women experience doctorates differently to men, given the gendered nature of domestic labour and a different form of work-life-PhD balance (Aitchison & Mowbray 2013; Brown & Watson 2010; Carter *et al*. 2013); at the experiences of working-class students (Gardner & Holley 2011; Holley & Gardner 2012); and at the experiences of students of colour (Crumb, Haskins, Dean & Avent Harris 2019; Felder, Stevenson & Gasman 2014). Many of the published studies that have looked at different intersections of issues of race, class, and gender, particularly and the experience of the doctorate have been prompted by concerns about student success, equity, access and social justice. To differing extents, they have tried to unpack aspects of this familiar narrative: the nature of students' doctoral experiences, the reasons for their struggles, and what those of us invested in enabling success at this level can do about it. These concerns about equity of access and success and socially just postgraduate education are global in nature, as they should be, and are part of the wider issues addressed in this book.

Students and supervisors from a range of national, linguistic, ethnic and cultural backgrounds constitute contemporary doctoral education in many contexts (for example, in Australia, South Africa, the UK and the USA). Differences in approaches to feedback, to managing authority, to engaging in debate may lead to successful or fraught supervision relationships, and in some contexts fears that these differences may impede student success may lead universities to aim for assimilation. For example, guiding international students into the host's ways of doing things (Manathunga 2007). This may contribute to difficult emotions for many students and supervisors which go beyond personal feelings and can be linked to the structural and cultural dimensions of doctoral education and support. Given increasing global movement within academia there is a need to explore the ways in which tensions between what students need and what they bring with them into their studies, and what universities and supervisors regard as 'appropriate' or 'successful' ways of working and being may create complex emotional labour that can have an impact on students' feelings about their studies, and academia more generally.

In this chapter, I want to pick up a particular strand in this wider body of research that is under-explored: the role of emotions in doctoral study and how we can better understand, theorise and incorporate emotions in both research candidature and in research supervision and support. This is a conceptual undertaking, starting with an initial exploration of dominant approaches to understanding emotions in the doctorate, before moving to propose a feminist sociological framework for understanding both the nature and the role of emotions. It is near to impossible to provide any singular definition of 'emotion' here, as how emotion is conceptualised and understood is largely dependent on the context in which it is being used or has meaning. In this chapter, following Sara Ahmed, Megan Boler and Arlie Russell Hochschild, the focus is less on what emotion is and more on what emotions do, and how we can understand the social and cultural dimensions of emotions as embodied, as powerful, and as collective, rather than limited to be of the mind and individually felt and experienced (see Ahmed 2014, Chapter 1 especially). The framework developed in this chapter represents an alternative language of description for this under-explored, often tacit dimension of doctoral education.

## UNPACKING A FAMILIAR NARRATIVE

The first step, following Ahmed (2014:1), is to look more closely at this "familiar narrative", and offer a "close and careful reading" instead of taking it for granted as a norm, or as just the way things are. An opening question, then, must be, "Why is *this* the familiar narrative?" When we think about doing a doctorate, why are some of the first emotions that come to mind fear, uncertainty, anxiety and feeling like a fraud (Imposter Syndrome)? Although several studies highlight that a doctorate brings both pleasure and pain – feelings of excitement, constructive growth and challenge, enjoyment of writing, alongside these "negative feelings" (Trafford & Leshem 2009:312) – the pain seems to be predominant, especially for students (see McAlpine & Amundsen 2009; Mewburn 2011). It is important to understand both the nature of the narrative and some of its key effects, because these are powerful forces in shaping doctoral learning, and this is a 'high stakes' space for universities, supervisors and students.

## PART THREE • TRAJECTORIES

Universities around the world invest substantial resources in doctoral education and have high expectations of 'output' at this level. This is largely because of pressure from governments to increase the number of graduates with doctorates, which many believe will, in turn, increase economic productivity and growth (Cloete 2015; Nerad 2019). The demand for more doctoral students puts pressure on universities to put in place sufficient resources, including the availability of research supervisors and other forms of support, particularly for doing and writing research. Students and supervisors are under pressure to succeed and this can create intellectual, physical, psychological and emotional stress that plays out in a range of ways across different university and departmental contexts. A logical deduction to draw from this global situation is that these stresses can have an impact on supervisor and student well-being, and on the timely completion of research projects. Slowed completion can lead to blockages in the 'academic pipeline', which can then cause further stress, including financial stress for students especially. Further, poor experiences can then be taken forward as 'baggage' that shapes current students' future supervision and research practice.

A great deal has been written, both in peer reviewed research and in more popular sources such as *Times Higher Education* and *The Conversation*, about different approaches to enabling both greater access and enhanced success at the doctoral level, from diverse contexts including Australia, New Zealand, Southern Africa, the USA, the UK, and Europe. This is, indeed, a global conversation. A great deal of this work focuses on aspects of doctoral study such as research supervision, giving students feedback on their thesis writing, supporting the writing of a doctoral thesis, and enabling students to grow intellectually as they progress through the PhD 'journey'. What is less overtly focused on is the nature and role of the emotion underlying all of that intellectual labour, and the ways in which emotion work, feelings and emotional labour can both enable and also powerfully constrain success at this level. This is intriguing, because it is an oblique focus or an 'elephant in the room' in many studies that overtly focus on the more intellectual or 'academic' dimensions of completing a doctorate successfully.

Emotion is referenced often in research on doctoral education, especially in relation to writing, feedback and supervision. Both in the titles of papers and in the research findings, emotions clearly play a central role in being a doctoral student and in being a supervisor (see, for example, Aitchison, Catterall, Ross & Burgin 2012; Doloriert, Sambrook & Stewart 2012; Strandler, Johansson, Wisker & Claesson 2014). These studies, among many others, explore different kinds of 'becoming' and behaviours that are considered valued by or appropriate in postgraduate scholarship. Students need to be able to 'manage' their emotions, but so do supervisors (Strandler et al. 2014). Key examples in published studies are of students needing to repress 'inappropriate emotions' with supervisors and peers, so as to appear in control (Aitchison & Mowbray 2013), especially in relation to feedback on their writing; on the other side of this, supervisors need to be mindful of offering feedback in ways that produce more 'positive' emotional and intellectual engagement (rather than making students feel stupid, fraudulent, or overly anxious and paralysed) (Aitchison et al. 2012). But what makes expressing, or even having, these feelings 'inappropriate?' What are 'appropriate' emotions?

Studies suggest that the kinds of emotions that are valued and ostensibly nurtured in doctoral education around the world are confidence, assertiveness, self-confidence, self-regulation, and proactivity (Gurr 2001; Stracke & Kumar 2010). The development of a scholarly identity is the focus of a relatively large body of research in doctoral education, and these studies suggest that students draw on significant personal, emotional and intellectual resources within themselves and within their study and home environments to do the hard work of developing a doctoral identity alongside researching and writing a doctoral thesis (McAlpine & Amundsen 2009; McAlpine & Lucas 2011). Many of these studies suggest that supervision plays a key role in both engendering the development of this identity and associated 'positive' or 'appropriate' emotions, and in undermining students' efforts to construct and assert a doctoral identity and voice.

Studies that do focus on the role of emotion in supervision (for example, Doloriert et al. 2012; Strandler et al. 2014) suggest that emotions are individually felt and experienced phenomena for both students and supervisors. Strandler et al. (2014) show that, while managing emotions effectively is part of developing a professional, scholarly identity, doing this as part of supervision is tricky. This is, at least in part, because emotions are viewed by many supervisors and students through a psychotherapeutic lens, as part of students' 'private lives'. In other words, if emotions are openly brought into the supervision space, supervisors will have to be either their students' therapist or their friend (see also Manathunga 2007), and neither of these roles feels appropriate or professional in this scholarly space. While emotions and feelings certainly can be linked to underlying mental health concerns (such as depression or anxiety) as well as personal issues (such as having a baby or getting divorced during one's candidature), conflating the creation of a space within doctoral education for emotion work and emotional labour with a supervisor becoming either a psychotherapist or a "mate" (Manathunga 2007:217) is problematic. This move obscures an understanding of emotions as "social and cultural practices" (Ahmed 2014:9), and as powerful mechanisms that position bodies, ideas and ways of being within particular hierarchies in education. It also limits critique of the ways in which doctoral education, and education more broadly, privileges some ways of being, ideas and bodies over others, which is a crucial part of socially just education.

Many studies talk about the 'negative' and 'positive' feelings and experiences associated with different aspects of postgraduate study, yet few really spend time theorising emotion in a way that enables the field to understand how emotions are generated by, and also engender, particular experiences of the doctorate. We know that these experiences are 'raced', gendered and 'classed', and this knowledge is important for developing and sustaining more socially just, inclusive and critical supervision and university support structures. But how we understand the social and cultural nature and effects of emotions in doctoral education is less well understood, and I argue here that this is a problematic gap in both research and related practice, especially given the increasingly diverse, global nature of doctoral education. This chapter adds to work in sociology, feminist theory and education that argues for reclaiming a sociological understanding of emotion and understanding its role in shaping education, specifically who gets access, how this access is managed, and the ways in which success is both enabled and constrained.

What I want to begin to understand is how we can more deeply understand why this familiar narrative of the doctorate has to consist, even when it is pleasurable and enjoyed by the student, of suffering, paralysis, frustration, anxiety, uncertainty, fear, and feelings of not being (clever, good, productive, engaged) enough. Further, I want to understand the ways in which dominant forms of supervision and research practice at this level work to elevate certain emotions and denigrate others, creating social and cultural spaces that privilege certain forms of participation and embodiment over others. Drawing on the work of Megan Boler, Sara Ahmed and Arlie Russell Hochschild, the remainder of this chapter will begin to build a feminist sociological framework for exploring, theorising, and more critically understanding the nature and role of emotion work and emotional labour in doctoral education.

## CONSTRUCTING THEORETICAL FRAMEWORK FOR RESEARCHING EMOTIONS

I propose a framework for researching emotions in doctoral education constructed from aspects of the work of three feminist sociologists: Megan Boler (*Feeling Power. Emotions and Education* 1999), Sara Ahmed (*The Cultural Politics of Emotion* 2014) and Arlie Russell Hochschild (*The Managed Heart. Commercialization of Human Feeling* 1983 [2012]). This section of the chapter is an exposition of pertinent aspects of these three texts, followed by a discussion that links them to the focus of my contribution, which is doctoral education.

### *The nature of the university and hierarchies of feeling: Megan Boler* and *Feeling Power*

Megan Boler's book, *Feeling Power. Emotions and Education*, begins with a personal account of a lecture she gave at different universities in the late 1990s on gender, power, emotion and education, about which she asked students in attendance to provide written feedback. The many different pieces of feedback showed Boler that many students, women especially, recognised intimately the "gendered rules of emotional conduct" (x) in the academy. But the feedback also indicated that these rules were largely tacit, unnamed and therefore unable to be critiqued, challenged, and reimagined.

These "gendered" rules that so many students so closely identified with exist because of a peculiar confluence of social, cultural and economic factors, especially in Western, capitalist, patriarchal societies (in which many academics teach, supervise, study and conduct research). Education at every level serves a crucial role in society: it "shapes our values, beliefs and who and what we become" (Boler 1999:xiv); in that society. This has been referred to in some studies as part of the 'hidden curriculum' – not overtly named and taught, but a powerful undercurrent pulling the knowledge, skills and aptitudes that are named and taught together for a larger purpose. Education thus frames particular emotions as appropriate and others as inappropriate, and this framing invokes much deeper sets of belief about how to be the 'right' kind of citizen and student.

In much of the Western world, this citizen and student is rational, objective, capable of reason, and master of their emotions and feelings. This, Boler argues (along with other feminist philosophers), is a result of the post-Enlightenment casting of reason, objectivity and rationality as appropriate and highly valued, and 'hysterical' outbursts of emotion, including passion, as inappropriate. Given that the prominent scientists, writers and thinkers in the years that marked the Age of Enlightenment were men, these appropriate emotions became associated with or perhaps were valued because of their association with hegemonic, privileged forms of masculinity. In valuing these masculine emotions as appropriate and conventional or 'the norm' we should all aspire to, we simultaneously devalue and denigrate their opposites, pathologising emotions that are feminised and thus rendered wholly inappropriate.

Boler argues that we have to confront and address emotions in our classrooms – and would add here supervision – if we are serious about social justice in education. This is important because of the way in which emotions have become a critical site of social control, within and outside of education. Think, for example, of how we teach students in different disciplines to make arguments and the kinds of 'rules' we invoke: you cannot say 'I', 'you must use this citation format', 'you need to change your tone', and so on. What does this feedback communicate about the dominant forms of scholarly identity we want our students to invest in and develop? What ideological beliefs underpin our notions of what it means to successfully acquire the valued identity (Boler 1999)? Boler suggests that this is far from a merely intellectual exercise; implicated in the ways in which we write our curricula, teach, supervise and assess our students' work are deep emotional investments that connect with the dominant sets of values and beliefs that our societies espouse in tacit, unnamed and unexamined ways. This is, to some extent, why some students may find the adoption and development of a particular form of doctoral identity relatively unproblematic and even comfortable, while others experience this process as a deeply jarring, even cruel, process that undermines and even fractures their sense of self, and self-worth.

From Boler's work, my proposed framework takes two important insights: the first is that education is, in Western, patriarchal, capitalist societies, marked by intense competition which valorises a particularly masculinised, heteronormative, middle-class form of hyper-individualism; and the second is that the result of this form of identity being placed at the top of social and educational hierarchies is that other forms of identity are relatively positioned in marginal, subordinate and even denigrated positions. The consequences of ranking forms of identity and assigning them different relative values are social injustice, narrowed access, and diminished success for students (and supervisors) who do not, or cannot, conform. Even though this hierarchy of identity or subject positions and attendant emotions is seldom named, made visible and opened for critique, we know it exists, because we all work to conform or resist the positioning in certain ways. We are aware of the powerful work done by emotions and the management of emotions, whether or not we have a name for all of it. This brings the framework to the next contribution, from the work of Sara Ahmed.

### *Emotions are not just private, personal feelings: Sara Ahmed* and The Cultural Politics of Emotion

Like Boler, Sara Ahmed is a feminist theorist, and she, too, understands education in Western patriarchal societies to be essentially, tacitly, masculine and heteronormative in terms of its underlying ideological orientations, beliefs and values. Adding to Boler's notion of a hierarchy of identity, Ahmed (2014:3) makes explicit the hierarchy between emotion and reason: emotion is "associated with women, who are represented as 'closer' to nature, ruled by appetite, and less able to transcend the body through thought, will and judgement". She further argues that this hierarchy between emotions and reason is displaced into a hierarchy between emotions, where some are elevated as being symbolic of the ability to cultivate the 'right' temperament or the appropriate form of identity, while others are signs of weakness or an inability to 'fit in'. In doctoral education, indeed education writ large, an appropriate scholarly temperament is evidenced through confident, reasoned engagement with ideas, and calm, reasoned interaction with peers; this presupposes the confident, assertive, self-regulated scholarly identity so valued by the field. Inappropriate would be, for example, losing your 'cool' and crying in a supervision meeting, expressing anger at unconstructive feedback, or becoming overwrought about aspects of writing or research (see, for example, Aitchison & Mowbray 2013).

Ahmed's fundamental argument is that emotions are "social and cultural practices" and as such resist both privatisation and pathologisation (see also Boler 1999). Part of the problem with privatising and pathologising emotion – particularly those emotions considered inappropriate by the dominant social and cultural context – is that we can then locate discomfort, an inability to 'fit in', struggle and resistance within individuals and put the onus on them to 'play the game' properly. We do not have to look too hard at social structures that set the game up in particular ways and that position bodies, values, beliefs and identities in competition with one another, and in relative positions of centrality or dominance (see also Boler 1999). If a student cannot produce writing or thinking that evidences an ability to 'play the game' of academic research and scholarship, an immediate response is to try and work out how to make the rules more apparent to them, rather than to question the rules in the first place and what kinds of emotional investments or "histories" they invoke and also reinforce (Ahmed 2014:7). This is a crucial point for doctoral scholarship, especially in the global South where current discourses on decolonisation in education are challenging educators and policymakers to reflect critically on where certain valued identities or subject positions come from, and what kinds of inclusion and exclusion are created when they are enforced as the 'norm' or the ideal to aspire to.

A key insight my framework draws from Ahmed's work, at this stage, is that, as social and cultural practices, emotions have histories. Having an emotion at a particular point in time that is assigned "affective value" (2014:11) in that space and time creates an impression, both on the person experiencing the emotion, and on others and the environment surrounding them. Over time, emotions accumulate value based on the impressions or traces they leave behind, as well as the ways in which they cohere or jar with the dominant hierarchies or positionings in play. This means that emotions can be anticipated as well as experienced: If a 'bad' emotion such as feelings of being fraudulent and not good enough (Imposter Syndrome) is experienced often enough within a particular space (academia) and this emotion is shared, it begins to accumulate a history and becomes part of grappling with the process of taking on a scholarly identity (for some, i.e. women or people of colour perhaps more than others, i.e. white men).

This means, for doctoral education, that before a student has even started their research or formed a relationship with their supervisor, they can feel anxious, worried that they are not good enough, afraid of their supervisor's criticism, nervous about being isolated and neglected, and so on. How do they know to feel these things? How do they 'know' this narrative before they have actually experienced it? Ahmed's work may help us to unpack the ways in which emotions 'circulate' and 'accumulate' in doctoral education spaces, and why some 'stick' more than others. Combined with Boler's work, we can start to ask, and answer, crucial questions about how different bodies, ideas, and ways of being are then positioned by the emotions that move, stick and accumulate within different national, disciplinary and university contexts, and what the effects of this are for access, success and social justice.

Part of our work as scholars and supervisors who want to be successful is to figure out which emotions are 'appropriate', 'inappropriate' and valued, and manage our own selves and emotions accordingly, both in private and in public, primarily to fit in, but as Boler and Ahmed both suggest, also to resist, reimagine and engender change. This brings us to the final part of the alternative framework, which draws in Arlie Russell Hochschild's concepts of emotion work, emotional labour, and feeling rules.

### *Emotion work, emotional labour and feeling rules: Arlie Russell Hochschild* and *The Managed Heart*

Hochschild's contribution to scholarship on emotions represented an important development of work on emotions which, up until she began publishing her work in the late 1970s, was largely focused on their psychological, personal and private dimensions. In essence, Hochschild makes three key contributions central to my framework.

The first is that emotion work has both internal and external dimensions. We engage in both 'surface acting' and 'deep acting' when we do emotion work, which is the work we do in our private spaces to make sense of and manage emotions (i.e. on our own or with immediate family). 'Surface acting' is when we read the situation, assess the appropriate or expected emotion, and then perform that emotion even if there is a "dissonance" (Aitchison & Mowbray 2013:862), or deception involved in that you do not really feel that way, such as smiling through a supervision meeting when you really feel angry and upset. 'Deep acting' is when you actually work to change how you feel so that what you truly feel and what you are expected to feel in a given situation or context aligns. What Hochschild highlights in this performance of emotion 'work' is the work itself: emotions are not animalistic, raw, unconscious things, nor are they overly performed and scripted, focused mostly on an audience external to ourselves. Rather, emotion work involves reflexivity, awareness of context and self, and acts of trying to feel as much as acts of simply feeling. Students and supervisors perhaps engage in emotion work both consciously and unconsciously. Becoming more aware of what kinds of work we are doing, why, when and in what circumstances would be an important part of theorising emotions as part of the shared doctoral education space, rather than as private, personal feelings that belong uniquely to each individual. If we can theorise emotion work in a more sociological way, we can begin to find ways to challenge and change this narrative, especially for students who do not or cannot conform to a dominant doctoral identity.

This notion of change, resistance and reimagination, also important in both Boler and Ahmed's work, is linked to Hochschild's next contribution, which draws on Erving Goffman's work on framing, to theorise feeling 'rules' and feeling 'frames'. In essence, Hochschild argues that certain events or situations invoke or are shaped by particular sets of 'feeling rules' which act to 'frame' both conventional and unconventional approaches to feeling emotion. Think, for example, of laughter at a funeral, or booing people at a university graduation ceremony. These events – funeral, graduation – are framed by the dominant emotions they invoke or engender – sadness, happiness and celebration. Thus, there are conventional approaches to what we 'should feel', expressed as a set of 'feeling rules'. You should, and must, for example, express sadness or grief at the funeral, and if you must laugh, it should be within certain limits, such as laughing at a funny story told by someone about the deceased (followed by a wave of sadness that this person is now gone). The funeral provides a frame within which certain social practices are considered appropriate, and we must, therefore, perform emotion work within ourselves to render the right kinds of emotions, which may involve both surface and deep acting (Hochschild 1979).

Like Boler and Ahmed, Hochschild links feeling rules and frames to ideological beliefs and values that operate normatively at deeper levels within society to shape what counts as 'conventional' and 'unconventional', that create and maintain rules around the 'should feels' and 'shouldn't feels' in different contexts, times, and spaces. This means, then, that we do not engage in emotion work and emotional labour (defined as the work to create a "publicly observable facial and bodily display" (Hochschild 1983 [2012]:7)) on our own. We do engage privately *and* publicly in emotion work and emotional labour because, as Ahmed also shows us, we share our emotions with others in "emotion-work systems" (Hochschild 1979:562). Within these systems, emotional labour in particular has exchange value. What Hochschild means by this, in essence, is that we manage our emotions out of a sense of expectation, or owing or being owed. She offers the examples of a graduate expressing happiness towards her parents at graduation as something she owes them in exchange for sacrifices they may have made to pay for her education, or an airline employee being polite and kind in exchange for the money passengers have paid for their airline tickets and flight experience. This exchange value is important to consider here, because there are certainly similar kinds of expectations attached to behaviour and becoming in doctoral education that are often unconscious, unnamed and unexamined, on the part of universities and supervisors especially.

Hochschild's concepts for feeling rules and frames and her sociological conceptualising of both emotion work and emotional labour enable a study interested in emotions in doctoral education to ask important questions about what kinds of frames dominate doctoral supervision and support in different contexts, and what sets of feeling rules are created and maintained. Who benefits and how? Who loses out and how? What is the import of this for such a high stakes endeavour? This is important work because, as all three theorists make clear, emotions are not comfortable things to talk about and shine a light on; they are messy and slippery and the boundaries between personal and private, and public and shared are challenged when the conversation turns to emotions and feelings. Yet, it is impossible to talk about writing, learning, thinking, building relationships, growing as a scholar and researcher – all core activities in building a doctoral identity – without talking about emotions, feelings, and how these operate as mechanisms of management and control within education.

## PULLING THE FRAMEWORK TOGETHER: STARTING POINTS FOR RESEARCHING DOCTORAL EMOTIONS

All three of these theorists are feminists and the value of feminist theory to the study this chapter marks the commencement of, is its offer of a language and tools with which to dig deeper into the ways in which feeling rules and social structures are raced, classed, gendered, and also biased around able-bodiedness and sexuality as well. Feminist scholars are often more comfortable in the messy spaces in between, in my humble opinion, and their work over the last five decades has tackled many difficult, uncomfortable questions and problems with criticality and care. This approach is at the heart of my proposed research into doctoral emotion work and emotional labour as well. Taken together, the insights I have drawn from the work of Boler, Ahmed and Hochschild work to create a powerful, novel language and set of conceptual tools within which to approach research that seeks to better understand the nature and effects of emotion within doctoral education, across disciplinary and national higher education boundaries.

The theoretical framework proposed in this chapter enables further empirical work that focus on issues related to access, success and social justice. Pulling these three threads together, we have a language now to ask more pointed questions related to how we conceptualise, enable, and continue to constrain wider forms of access, success and social justice in doctoral education, in our own and across different local and global contexts. As just a few examples:

- When we admit students into doctoral programmes, what are we recognising in them – their writing, their presentation of themselves, their applications – and what emotional investments or attachments does this point to?
- When we construct doctoral programmes, especially those that have formal, taught elements or structures, what kinds of engagement do we expect, and why? Are our expectations 'neutral' as we may suppose them to be, or are we invoking deeper, unnamed and unexamined ideological beliefs about what it is to be a 'good' scholar?
- What is the effect of imposing a dominant ideology and identity on students who do not live in this ideal body, speak this ideal language, perform this ideal identity? In what ways can the 'ideal' be reimagined, and what might we have to confront and examine within ourselves and the structures we are invested in to do this emotion work?
- What bodies and ways of being are privileged in different contexts and programmes and what underpins this? What might the effects be on scholars who cannot, or do not, 'fit in' – both students and supervisors?

By collectively challenging accounts that restrict discourses on emotions to the private, individualised and psychological sphere, Boler, Ahmed and Hochschild together offer me, as both a researcher and a supervisor, a way to look at how emotions are part of structuring, maintaining and enacting a shared doctoral education and support space. There must be space for emotion work and emotional labouring within doctoral supervision and support, and we need to take the sociological and political nature and role of emotions seriously if, as Boler argues, we are serious about socially just educational praxis. We need more research that critically unpacks, critiques, and reimagines education in ways that truly widen and deepen what we consider to be success in academia. To do this research we need the kind of critical social theory I am drawing on here, and a willingness to look at ourselves just as hard as we look at others.

## REFERENCES

Ahmed S. 2014. *The cultural politics of emotion*. 2nd ed. Edinburgh: Edinburgh University Press.

Aitchison C, Catterall J, Ross P & Burgin S. 2012. 'Tough love and tears': Learning doctoral writing in the sciences. *Higher Education Research & Development*, 31(4):435-447. https://doi.org/10.1080/07294360.2011.559195

Aitchison C & Mowbray S. 2013. Doctoral women: Managing emotions, managing doctoral studies. *Teaching in Higher Education*, 18(8):85-870. https://doi.org/10.1080/13562517.2013.827642

Boler M. 1999. *Feeling power: Emotions and education*. London and New York: Psychology Press.

Brown L & Watson P. 2010. Understanding the experiences of female doctoral students. *Journal of Further and Higher Education*, 34(3):385-404. https://doi.org/10.1080/0309877X.2010.484056

Carter S, Blumenstein, M. & Cook, C. 2013. Different for women? The challenges of doctoral studies. *Teaching in Higher Education*, 18(4):339-351. https://doi.org/10.1080/13562517.2012.719159

Cloete N. 2015. Nurturing doctoral growth: Towards the NDP's 5000? *South African Journal of Science*, 111(11-12):1-3. https://doi.org/10.17159/sajs.2015/a0127

Crumb L, Haskins N, Dean L & Avent Harris JR. 2019. Illuminating social-class identity: The persistence of working-class African American women doctoral students. *Journal of Diversity in Higher Education*. https://doi.org/10.1037/dhe0000109

Doloriert C, Sambrook S & Stewart J. 2012. Power and emotion in doctoral supervision: Implications for HRD. *European Journal of Training and Development*, 36(7):732-750. https://doi.org/10.1108/03090591211255566

Felder PP, Stevenson HC & Gasman M. 2014. Understanding race in doctoral student socialization. *International Journal of Doctoral Studies*, 9:21-42. https://doi.org/10.28945/1947

Gardner SK & Holley KA. 2011. "Those invisible barriers are real": The progression of first-generation students through doctoral education. *Equity & Excellence in Education*, 44(1):77-92. https://doi.org/10.1080/10665684.2011.529791

Gurr GM. 2001. Negotiating the "Rackety Bridge" – A dynamic model for aligning supervisory style with research student development. *Higher Education Research & Development*, 20(1):81-92. https://doi.org/10.1080/07924360120043882

Hochschild AR. 1979. Emotion work, feeling rules, and social structure. *American Journal of Sociology*, 85(3):551-575. https://doi.org/10.1086/227049

Hochschild AR. 1983 [2012]. *The managed heart: Commercialization of human feeling*. Updated ed. Berkeley: University of California Press.

Holley KA & Gardner S. 2012. Navigating the pipeline: How socio-cultural influences impact first-generation doctoral students. *Journal of Diversity in Higher Education*, 5(2):112. https://doi.org/10.1037/a0026840

Manathunga C. 2007. Supervision as mentoring: The role of power and boundary crossing. *Studies in Continuing education*, 29(2):207-221. https://doi.org/10.1080/01580370701424650

McAlpine L & Amundsen C. 2009. Identity and agency: Pleasures and collegiality among the challenges of the doctoral journey. *Studies in Continuing Education*, 31(2):109-125. https://doi.org/10.1080/01580370902927378

McAlpine L & Lucas L. 2011. Different places, different specialisms: Similar questions of doctoral identities under construction. *Teaching in Higher Education*, 16(6):695-706. https://doi.org/10.1080/13562517.2011.570432

Mewburn I. 2011. Troubling talk: Assembling the PhD candidate. *Studies in Continuing Education*, 33(3):321-332. https://doi.org/10.1080/0158037X.2011.585151

Nerad M. 2019. Are they converging? Postgraduate education worldwide: Trends and future challenges. Keynote address, 7th Postgraduate Supervision Conference, Stellenbosch. 26-29 March 2019.

Stracke E & Kumar V. 2010. Feedback and self-regulated learning: Insights from supervisors' and PhD examiners' reports. *Reflective Practice*, 11(1):19-32. https://doi.org/10.1080/14623940903525140

Strandler O, Johansson T, Wisker G & Claesson S. 2014. Supervisor or counsellor? – Emotional boundary work in supervision. *International Journal for Researcher Development*, 5(2):70-82. https://doi.org/10.1108/IJRD-03-2014-0002

Trafford V & Leshem S. 2009. Doctorateness as a threshold concept. *Innovations in Education and Teaching International*, 46(3):305-316. https://doi.org/10.1080/14703290903069027

# WORKING TOGETHER BEYOND THE PHD

Gina Wisker, Gillian Robinson and Shosh Leshem

## INTRODUCTION

Most work on supervisors' and doctoral students' relationships focuses on the PhD journey, which (ideally) builds sound working interactions, good research practices, and a thesis which makes a valuable contribution to knowledge. Working intellectual interactions between supervisors and postgraduates can develop in both positive and negative ways during the supervisory relationship term, and for those seeking academic careers, ongoing work with a supervisor can be a useful first step in entering the research and writing conversations in which the supervisor might already have a role. Not all graduates wish to pursue working, writing and publishing with their supervisor, perhaps because they do not seek an ongoing academic relationship and perhaps because they have not undertaken the PhD in the first place intending to become an academic themselves. However, there are some problematic relations between students and supervisors, during and after graduation, and some issues regarding intellectual property. Autoethnographic and other narrative interviewing with doctoral graduates (including the researchers) reveals insights that boundaries of the PhD process are often artificially limited, and that working intellectual interactions between supervisors and graduate doctors continue in various ways, for better or for worse, after graduation. Some positive co-working produces co-written, co-owned publications and work on funded or unfunded projects, while the less positive examples could be described as less than benign neglect (Gurr 2001), and in worst case scenarios, intellectual property theft.

This chapter considers the practices of supervisors and doctoral graduates working beyond graduation, looking at successful mutually beneficial practices, and some more problematic behaviours. It aims to offer useful examples of continued working together which is based on productive supervisor-student interactions. Our recent 10-year reunion with an international PhD cohort with whom we have worked as 'guardian supervisors' (Wisker, Robinson, Shacham 2007), and other recent work facilitating courses on writing for academic publication and supervision, prompted our interest in supervisors and doctoral graduates working together. Some insights also emerged from anecdotal and individual examples of co-working, and of seeing the results of poor working practices after graduation.

We use theories of academic identity (Henkel 2005a, 2005b; Clegg 2008), communities of practice (Lave & Wenger 1999), and some Gothic images of 'lightside' and 'darkside' behaviours (Wisker, Robinson & Bengtsen 2017; Wisker & Bengtsen 2018) to focus on the processes and practices of supervisors and PhD doctoral graduates working together productively or experiencing troubled relationships and dubious practices beyond the PhD process. Our interest in this topic on students and supervisors began through following up a large cohort of PhD students, through writing or not writing with our own supervisors, and through working with supervisors and doctoral students with whom we had not previously been involved, who spoke in supervision and writing workshops of their working relationships, supervisor/doctoral student, ex-supervisor/doctoral graduate, and agreed to be interviewed on the project.

Early research based on narrative interviewing with supervisors and doctoral graduates has brought to the surface worrying examples of problematic, non-productive, one-sided, even predatory attempts at continued working practices, and a range of productive, ongoing interactions. The productive examples include co-writing of articles or books from the PhD (Ivanic 1998; Wisker 2015a); ongoing and future co-conducted research projects; co-presenting and continuing to co-write from future projects; supporting the careers of early career researchers through joint bid writing and inclusion in funded projects; and references, mentoring, and employment in a teaching function. There are also examples of established academics and professionals inviting ex-supervisors to join projects or offer consultancies. Data from our sample and this early ongoing work shed new light on the 'boundaried' doctoral student-supervisor relationship, indicating ways of building productive, ongoing working partnerships that are more between equals, working together to support the development of the early career researcher's sense of a productive, respected academic identity, where these can be felt as fragile, transitional and tenuously held (Henkel 2005a; Acker & Haque 2010). Positive relationships offer opportunities to maintain effective communities of practice and enhance researcher academic identities throughout the academic and professional research career.

## LITERATURE REVIEW

There is plenty of literature indicating that the academic career is not open to all graduates because of the scarcity of positions (Acker & Haque 2010), the inappropriate fit with skills and lifestyles, and graduates desiring and working towards different kinds of employment than that offered by academe (Sekuler, Crow & Annan 2013). Not all postgraduates wish to continue in academic careers, instead working in government or industry (Mendoza 2007; Gardner & Mendoza 2010), or returning to or entering professional practice for which the PhD has been a useful stepping-stone. Much of the literature focusing on supervisors and postgraduates working together, whether during or after the PhD, in ongoing research and/or writing relationships, concentrates on the problems this state of affairs brings to the fore. Essentially, they are problems of power imbalances and ownership, where postgraduates and graduates might be flattered, side-lined or provoked into working with their supervisor beyond the PhD examination to get work published. Where this work is credited appropriately to whoever and in what proportion it was produced, then this can be a relationship of mutual benefit. The insight a supervisor has into publishing politics and practice, the contacts, the continuation of a supportive relationship where the balance of power sits with the two as equal colleagues, and the success of the student or ex-student can at the very least enable work to be published which otherwise might not see publication. Kamler (2008) argues that publishing from the PhD work is considered important. Publications measure performance and can underpin promotions and research funding, and professionally she cites two international surveys by Dinham and Scott confirming a "connection between publishing support and increased productivity" (Dinham & Scott 2001:284). Kamler's work focuses largely on positive examples of working together during the PhD and co-publishing as a part of that process. Not everyone has such positive examples, and some emphasise the difficulties in sharing work as equals in an unequal relationship both during and after the PhD process. In relation to earlier work conducted by two of the authors, we label the positive relationships and activities 'lightside' and the negative unproductive relationships and activities 'darkside' (Wisker et al. 2017; Wisker & Bengtsen 2018) – a continuum characterising relationships between postgraduates and their supervisors, or others related to their work, which we have elsewhere identified as Gothic because of the silences, absences, hidden experiences and the ways in which the Gothic, a cultural and imaginative critical construct, reveals instabilities beneath taken for granted or complacent behaviours and norms.

Using Bakhtin's notion of the superaddressee or third listener, Midgley, Henderson and Danahar (2010:87) look at issues of "risks of miscommunication, exploitation and learned dependency". Focusing on research collaboration, they note Olson and

Clark's (2009) view of leader-scholar communities for success in situated research, cite Waters (2008) who, while recognising that there is largely a master-apprentice model, when supervisors and students or graduate students work together, urges shared responsibility between supervisors and institutions for providing 'opportunities' for reducing doctoral students' isolation, and for research collaboration between doctoral students and supervisors, for example, through using learning technologies.

However, there are darker sides to this matter, and a variety of problems mostly related to power imbalance, where supervisors might be holding students back from useful research experiences and sharing of their work, using them as technicians rather than supporting their development as independent researchers. There are also cases of theft of students' intellectual property and capital, although, from comments gleaned anecdotally in the many international supervision workshops we have facilitated, separately or together, it seems that supervisors often find it difficult to determine who had the ideas, who did the work, or who produced the wording. Therefore, contexts of co-creation, a feature of good supervisor-student relations, it is often not clear cut who owns what. Martin (2013) defines such negative behaviours as exploitation and looks at the damage done to the student through being "denigrated", and "their contributions to research projects dismissed as small, unoriginal or insignificant". Martin looks at work during the PhD rather than beyond it, while working together beyond the PhD is the focus of our chapter. The issues of silencing, theft and misappropriation (supervisor of student work), under-estimation and absence of recognition (student of supervisor input) can happen at any point. However, we argue that there are many benefits of empowerment and recognition of the right to speak bound up with writing together during and beyond the PhD, and a personal professional dialogue (possibly a long-term, ongoing working relationship and dialogue) between equals is in many cases likely to result from researching and writing together on work which is then published.

Previous research which we have conducted looks at other elements of the 'darkside' of the supervisor-student relationship (Wisker et al. 2017; Wisker & Bengtsen, 2018) and at the importance of publishing from the PhD, which often involves working closely with a supervisor (Wisker 2015a, 2015b). Publishing together appears to be a popular form of establishing and maintaining working and practising, which can introduce the graduate or postgraduate into a community of research writing practice (Lave & Wenger 1999), such as forming a project team.

Much of the continued working together of supervisor and graduated student is historically that of co-writing, a way of ensuring the research gets out into the world, and of recognising the participation in its construction and expression of supervisors, students and any wider research team. One of the authors of this chapter (Wisker 2015b) considers working together beyond the PhD as a continued production of references, advice in conferences and co-presentation, co-publishing, and mutual invitations onto future projects. If this begins to look community-oriented and mutually beneficial there is also literature aligned with the issues of breakdowns in supervisor relations and student isolation, and then of what seems equal, student and supervisor working together, being revealed as a problem over intellectual property and what can be considered supportive – the supervisor's continued care – being alternatively seen as exploitative.

A range of exploitative practices can leave students threatened, uncomfortable, or unable to complain, since professional contexts often favour those in power and official channels focus on procedures. This could challenge their likelihood of success in academe and/or other work contexts after graduation, and damage their sense of academic identity (Henkel 2005a, 2005b; Clegg 2008). Martin's (2013) examples show dismayed, disillusioned, depressed postgraduates, shocked that their work has been stolen and their contributions marginalised in this way. In earlier work, two of the authors and a colleague began to recognise support practice outside the supervisory relationship as positive and negative, the negative being more a case of being underhand, informal and perhaps a substitution for the student's work. But we can also use the characteristics of 'darkside' and 'lightside' from this earlier piece (Wisker, Robinson & Bengtsen 2017) to characterise the same interactions between students and supervisors beyond graduation, when they do or do not continue to work together, and to determine a range of effective and mutually empowering, beneficial, constructive practices of working together.

## METHODOLOGY AND METHODS

The issue of doctoral graduates and supervisors working together after graduation emerged from our experience, observation and discussion with a cohort of graduated PhDs as mentioned at the start of this article in order to respect the richness of our own experiences, as well as the experiences of participants who agreed to be part of the research, we adopted two related narrative approaches to our research. First (see a below), we used autoethnographic narrative, where we told our own stories of working with our supervisors after graduation, and of perceiving others working with their supervisors after graduation, sometimes in terms of writing and publishing together, where we were in a position either supporting this process (as guardian supervisors, as editors, as colleagues) or noting the problems it produced.

Next (see b below), and more conventionally, we conducted semi-structured, open-ended narrative interviews with a total of 12 doctoral graduates in Israel (6), South Africa (4) and the UK (2), (2016-2019). The participants from Israel were invited to respond to an email invitation we developed, built on previous knowledge of the students' and supervisors' joint ongoing work. Their interviews were conducted by email or face to face. The participants from South Africa and the UK were invited to respond to questions about co-working beyond the PhD, which formed part of discussions in a suite of workshops for supervisors, postdocs, doctoral students and teachers, focusing on writing for publication. Their interviews were face to face. The interview questions with doctoral graduates sought to answer the following questions:

- When does the role as supervisor finish?
- Did you continue to work with your supervisor after the exam or the exam and viva?

If yes:

- Who initiated the collaboration?
- What was the nature of the collaboration (conferences, papers, books, consultations, bids, other)?
- Who benefited from the collaboration?

We also sought further comments and accounts of individual critical incidents.

This early research was built on autoethnographic narratives in the form of semi-structured, open-ended narrative interviewing conducted by the three researchers/authors (following Goodson 2010) using a voice recorder. It was transcribed and thematically analysed, then re-storied into short case studies. No single example could be attributed to individuals. In conducting interviews we each explained our own positionality and were careful to remain neutral in the use of set questions and not to let our positionality affect either the questioning or the analysis of the data and construction of findings.

Research was given ethical approval from one of the three universities in which the authors are based, all participants were fully informed about the research and their right to withdraw, and all who took part in the research gave informed consent. Autoethnographic narratives and interviews with the participants who responded face to face were taped and transcribed and the email interviews were included in the data for analysis. Data were kept on the password-protected PCs of the three researchers, and pseudonyms were allocated to respondents.

## FINDINGS

First, we share the autoethnographic narrative of one of the researchers, since it was built out of an experience that partly initiated the research.

## Case 1 from the autoethnographic narrative responses. Publishing together beyond the PhD

As an editor, one of us receives a range of informal contacts about potential papers. We refer to the person in this introductory story as 'K'.

> One paper came in from X country and the author (K) and I discussed it by email. I had a quick look; it was not suitable for the journal. He then sent in another suggestion, an abstract, which sounded as though it would fit the journal, so we proceeded with the reviewing process and, finding it near perfect, took it. After it was reviewed, I was sent the paper to look over, as it is unusual to have so few corrections, but it was very good. Upon acceptance he immediately said he had several other papers we could consider, so I said to send them. This paper went into production, and was published first online. Suddenly I was contacted in great annoyed distress by the PhD student whose work it actually was. He had published her work without consulting her, and without even adding her name. A long process took place to ensure that her name was added online and in the hard copy of the journal. The next paper he offered me I turned down, and I would be reluctant to consider anything from him again, but if you look him up, you will see he is a prolific, published author of a range of vaguely connected topics, no doubt all stolen from his PhD students.

This example of working, or rather not working, with your supervisor after completion is the 'darkside', the rock bottom, perhaps, of the process, but we include it so we can also share the many positive examples we have found.

## The interviews

The analysis of the data brought to the surface a range of ongoing 'lightside' and 'darkside' interactions (Wisker *et al.* 2017) of supervision, working on projects, career work, and in the main, joint publishing and we report on these extremes rather than the many 'grey' interactions which are more of a mixture of the supportive and positive (lightside) on the one hand or the absent or appropriating behaviours (darkside) on the other. We report here in two forms: (1) the emerging themes, and then (2) through restoried narrative case studies, which we developed from building narratives around specific responses from these narrative interviews.

## DATA ANALYSIS: THE CONTINUUM OF SUPERVISORS AND GRADUATED STUDENTS WORKING TOGETHER – FROM THE 'LIGHTSIDE' AND THE 'DARKSIDE'

Data from our sample in this early ongoing work shed new light on the 'boundaried' doctoral student-supervisor relationship, particularly the relationship beyond graduation. It indicates some negative examples of quite problematic disempowering practice, which verges on intellectual property theft, as well as positive examples of ways of building productive, ongoing, working partnerships that are more between equals, and which offer opportunities to maintain effective communities of practice and enhance researcher academic identities throughout the academic and professional research career.

Themes are reported first and then case studies, which also exemplify, amplify and enrich those themes through the stories presented. Supervisors are labelled alphabetically, graduated students numerically. Figure 12.1 represents some themes emerging from the data on the continuum of supervisors and graduated students working together, from the 'lightside' to the 'darkside'.

*The 'lightside' of ongoing relationships include:*

> Onwards working with the supervisor: a variety of interactions including continued contact, advice and support;
>
> Loose working relationships producing generously co-authored work (when neither author is there for ornamental purposes alone); and
>
> Over time, an ongoing positive working relationship producing good outputs, appropriately acknowledged, and new work.

*The 'darkside':*

> Lack of contact with graduate and lack of further support, including networking support, when it is sought; and
>
> Silent, unacknowledged theft of the candidate's work.

*Light and dark:*

> No continued relationship and a great sense of relief at that.

# CHAPTER 12 • WORKING TOGETHER BEYOND THE PHD

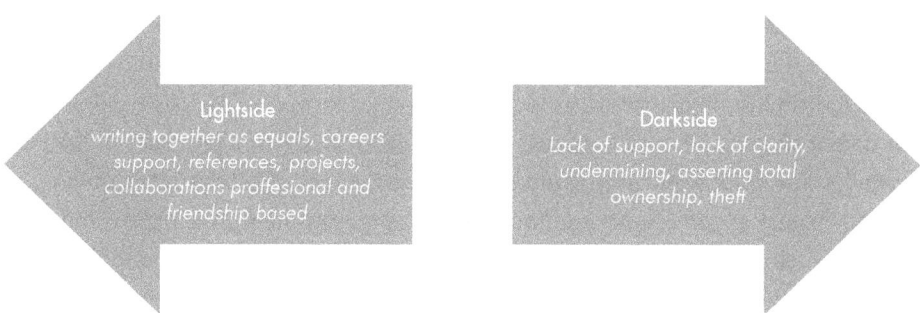

**FIGURE 12.1** The continuum of supervisors and graduated students working together: From the 'lightside' to the 'darkside'

## ONWARDS WORKING WITH THE SUPERVISOR AND GRADUATED STUDENT

Different perspectives about the supervisor's role after graduation emerged from our interviews. Some felt that the role is one of supporting and enabling the graduated student to develop and achieve their projects and their thesis and that the supervisor's role ends when the student graduates. Others, however, believed the relationship does not end with graduation and the supervisor could or should assist with publishing, references, careers and networking (Wisker 2012, 2015a). The continuation of a working relationship might well be based on an ongoing personal/ professional relationship (Wisker 2012) and be more a matter of individuals getting along well together in a working relationship rather than a behaviour that is common across all of a supervision relationship. Respondents noted that, with some students, it clicks, while with others it ends formally after graduation. They noted examples of writing together, and of a mix of formal and informal relationships throughout the supervisory process. Both graduated students and supervisors spoke of consulting the supervisor and some of building friendly relationships, remembering birthdays, and significant holidays. When asked why they think some relationships just develop naturally and some just do not 'click' one of the supervisors responded:

> I think it is the personality, you just click with students, you think this is a journey that I can continue afterwards. It is more natural than with other students. It's a formal relationship but it is much more informal after the production of the thesis. (Sup C)

**PART THREE • TRAJECTORIES**

Some of the emerging themes highlight continued positive working practices, which often began as fragmented relationships during the student-supervisor journey, and some indicate continuation of a lack of working practices. Discipline differences, the career stage of the postgraduate or graduate, and different practices at different stages in the initial supervisor-student relationship might affect the establishing and maintaining of ongoing working practices (or the lack of them). We discovered ways in which such ongoing working practices were initiated and nurtured, and the forms they took. We also discovered some very negative non-relationships or relationships and practices ranging from benign neglect (Gurr 2001), completely ignoring the student or graduate, to predatory behaviours.

Writing and publishing together is a key area of ongoing working practices. However, some graduated students and supervisors never even consider working together, while others work together and co-research, co-publish and network from the early moments of the relationship. Discipline-related practices are seen to affect this. It is rare to co-publish articles in literature, for example, while it is common in the sciences, and social scientists write together with supervisors, students and others involved in projects, as well as on their own.

Career stage is also a factor in the ongoing relationship. Mid-career professionals often do not need this ongoing relationship; perhaps because their aims in undertaking a doctorate could be professional development, promotion within and beyond their current place of work, rather than building up research relationships and co-publishing. Early career researchers, however, might well need co-researching, networking and co-publications as the next step in their research career journey.

Some positive practices emphasising equality and balance between graduated students and supervisors ('lightside') have emerged. These include co-writing of articles or books from the PhD; ongoing and future co-conducted research projects; co-presenting and continuing to co-write from future projects; supervisors supporting the careers of early career researchers through joint bid writing and inclusion in funded projects; and supervisors contributing references, mentoring, and offering employment in a teaching function.

There are also examples of professional and personal relationships and of established academics and professionals inviting ex-supervisors to join projects or offer consultancies.

Some less than positive practices ('darkside') have also emerged. These include supervisor lack of support and clarity of direction hampering student development (during the supervisory relationship), followed by the supervisor claiming total ownership of the work produced; and supervisors publishing student work without consultation, and under the supervisor's name alone.

### Loose working relationships producing generously co-authored work (when neither author is there for ornamental purposes alone)

We enquired about how working relationships began and identified stages and practices, including initiation in which the supervisor is quite supportive and encourages the student to publish, as sometimes the student feels insecure, or even wants to forget about the thesis and does not want to do any additional work, as they do not see the benefit of it. Another form of support from the supervisor is guiding the student with possible topics or suitable journals, but usually leaving it open to the student to make the final decision, as one of the supervisors commented on who initiates the working together:

> Mostly it's not the candidate, mostly it's me that encourages. (Sup A)

> Most of them are happy about it ... some of them feel intimidated. (Sup B)

Asked about what they work on together, two of the supervisors responded as follows:

> If I see that a student has done really good work that is of publishable quality, or if an external examiner report comes back and recommends it, I would contact the candidate and suggest we look at journal publication and conferences. So mostly it is not the candidate, mostly it is me that encourages them to do that, but not all of them. (Sup A)

> Usually I would recommend what we could work on based on their dissertation ... But I kind of leave it open to the candidates ... It's a kind of a question like, "I think we could do this but what would you like to do?" I try and guide them because they're not as experienced and they don't really know what to do. (Sup B)

At other times, the student initiates the ongoing relationship, suggests a topic and consults the supervisor:

> I thought of a topic and she came back and said, "This is definitely something that we need to explore," and thereafter we worked together and published that. So, we've got a good relationship ... (Stu 1)

### Over time, an ongoing positive working relationship producing good outputs, appropriately acknowledged, and new work

There are various motives for continuing to work together after graduation. Some of them relate directly to career progression, including promotion for both supervisor and candidate, status, career development, adding to CV, institutional requirements to publish with the supervisor, and a desire to continue a productive intellectual/research/writing relationship.

One of our graduate respondents commented that continued working was expected:

> When I finished mine, it was expected of me to publish with my supervisors, that was the institution's sort of requirement, that you must publish at least one article with your supervisor. (Stu 2)

Some supervisors and graduated students publish together once, regularly, or on a long-term basis. For some this approach is related to the graduate's need to be published and there will also be a time limit (Thomson 2016). While good personal professional relationships were reported as a feature of some of the supervisors and students working over time, this did not always lead to continuation of the working relationship, since in some cases the student did not want or need to publish, or the research areas of each were not close enough to consider such publishing, or it was not felt that this relationship should continue beyond graduation. One of the reasons for students not engaging with the supervisor to publish or continue research is that work demands usually do not allow time to pursue such a relationship after graduation, or that having achieved the qualification, the student sees no benefit in a publication, possibly a stance taken by those who neither intend nor are already in any kind of academic career. Ongoing research might well not be a priority and publications are not always significant currency in the world of professional practice, at least in some contexts, either cultural or disciplinary.

Some supervisors commented that they would choose with whom to pursue the relationship after graduation. They would choose students who can also work independently and would not need much support.

### Ongoing: Working beyond the supervisory process – a range of other practices

Networking is also involved, where the supervisor informs the graduated student about different conferences or people with whom it is worth networking, and they also present jointly at conferences. Some become involved with co-working on projects, which is not a one-way process, since graduated students invite supervisors or the supervisor invites the graduate student onto projects. Supervisors are often involved in supporting the continued career of the graduated student, even if they do not continue to work together or co-publish, so they provide references, and they might be involved in co-editing or co-running conferences. In due course the graduated student becomes a supervisor themselves, although, again, that was not always the case with mid-career professionals whose engagement with this stage of academic work was a step to enhance their own career rather than a further step into an academic career. So, in such cases the ongoing actions resulting from any project and ongoing work with a supervisor were less likely to be academic in focus (i.e. publishing, writing and conferences.)

## DARKSIDE – SOME NEGATIVE INTERACTIONS AND STALLED RELATIONSHIPS

However, not all the interactions are constructive, and one example of a student's initiation of a working relationship beyond the PhD was met with silence:

> I asked my supervisor, "Would you please comment on it and give me suggestions for changes and comment on anything that you think would improve the quality" and I never got a response from her. (Stu 4)

**We developed these darkside examples into short case studies based on the narrative interviewing**

While these are particular to our respondents, some of the themes they exemplify are familiar across a range of stories offered by participants in our supervisor and writing workshops, and across the large cohort of graduates and the range of individuals with whom we are familiar, as well as those we specifically interviewed.

### *Case 2: Graduate student case E*

Beyond the working supervisory relationship, this graduate wrote an article from their research and sent it to the supervisor to comment; however, the supervisor did not respond. They sent some more reminders saying that adding the supervisor's name required their input, but still received no response. They published the article without the supervisor's name on it – in the end – and felt quite proud of themselves for persevering.

Two years later the supervisor suggested they write a joint article on the methodology, but this time the candidate refused and did it on their own.

> I was disappointed that I didn't get the support I would have got from X. Any kind of support at the stage would have been really fantastic, and there was no guidance from X. I did it all on my own. And then about two years after that. X says, "Oh, I noticed that your methodology chapter was very exciting, it was very interesting, and the examiners have commented on the uniqueness of your methodology. Is there a way of us publishing that together?" And I thought, well I don't want to go through the same process of me doing everything and you will not comment on it and then I must put your name on it, and I just ignored it. And then I thought I will do that on my own and not put you on it because when I gave you the opportunity you were not prepared to do it so why should I go through the same process of being rejected now?

This example emphasises a range of issues, including lost opportunities (to work together), a threat to academic identity, and, on the positive side, the graduate eventually feeling independent and empowered enough to publish on their own, having earlier followed all the expected steps to include the supervisor.

### Case 3: Graduate student case F

F's supervisor was unresponsive during the process of her PhD and there was no connection with him after she had finished. However, several years later he contacted her out of the blue to ask if he could use her work, as he needed publications to give him credibility for a new academic post. F was shocked and refused his request.

Two other cases, Cases 4 and 5, shed further light on a darkside of supervisor practice.

### Case 4: Graduate student case G

During the process of her PhD research, G discovered her supervisor had published an article based on her work without acknowledgement and that he had even omitted her name on the publication. She was so upset she did not want to continue with her PhD.

### Case 5: Graduate student case H

H, a master's student, graduated and the supervisor decided to publish their work under their own name with no reference to the student. Their arguments for doing so were that the work gets out into the world; the supervisor gets a publication; the student is not interested, it seems, in writing now. Of course, one reading of this is that the work does at least get shared with the world and does not just sit on a shelf somewhere. The supervisor would have had a stake in the work and probably was the source of much thinking, advice, rewriting and so on. However, in this case there is no recognition of the student who conducted the work and wrote the dissertation. Intellectual property is a major issue here, and in this instance it is theft: the student is silenced, their work stolen and they receive no credit.

There are many issues in these complex, dark relationships and they concern ownership, such as whether it was the student's work or the supervisors' work, or whether it was that flexible, generous, interactive work called 'co-production'. What each of the negative examples shows is that one cannot assume either the establishment of cooperative learning, or an ongoing, mutually beneficial community of practice (Lave & Wenger 1999; Wisker, Robinson & Shacham 2007) in research and writing of which the supervisor and graduated doctor are active members.

## FURTHER DISCUSSION

Establishing a scholarly relationship between a doctoral student and the supervisor is a long, sensitive, essential process. We become aware of each other's concerns about research ethics, methods and writing, time management, and a range of personal behavioural traits. Like dancers rather than synchronised swimmers, we match each other's moves so that we can work together. As supervisors, we can find the exactly appropriate way to engage with a doctoral student's issues, be they personal or conceptual, about identity or writing, or confusion over theorists, so that in our dialogue we can offer the most appropriate support and the right ways of working. Some of our work on dialogues has indicated a range of such interactions and so has suggested that there are stages in the supervisory and doctoral journey where, as a supervisor, we choose the language to use and the mode of interaction in relation to the issues, the stage and that particular student. In short, we learn, like dancers, to dance together, and each supervisor-student dance is a little different to the next. Comparison with dancing sounds slightly intimate and lovely, but one must also remember flamenco and some of the more violent, separated dances, as well as the stately choreographed moves of line dancing and ballroom dancing. There are rules to the ways we work together to enable the student to be guided in the way they can work, not overwhelmed or shut out. We learn how to work together, and we also learn how to write together, because the constant, interactive feedback in good supervisory relations is modified by the different students and the different stages they are in, and is intended to support the development of their work. So, we are like critical friends: we guide, we suggest ideal wording, complex thinking, cutting back and shaping. We might feel when we have stopped working with a student and their work is through the process that much of it comes straight from our experience and even sounds like our work, but it is not, it is theirs; we have mentored support, but the work is theirs. Supervisor and student have constructed it, working together, probably building on it in the years of a harmonious and contested, challenged, but ultimately shared successful practice.

Some supervisors do not do this, of course, as in the example we started with. Some supervisors merely steal their students' work, believing they kind of did it all anyway, and some students would never want to see or hear from their supervisors again – if they saw or heard enough from them during the process in the first place – since many relationships are tenuously held until doctoral completion and many are unsuccessful (Wisker & Robinson 2014).

The relationship of working together after doctoral achievement is probably one that will change from father-doctor (the German version), to equal partnership. The moments of this change can be everything from invisible to smooth, recognising the autonomy and the new equality of the doctor. The doctor-doctor relationship of equals has grown from the student -supervisor relationship. Many of us have mentors, even when we have published regularly for years. Perhaps it is this kind of relationship – more a mentoring between equals and a continued working practice based on shared decision-making and shared ownership of the processes and products – that is the positive outcome sought for ongoing working together rather than the hierarchical relationship underpinning and informing supervisory relationships.

It is a complex process – not everyone wishes to, or can, work together after graduation. We discovered some rather underhand, problematic, lack of ongoing relationships when it might perhaps have been supportive and useful to both parties to remain in touch to help launch the student, for example. We also discovered straightforward unethical behaviour. However, we found several examples of positive, ongoing interactions of co-researching for publications. We discovered a range of nurturing co-production relationships. As a norm, some relationships often continued insofar as supervisors provided references, and continued to enable networking. For some, the hierarchical relationship of supervisor and student ceased as such with graduation and then morphed so that the relationship actually developed differently, further, into something productive between equals, and continued insofar as they remained colleagues or friends, co-researched and co-published together.

## CONCLUSIONS

There is a range of research that considers doctoral graduates, their plans for employment and their entrance (or otherwise) into the academic workplace. The literature tells us that academic identity development can be clouded by the knowledge that, indeed, there are shrinking opportunities for those who seek academic employment (Henkel 2005a, 2005b; Clegg 2008; Acker & Haque 2010), and we know that networking, links with academic communities, publishing and co-publishing are key practices in enabling that access, transition and success. Thus, for many graduates, productive, positive, ongoing working relationships with supervisors could or should be a natural development. Most work on supervisors' and doctoral students' relationships focuses on the PhD journey, which (one hopes) builds sound working interactions, good research practices, and a thesis that makes a valuable contribution to knowledge. There is also a body of work and a wide range of anecdotes that highlight the negative interactions and the lack of care shown by some supervisors towards their postgraduates during the student-supervisor relationship. There is very little work on supervisors' and students' work beyond the PhD, the positive and negative experiences where intellectual property, varied kinds of relationship, from master-apprentice to collegiate equals involved in co-production, are the focus. Our work sheds light on the positive and negative experiences, the lightside and darkside of postgraduates and graduated doctoral students working with their supervisors, and raises issues of academic identity development, ownership, and duty of care. Much of our work here focuses on the darkside of interactions after graduation; however, it is useful to return briefly to the autoethnographic engagement that began our work together here. As authors we are all very positive about our own supervisors and their generosity, insights and individually modulated perseverance in 'nudging' us when we were stuck, or had not quite achieved the level of thought and understanding, the level of expression, which could do our work justice. We are also positive about the various ways in which our supervisors continued to work directly with us (co-writing, co-presenting) and/or maintained communicative links, thus supporting our careers. There is much to celebrate and nurture here, as well as much to ensure the process is more regulated and managed, more equitable.

## REFERENCES

Acker S & Haque E. 2010. Doctoral students and a future in academe? In: L McAlpine & G Åkerlind (eds.), *Becoming an academic: International perspectives*. Basingstoke: Palgrave Macmillan. 96-124. https://doi.org/10.1007/978-0-230-36509-4_5

Clegg S. 2008. Academic identities under threat. *British Educational Research Journal*, 34(3):329-345. https://doi.org/10.1080/01411920701532269

Dinham S & Scott C. 2001. The experience of disseminating the results of doctoral research. *Journal of Further and Higher Education*, 25(1):45-55. https://doi.org/10.1080/03098770020030498

Gardner S & Mendoza P. 2010. *On becoming a scholar: Socialization and development in doctoral education*. Sterling, VA: Stylus Publishing, LLC.

Goodson I. 2010. *Narrative learning*. London, New York: Routledge. https://doi.org/10.4324/9780203856888

Gurr G. 2001. Negotiating the 'rackety bridge' – a dynamic model for aligning supervisory style with research student development. *Higher Education and Development*, 20(1):81-92. https://doi.org/10.1080/07924360120043882

Henkel M. 2005a. Academic identity and autonomy in a changing policy environment. *Higher Education*, 49:155-176. https://doi.org/10.1007/s10734-004-2919-1

Henkel M. 2005b. Academic identity and autonomy revisited. In: I Bleiklie & M Henkel (eds.), *Governing knowledge: A study of continuity and change in higher education: A festschrift in honour of Maurice Kogan*. Berlin: Springer Verlag. 145-165. https://doi.org/10.1007/1-4020-3504-7_10

Ivanic R. 1998. *Writing and identity: The discoursal construction of identity in academic writing*. Amsterdam: John Benjamins. https://doi.org/10.1075/swll.5

Kamler B. 2008. Rethinking doctoral participation practices: Writing from and beyond the thesis. *Studies in Higher Education*, 33(2):283-294. https://doi.org/10.1080/03075070802049236

Lave J & Wenger E. 1999. Legitimate peripheral participation in communities of practice. In: R McCormack & C Poechter (eds.), *Learning and knowledge*. London: Paul Chapman Publishing. https://doi.org/10.1016/B978-0-7506-7223-8.50010-1

Martin B. 2013. Countering supervisor exploitation. *Journal of Scholarly Publishing*, 45(1) October:74-86. https://doi.org/10.3138/jsp.45-1-004

Mendoza P. 2007. Academic capitalism and doctoral student socialization: A case study. *The Journal of Higher Education*, 78(1)January:71-96. https://doi.org/10.1353/jhe.2007.0004

Midgley W, Henderson R & Danahar PA. 2010. Seeking superaddressees: Research collaborations in a doctoral supervisory relationship. In: CH Arden, PA Danaher, L De George-Walker, R Henderson, W Midgley, K Noble & MA Tyler (eds.), *Sustaining synergies: Collaborative research and researching collaboration*. Mount Gravatt, Qld, Australia: Post Pressed. 87-102.

Olson K & Clark CM. 2009. A signature pedagogy in doctoral education: The leader-scholar community. *Educational Researcher*, 38(3):216-221. https://doi.org/10.3102/0013189X09334207

Sekuler AB, Crow B & Annan RB. 2013. *Beyond labs and libraries: Career pathways for doctoral students*. Toronto, ON: Higher Education Quality Council of Ontario.

Thomson P. 2016. When is it too late to write from the PhD? March 31. https://bit.ly/3tNo0t2

Waters EG. 2008. The learner connection model: Can doctoral students make it alone? In: G Richards (ed.), *Proceedings of world conference on e-learning in corporate, government, healthcare, and higher education*. Chesapeake, VA: Association for the Advancement of Computing in Education. 3534-3539.

Wisker G. 2005, 2012 (2nd edn). *The Good Supervisor*. Basingstoke: Palgrave Macmillan. https://doi.org/10.1007/978-1-137-02423-7

Wisker G. 2015a. *Getting published*. London: Palgrave Macmillan. https://doi.org/10.1007/978-0-230-39211-3

Wisker, G. 2015b. Publishing while completing your PhD. DoctoralWriting SIG. https://bit.ly/3vfd0Vn

Wisker G & Bengtsen SE. 2018. Crisis, catharsis, and creation – A gothic approach to doctoral supervision. Paper presented at SRHE Conference 2018: The changing shape of higher education: Can excellence and inclusion cohabit? Newport, 5-7 December.

Wisker, G. & Robinson, G. 2014. Picking up the pieces: Supervisors and doctoral 'orphans'. *International Journal for Researcher Development*, 3(2):139-153. https://doi.org/10.1108/17597511311316982

Wisker G, Robinson G & Bengtsen SE. 2017. Penumbra: Doctoral support as drama: From the 'lightside' to the 'darkside'. From front of house to trapdoors and recesses. *Innovations in Education and Teaching International*, 54 (6):527-538. https://doi.org/10.1080/14703297.2017.1371057

Wisker G, Robinson G. & Shacham M. 2007. Postgraduate research success: Communities of practice involving cohorts, guardian supervisors and online communities. *Innovations in Education and Teaching International*, 44 (3):301-320. https://doi.org/10.1080/14703290701486720

# PART FOUR

REFLECTIONS AND DIRECTIONS

# REFLECTIONS ON COVID-19 AND THE GLOBAL SCHOLAR

Peter Rule

## INTRODUCTION

Covid-19 came with its various waves and mutations during the production of this book, and the first anniversaries of lockdown in many countries coincided with its finalisation. In addition to the direct and devastating impact of illness and mortality, the pandemic seemed to change everything about the way that students and academics – and society as a whole – went about daily life. The critical moment of the pandemic presents a kind of *kairos*, or moment of truth, to higher education, bringing into question the very nature of higher education and its role in society. This context further sharpens the questions raised by Sioux McKenna (Chapter 5) in this book: "Is postgraduate education good for the public, many of whom will never venture onto university premises? Or is it at times a public bad?"

We therefore conclude this book by reflecting on some of the impact and implications of Covid-19 for the global scholar in relation to postgraduate studies and supervision. We use the conceptual lenses of horizon, currency and trajectory introduced in the Introduction, and draw on insights from the preceding chapters. While there is some published research on these topics in peer-reviewed journals, still emerging because of the time lag, we also draw on the considerable literature in higher education newspapers and magazines.

## COVID-19, CURRENTS AND CURRENCIES

In Chapter One, we introduced currency as a lens for understanding the theme of the global scholar and its implications for supervision and postgraduate studies, distinguishing currency as *academic exchange value*, as *academic mobility*, as *immediate relevance* and as *intellectual charge*. One of the most salient features of the pandemic for the academy has been the restriction of academic mobility. Academics have been confined to domestic workstations. Even travelling to work, never mind local and international conferences, has been ruled out for many at some stage/s. Students have been barred from campus or, if already there, in some cases barred from leaving campus. The promise of social, cultural and academic freedom which student life offers has been replaced by restriction, confinement, isolation and intense frustration. It has prevented scholars and students from inhabiting each other's geographical, social and cultural spaces, and by extension, the potential learnings and transformations that result from contact and interaction. On the other hand, the proliferation of virtual conferences, webinars, courses and online forums has offered novel (and often much more accessible and affordable) opportunities to scholars and students to "move", learn and interact – provided they have computer and internet access. Rapidly developing virtual environments have given students and academics the flexibility (if not the choice) to work and study from home.

The kinds of mobility that Rebekah Smith McGloin discusses (Chapter 7), particularly that of international students, have been severely disrupted, leaving many students in limbo. Attracting international students, especially postgraduate students, has become a significant stream in the financial lifeblood of many universities, as Anna Morozov and Cally Guerin (Chapter 6) point out. Covid-19 has at least temporarily threatened this flow with implications for the financial sustainability of institutions. Initial indications are that Covid-19 has significantly decreased the mobility of international students; for example, numbers enrolling at anglophone universities in 2020-21 nosedived, with the prospects for recovery uncertain (Bothwell 2021). In addition to students, the recruitment of international academics, whom universities prize in promoting innovation and international perspectives and collaborations, has been disrupted. International students and academics also contribute to the metrics that inform university rankings and their international reputations as academic destinations of choice.

Morozov and Guerin differentiate among temporary, permanent and circular forms of academic mobility. Covid-19 has severely curtailed temporary and circular mobility, and perhaps in some cases forced temporary stays into more permanent ones. As more postgraduate students stay at home and study remotely at local or foreign universities, concerns arise regarding their orientation, acculturation and continuing support.

Perhaps in the absence of high-speed and long-distance travel, which had become such a taken-for-granted feature and "perk" of academic life, the authentic mobility of the moment lies in the movements of our minds to new and creative thoughts and ways of thinking and doing. Sioux McKenna's call (Chapter 5), in a context of "crass consumerism and the accumulation of wealth amid environmental ills" – for focusing on the quality and processes of knowledge rather than the metrics of production, for time to read and reflect, for being vulnerable, compassionate and kind (to our students and to ourselves as supervisors and academics) and for promoting collaboration and shared spaces – is especially prescient here.

There is no doubt that Covid-19 has been a blow to the internationalisation and academic mobility of higher education, although the extent and duration of this is yet to be definitively ascertained. From a wider global perspective, academic mobility contributes to how and what we learn as a species, particularly in a time of crisis: "brain circulation" and "talent flow" are crucial to the process of human learning in this generic sense. It seems inevitable that Covid-19 will, at least in the short term, push higher education institutions into a more parochial and inward-looking orientation. In this context, the currents of xenophobia and 'othering', evident in the attacks on Asians in various parts of the world and the stigmatised nationalistic labelling of the virus and its mutations – the "Chinese"/"South African"/"UK"/"Brazilian" variant – endanger the inclusive international ethos of higher education.

Vaccination aptly illustrates the contending international and parochial tendencies of the pandemic. On the one hand, the development of vaccines is a testimony to the internationalisation of higher education and global research, as vaccines are developed by multinational teams, and manufactured and tested in a variety of global contexts. The Covid-19 Vaccines Global Access (COVAX) facility, that works towards fair and speedy distribution of vaccines to all countries, and the World Health Organisation's (WHO) efforts to prepare and support countries in vaccinating their populations typify this tendency (Ministry of Social Affairs and Health, Finland 2021). The vaccine itself is an example of a highly mobile product to which research institutions significantly contribute. On the other hand, the global distribution of vaccines is hugely uneven, with rich countries speeding ahead in vaccinating their populations and middle-to-low income countries left behind (Karrim 2021). The hoarding of vaccines by developed countries and the priority given by 'big pharma' companies to profit and intellectual property rather than to global herd immunity (as well as criminal syndicates peddling fake vaccines) show the malignant side of the political economy of vaccination.

The pandemic's impact on the economy has negatively affected postgraduate students in various ways. According to the Pew Research Center, drawing on World Bank data (Kochhar 2021), the economic downturn precipitated by the pandemic has shrunk the global middle class and increased the ranks of the poor, making higher education unaffordable for many prospective students. Besides increasing unemployment and poverty, it has also resulted in cuts to research budgets. In South Africa, for example, such cuts are "likely to affect adversely postgraduate and PhD training" and have raised concerns about the country meeting targets in research and development (Van Schalkwyk 2021:50). Ironically, there has been an increase in the availability of funding for research related to Covid-19 and its impact, thus creating opportunities for some scholars and postgraduate students (Soudien 2021).

Covid-19 has affected the ways that postgraduate students conduct their research. In their research proposals and ethical clearance applications, students have had to take the new Covid-related circumstances into account. In the natural sciences, students have struggled with access to laboratory facilities and with site visits. In the social sciences, students have had to revise their data collection strategies to accommodate Covid-19 regulations, for example, by changing from face-to-face to remote interviews and focus group discussions, or by reverting to non-empirical research designs (Hedding, Greve, Breetzke, Nel & Jansen van Vuuren 2020). In educational research, classroom observation has become much more difficult or changed in modality as teaching and learning have shifted online. Because Covid-19 has altered their employment status or residential location, making it impossible to pursue their original research plans, some students have had to suspend their studies or revise their research projects entirely and start again. The Covid-19 context also has implications for examining theses. In addition to the quality indicators that Margaret Kiley (Chapter 4) discusses, examiners might need to consider the ethical and methodological appropriateness of the study in pandemic circumstances – difficult to benchmark given how these circumstances vary across time and space. Every thesis written under Covid-19 is also a unique account, at least implicitly, of Covid-19 itself as it impacted on the researcher and the study.

The psychological impact of Covid-19 and its associated lockdowns has been dire, affecting society at large and not just education: loneliness, isolation and depression, not to mention the pressure on students and academics who are parents or caregivers (disproportionately affecting women) to juggle the balls of housework, income generation, home schooling and health concerns, among others, with their academic work. A global survey of students found that Covid-19 affected the mental health of a high percentage of students worldwide who are especially worried about employment prospects in a constrained labour market and worsening economic inequalities (Kigotho 2021). Psychological stress has been particularly acute among medical students working at the frontline of the pandemic (Imran, Masood, Ayub & Gondal 2020).

The pandemic has had a significant impact on the well-being of academics, as well as students. A survey found that academics were negatively affected by increased workload, technological challenges and heightened anxiety about online teaching (Jump 2021). While academics have continued to meet online, meetings are formal and time-bound; they have lost the informal collegiality of the tearoom and spontaneous corridor chats (Van Schalkwyk 2021). The challenges of managing time, space and relationships in a context where work and domesticity have collided and "roommates vie for Wi-Fi bandwidth and office space" (AbuJarour, Ajjan, Fedorowicz & Owens 2020:3) have taken their toll on mental health and domestic relationships. As one academic put it, "It's not working from home. I can do that. It's working while at home with kids and my spouse during a pandemic that's the problem" (AbuJarour, Ajjan, Fedorowicz & Owens 2020:7).

The affective dimensions of Covid-19 and lockdown are highly relevant to supervision. Some students have stalled, suspended their studies or dropped out during this time. Many have experienced depression, anxiety and emotional burnout which have disrupted their studies. The kinds of issues raised by Sherran Clarence (Chapter 11) regarding supervision and affect, which have been somewhat neglected in the scholarship, are especially pertinent in this context. She reflects that "doing a doctorate can be a lonely, isolated, frustrating, uncertain, difficult business" – all of these affects have been aggravated by the circumstances around Covid-19. Where students and supervisors might have previously met face-to-face, they have had to adapt to virtual supervision. The affective dimension of supervision, not only for students but also for their supervisors, is an emerging current of research which warrants greater attention.

The pandemic's impact on the delivery of higher education has become a new "current" in the sense of intellectual charge in academic discourse. In particular, its impact on and implications for teaching, learning and assessment have been on the minds of students, practitioners, researchers and curriculum developers. IT specialists have become central to these processes as online learning has shifted from a supplementary to a mainstream mode of delivery in previously contact institutions. Stellenbosch University, for example, moved to an approach termed Emergency Remote Teaching, Learning and Assessment (ERTLA) during the period of lockdown. This involved a rush to migrate face-to-face offerings into online formats in order to continue with teaching and learning under lockdown conditions and prevent the university from losing the academic year. 2021 has seen a further shift from ERTLA to Augmented Remote Teaching, Learning and Assessment (ARTLA), which builds on the resources and expertise developed under ERTLA but combines contact tuition for smaller groups of students with online elements. This exemplifies an accelerating international trend at contact institutions towards integrating online teaching, learning and assessment into the curriculum.

However, the transition to online learning has been uneven across universities and national contexts. While well-resourced institutions have managed adequately and even boosted their capacity for remote teaching and learning, many poorer universities have struggled, and some have closed down temporarily. A variety of factors has contributed to this including "inadequate information technology infrastructure, limited expertise for online teaching and learning methods and the inability of institutions to provide computers and data to students" (Kupe & Wangenge-Ouma 2020). This indicates the potential for Covid-19 to exacerbate existing inequalities within higher education, not only between countries but also between institutions within the same country.

Besides modes of delivery, Covid-19 might also have had an impact on the actual content of the curriculum, perhaps as a topic, certainly as a curricular context. Sunil Maharaj from the University of Pretoria argues that the changes brought about by the pandemic offer "an opportunity to embrace best practices associated with the Fourth Industrial Revolution" (Maharaj 2021). The various aspects of Covid-19 and its impact have begun to feature prominently on research agendas and calls for funding. The changing modes, methods and content of higher education in the context of a pandemic are currents that warrant further study.

## COVID-19 AND TRAJECTORY

Covid-related circumstances have affected not only what students and academics do and where they go, but also their understanding of who they are. This links to the theme of trajectory which we define in the Introduction as the particular course that the career of an individual or group takes. Such trajectories are intensely personal, informed by factors such as individual talent, self-efficacy, personality and resourcefulness. They are also social and determined by external factors, among which Covid-19 now significantly figures. The intersectionality of Covid-19 means that trajectory plays out differently according to other elements of identity such as race, gender, nationality, class and age. The way that Covid-19 affects the trajectories of academics and postgraduate students is thus often a complex of personal and social factors.

Academics might now ask themselves: who am I as an academic when I have no face-to-face contact with students and no physical presence in classrooms and on campus? In this context, new elements of academic identity have emerged:

academics have added aspects such as graphic design, videography, learning design and even acting to their conventional identities (Rivers & Holland 2021). One's digital presence becomes a new domain of practice in which one constructs and exercises identity. Observing a digital recording of oneself and one's students on Zoom or Teams can be a strange and sobering experience as the "subjects" of teaching and learning become "objects" or elements in a stored digital record. A new career trajectory as online teacher has emerged for many academics, including new skills of online facilitation and delivery, and technical competencies. For some, this trajectory was already well established and has been refined and augmented by new technological affordances, for others it has been novel and disorienting.

The kinds of career trajectories that Roxana Chiappa describes in the Chilean context (Chapter 10) of postgraduate students studying overseas and returning to take up academic posts at home have been disrupted by Covid-19. Uncertainties around visas, access and travel options to (and from) the destination country might persuade students to postpone or cancel their study plans or to consider pursuing postgraduate studies at home; if already studying elsewhere, they might consider the possibility of a career in the host country, at least for some time. Student exchanges and study visits, which can play a vital role in study trajectories and personal development, have been cancelled or curtailed. Maresi Nerad (Chapter 1) calls for academics to engage in "collective thinking" on the future of these activities given the current circumstances. While acknowledging the value of such exchanges "to ignite or maintain the flame of intellectual curiosity", she also problematises them (and perhaps academic travel generally), "knowing that we also contribute to increasing carbon footprints and thus climate change".

Covid-19 means that academic trajectories that were once normative might become much more problematic and less common, especially if the pandemic lasts for several years or if pandemic waves become the "new norm" as the relation between the human and the non-human world shifts in fundamental ways. Is it possible that "Pandemic Studies" will emerge as a new interdisciplinary field to join and interact with other established interdisciplinary fields such as Environmental Studies and Peace Studies? This might open up new possibilities for "the interdisciplinary PhD" to add to those which Karri Holley discusses in Chapter 9.

## COVID-19 AND HORIZON

In the Introduction we offered Gadamer's notion of horizon as a spatiotemporal lens for understanding the global scholar and its implications for postgraduate studies and supervision. We suggested that the notion is particularly useful for understanding supervision: students and supervisors engage each other's horizons as they relate and interact on the project of the thesis. The Covid-19 pandemic has simultaneously narrowed the horizons of students and academics by "locking them down" to their domestic workstations and underscored a shared global horizon characterised by the rapid spread of the virus and the significance of virtual (in the circumscription of physical) connectedness.

New digitally enabled horizons have opened up – Zoom, Teams, Skype and other affordances have changed the way we meet, relate and exchange ideas. This strange simultaneous shrinking of the physical and expanding of the virtual horizon has created a semi-permanent state of (dis)connectedness in which we are continually present/absent with a sense of con/fusion about who and where we are.

The Covid-19 pandemic has changed the global and local horizons in other astonishing ways. It has given us a glimpse of a world free from the chokehold of fossil fuels, as urban pollution rapidly diminished and blue skies returned to previously smog-bound cities, at least for a while. Besides reduced air pollution, remote sensing data recorded by the NASA/Goddard Space Flight Center, from before and during the pandemic, indicated that water quality was improving and snow becoming more reflective because of reduced pollution (Bates 2020). There was also a glimpse of the non-human world (re)claiming Earth so long dominated and decimated by human activity: curious goats, wild pigs, civets, cougars and monkeys explored urban streets unimpeded. A peculiar reversal occurred as humans and their artefacts became objects of observation and exploration to the non-human world.

The horizon of 'science' has been prominent in the debates around Covid-19. In particular, the contestation between 'science' (seen as good, progressive, rational, evidence-based, credible), on the one hand, and myths, lies and disinformation (seen as ignorant, populist, conspiratorial, irrational and dangerous), on the other, has been fierce. 'Science' has generally fared well through its advocacy of prevention methods, its development of vaccines, its administration of surveys and provision of metrics (Soudien 2021). Governments that have "followed the science" have tended to cope better with the pandemic than those that have ignored or vituperated scientific advice. However, what is sometimes overlooked is the contribution of 'science' to the conditions that make a global pandemic possible: the means of international travel, the objectification and exploitation of the non-human world. More widely, science, in its collaboration with capitalism, has shaped and powered the monstrous mentality of unbridled consumerism and accumulation, limitless growth and exploitation of the human and natural world which has resulted in a new mass extinction and dangerously affected the global climate. While Covid-19 draws attention to the achievements of science, it should also draw our critical attention to its weaknesses as we assess its potential contribution to a just and sustainable future for the homo sapiens and other species and for the planet.

The pandemic revived the longing for a better world by giving us a glimpse of new horizons, less cluttered and marred by overconsumption, pollution, waste and degradation. It created a pause for reflection and reorientation which might have profound implications for our pursuit of knowledge in more just, sustainable and creative directions. As Arundhati Roy puts it, "Historically, pandemics have forced humans to break with the past and imagine their world anew. This one is no different. It is a portal, a gateway between one world and the next" (Roy 2020). The danger is that this opportunity will be lost in the scramble to get back to "business as usual" – already, indications are that air pollution is returning to pre-Covid levels. Is it possible to harness the mind-opening *kairos* of the Covid-19 pandemic to inform the trajectory of the global scholar and to re-imagine postgraduate studies and supervision?

## NEW DIRECTIONS

Here we suggest four new directions for research, theory and practice in postgraduate studies and supervision in the light and the shadow of Covid-19.

### Rethinking teaching, learning and assessment as virtual activities

This was already happening pre-Covid but has been given huge impetus by the imperative to continue with teaching, learning and assessment under pandemic conditions at all levels within the education system. It is an area that has been developing rapidly in open and distance learning institutions but is now also becoming mainstream in contact institutions. Higher education faces major challenges in developing appropriate IT infrastructure (including data and equipment for students and academics where needed) as well as in enhancing the capacity of academics and students to engage optimally with new digital forms of teaching, learning and assessment, and in finding the right balance between virtual and face-to-face (where this is possible) interactions. A survey by AbuJarour, Ajjan, Fedorowicz and Owens (2020) found that academics' access to appropriate hardware, software and Wi-Fi significantly affected their productivity in working from home. However, engagement with online learning is not simply a technical matter.

As Blewett (2018:265) argues, online learning should not be viewed as a "tool" to replicate offline learning, but rather as an entirely different system of affordances which requires "new and different pedagogies". One danger for postgraduate studies is that the shift to online learning will affect the quality and depth of engagement between lecturers/supervisors and students, particularly regarding the relationality of learning which is so important at this level (O'Regan 2020). Another is that it will aggravate existing social inequalities between digital "haves" and "have nots" in higher education. It is important to find ways of sharing and nurturing best practices in online teaching, learning and assessment in order to solicit regular formative and summative feedback from students in the online environment, and to create "communities of practice" in a virtual environment, as we elaborate below.

### Rethinking scholarly community and identity

How do we foster academic community in a digital environment? We need to recognise that the "turn" to digital learning is not only a technical matter but also a social and cultural one that affects identity. Postgraduate students, especially those returning to study in mid-career, often struggle to reconcile their identities as practitioners, citizens, family and community members with being a student. To these identities they are now compelled to add a digital academic persona, with the associated technical competencies, and project it appropriately to peers, lecturers, supervisors and even examiners in some cases.

Similarly, academics are required to add new technological dimensions to their professional academic identities. Many students and academics have been forced into a "sink or swim" approach in the Covid-19 era. While this can have positive spin-offs such as accelerated learning, new proficiencies and affirmed self-confidence, it can also lead to burn-out, drop-out, paralysis and a waste of human potential. How we support students and academics in their identity work, and how we create enabling virtual communities to enhance the academic project, are highly pertinent challenges. Peer networks, accessible support personnel, mentoring relationships and opportunities for formative performance reviews can all play a role here. Safe digital spaces that allow postgraduate students to find, explore and exercise their digital voices and identities are especially important. In this regard, Blogs have started to play an increasingly important role for both students and supervisors in building and sustaining a sense of community (for example: https://bit.ly/3sPwApR and https://bit.ly/3gCShH8).

### Living and learning up to the transformative moment of Covid-19

The *kairos* moment of Covid-19 challenges us to rethink our roles in higher education not only as academics and students but also as national and global citizens in a troubled and troubling world. The pause in mobility which Covid-19 has enforced offers an opportunity to reflect, question and reorient. Many postgraduate students and academics have been forced to reassess the relation between home and work in very practical ways, including new ways of managing space, time, energy and relationships. More broadly, how can we contribute to a more just, sustainable and healthy world both in our individual daily lives and in our various collectives? As global scholars, this might include not only what and how we teach, supervise and research, but also why we do so in relation to the pressing local and global challenges that Covid-19 has highlighted. More than ever, Covid-19 has raised the question of what makes higher education a public good rather than a public bad. This requires a response at multiple levels including the personal, departmental and institutional, taking into account both local and global contexts.

### Troubling connectedness

It is interesting that the predominant sense of the term "connectivity" is digital: "the ability of a computer, program, device, or system to connect with one or more others" (Cambridge Dictionary 2021). Covid-19 has demonstrated in a direct and often traumatic way how we are virally connected, that our destiny as a species is indissolubly collective. The pandemic shows that what happens to one person, one city, one nation or one university can have implications for all. It illustrates that "going viral" is not just a metaphor for memes and Tweets but is a matter of our shared physiology, of life and death. It underlines that we are connected not only to each other but to the non-human world, that our misuse or abuse of animals has consequences both for the human and non-human world, which is a shared and interconnected world. Controlling the virus has required "disconnecting" from others: staying at home, wearing masks, social distancing, washing hands and sanitising. Yet, it has highlighted that as social beings we need to "connect" physically and emotionally, and that we suffer when this is not possible. Lockdowns have also highlighted how we need to "get out" and connect with the natural world. This has profound implications for the perspectives that we bring to and develop through our teaching and research and runs counter to a discrete, atomistic, unconnected way of thinking and acting.

## CONCLUSION

The chapters of this book shed light on the notion of the global scholar and its implications for postgraduate studies and supervision. We used the framing concepts of currency, trajectory and horizon to connect the various threads that weave through the book. However, Covid-19 has profoundly challenged the construct of the global scholar as a free-ranging mobile academic, attending to an individual career trajectory and constantly exploring and expanding his or her horizons. In its imposed deprivations, it has underscored the importance of being connected to each other and to the world, and of rethinking our relation to both. Perhaps, given the privileges of connectivity and connectedness that scholars and postgraduate students often enjoy – the connections of ideas, disciplines, technologies, systems, people and social networks – they have an important contribution to make in understanding and fostering our interconnectedness in creating a more just and sustainable future, and ensuring that higher education is truly a public good.

## REFERENCES

AbuJarour S, Ajjan H, Fedorowicz J & Owens D. 2020. How working from home during Covid-19 affects academic productivity. *Communications of the Association of Information Systems*. https://bit.ly/3sLK8CM [Accessed 24 March 2021].

Bates S. 2020. Environmental impacts of the Covid-19 pandemic, as observed from space. *Science Daily*, 8 December. https://bit.ly/3gBEUHm [Accessed 5 March 2021].

Blewett C. 2018. From traditional pedagogy to digital pedagogy. In: MA Samuel, R Dhunpath & N Amin (eds.), *Disrupting higher education curriculum*. Rotterdam: Sense. 265-287. https://doi.org/10.1007/978-94-6300-896-9_16

Bothwell, E. 2021. Will international recruitment survive Covid-19? *Times Higher Education*, 4 March. https://bit.ly/2PjXOHr [Accessed 5 March 2021].

Cambridge Dictionary. 2021. Cambridge: Cambridge University Press. https://bit.ly/3nihRlX [Accessed 24 March 2021].

Hedding DW, Greve M, Breetzke GD, Nel W & Jansen van Vuuren B. 2020. Covid-19 and the academe in South Africa: Not business as usual. *South African Journal of Science*, 116(7/8). https://doi.org/10.17159/sajs.2020/8298

Imran N, Masood HMU, Ayub M & Gondal KM. 2020. Psychological impact of Covid-19 pandemic on postgraduate trainees: a cross-sectional survey. *Postgraduate medical journal*, 0:1-6.

Jump P. 2021. Times Higher Education's Digital Teaching Survey results. *Times Higher Education*, 4 February. https://bit.ly/2S3bmbh [Accessed 5 March 2021].

Karrim A. 2021. 'The loss of humanity': South Africa and the Global South's battle for Covid-19 vaccine justice. *News 24*, 26 March. https://bit.ly/3aC39Ba [Accessed 26 March 2021].

Kigotho W. 2021. Most students say their mental health suffered in pandemic. *World University News*, 5 March. https://bit.ly/3aBb9Tg [Accessed 5 March 2021].

Kochhar R. 2021. In the pandemic, India's middle class shrinks and poverty spreads while China sees smaller changes. Pew Research Center, 18 March. https://pewrsr.ch/3sJpsuV [Accessed 19 March 2021].

Kupe T & Wangenge-Ouma G. 2020. Post Covid-19: Opportunity for universities to have a rethink. *The Conversation*, 15 November. https://bit.ly/3tP4xYS [Accessed 5 March 2021].

Maharaj S. 2021. New game, new rules in the post-Covid-19 world. *World University News*, 4 March. https://bit.ly/32KLZ08 [Accessed 5 March 2021].

Ministry of Social Affairs and Health, Finland. 2021. *Covid-19 vaccines and international cooperation* (Updated 22 February 2021). https://bit.ly/3aBF51u [Accessed 24 March 2021].

O'Regan MA. 2020. Learning at a distance but not a distance learner: Meeting the needs of a diverse body of students post Covid-19. *All Ireland Journal of Higher Education*, 12(2):1-9. https://bit.ly/3exQkJz

Rivers C. & Holland A. 2021. Who am I now? How the academic identity changed through Covid. *Times Higher Education*, 23 February. https://bit.ly/3tOAeSf [Accessed 5 March 2021].

Roy A. 2020. Arundathi Roy: 'The pandemic is a portal'. *Financial Times*, 3 April. https://on.ft.com/2PhR5O2 [Accessed 26 March 2021].

Soudien C. 2021. The role of South Africa's social scientists in Covid-19 responses: why it matters. *The Conversation*, 10 March. https://bit.ly/2QOLQG5 [Accessed 29 Marc 2021].

Van Schalkwyk F. 2021. Reflections on the public university sector and the Covid-19 pandemic in South Africa. *Studies in Higher Education*, 46(1):44-58. https://doi.org/10.1080/03075079.2020.1859682

# INDEX

## A

Academic ix, 1-3, 6-11, 18-22, 25, 27, 29, 34, 36-37, 44, 59, 63, 65, 69-70, 74, 90, 101, 106, 108, 110, 113-117, 121-123, 132, 133-136, 138-139, 142-144, 149, 153, 155, 163, 176-179, 181-185, 190-209, 213, 218, 221, 223, 231-233, 238, 240, 242-244, 246, 253-264, 267-269

    Academic identity 232, 235, 244, 246-247, 258

    Academic literacy 100

Access 23, 26, 28-29, 65, 76, 102, 105, 109, 139, 141-144, 153, 189-191, 195-196, 204, 207, 216, 218, 220, 222, 224, 227, 246, 256, 259, 261, 267

    Access to funding 104

    Access to information 198

    Epistemological access 109

    Internet access 123, 254

Africa 4, 19, 24, 27, 44, 51, 53, 55, 59-60, 65, 67, 74, 77, 86, 133-134, 149-155, 159, 165-166, 168, 218, 267, 269-271

Agency 9-10, 68, 101, 106, 115-116, 132, 135

Ahmed, Sara 217, 219-220, 222-227

Arts 6, 22, 29-30, 268

Asia 21, 51, 55, 86, 131, 133, 139, 255, 271

Australia 17, 21-22, 27, 52, 54, 69-72, 84-85, 89, 113, 131, 133-135, 183, 189, 216, 218, 268-270

## B

Benchmarking 4, 83-91

Boler, Megan 217, 220-227

Boundaries 1-2, 8, 20, 30, 38, 121, 177-178, 181-182, 184, 216, 226-227, 231

Brain 115-116, 132, 271

    Brain circulation 7, 115-116, 134, 255

    Brain drain 7, 24, 115-116

    Brain networking 7

    Brain retain 7

Brazil 20, 24, 131, 133-134, 143, 209, 255

## C

Capabilities 67, 70, 77, 104

Chile 11, 20, 189-193, 195, 196-209, 259, 267

Citizenship 104, 110

Collaboration 1, 12, 24, 28, 31-32, 44, 51, 56, 59, 71, 73, 109, 113, 131, 139, 150, 154-155, 158, 163, 168, 233-234, 236, 239, 254-255, 260, 270

Community 10, 12, 60, 66-67, 77-78, 107, 109, 119-120, 122-124, 131-132, 155, 179-180, 234-235, 244, 262

    Academic community 1, 134, 145, 262

    Community engagement 1, 6

Conceptual ix, 2, 33, 43, 45, 51, 71, 98, 110, 113, 163-164, 217, 226-227, 245

    Conceptual framework 11, 32, 194

    Conseptual lense 2-3, 6, 12, 253

Covid-19 v, 1, 4, 7, 12, 253-258

Currency ix, 2, 6-10, 12, 23, 60, 66, 95, 242, 253, 263

    Currency as immediate relevance 7

    Currency as intellectual charge 8

    Currency as mobility 3, 7

Curricula  64, 66, 105-106, 152, 154, 177-179, 222, 258, 268
Curriculum  56, 66, 68, 99, 160, 177-178, 183-184, 257-258
   Doctoral curriculum  30, 178
   Formal curriculum  78
   Hidden curriculum  122-221
   Informal curriculum  120

## D
Decolonisation  2, 67, 75, 77-78, 223, 268
Digital  1, 7-8, 113, 116-117, 119, 122, 158, 259-263
   Digital academy  113, 116-117, 123
   Digital communication  117, 119
   Digital literacy  69
   Digital technologies  10, 12, 113, 116, 119, 121-123
Digitalisation  2, 157
Doctoral  ix, x, 3-4, 9-12, 17-32, 34-38, 43-46, 48, 50-60, 63-65, 68-71, 74-76, 83-91, 109, 113, 117-123, 131-138, 140, 143-145, 149-160, 162-168, 175-185, 189-191, 194, 197-199, 207-208, 215-220, 222-227, 231-232, 234-236, 238, 245-247, 267-272
   Doctoral community  134, 143-144
   Doctoral examination  4, 83, 89
   Doctoral journey  11, 68, 245

## E
Early career researchers  2, 10, 19, 34, 72, 78, 121, 132, 156, 179, 232, 240
East Africa  9, 150, 154, 159-160, 165-167, 269
Emotion  11, 122, 142, 144, 215, 216, 217, 218, 219, 220, 221, 222, 223, 224, 225, 226, 227, 257, 263
   Emotional labour  217-220, 224-227
   Emotion work  218-220, 224-227
Equity  4, 29, 104, 216
European Union  9, 136, 206

## F
Fees Must Fall  101
Fourth Industrial Revolution  103-104, 189, 258

## G
Gadamer, Hans-Georg  3, 259
Germany  17, 20-21, 24, 86, 133-135, 160, 190, 202, 204, 270-271
Global  v, ix, 1-9, 11-12, 18-20, 22, 28, 34, 36, 38, 43-44, 51, 58-59, 63-68, 70, 74, 77, 83, 90, 97, 102-103, 113-116, 132-136, 143, 151, 155, 159, 164-166, 178, 180, 184, 216-218, 220, 253, 255-256, 259-261, 263
   Global citizen  1, 12, 17, 116, 262
   Global North  7, 20, 22, 24, 44, 50, 59, 132, 139, 143, 145, 154
   Global South  1, 7, 24, 132, 139, 143, 145, 223
   Global warming  2, 7, 132
Globalisation  2-4, 19-20, 99, 102, 131, 137, 157-158
Graduate attributes  69, 163-164, 168

## H
Hannover Recommendations  132, 140, 143
Hochschild, Arlie Russell  217, 220, 224-227
Horizons  2-4, 7-9, 11-12, 15, 30, 60, 253, 259-260, 263-264
   Fusion of horizons  3, 5
   New horizons  4, 261
Human Capital Theory  9, 98-107, 110, 208

## I
Innovation  20-21, 23, 29-30, 43, 48, 51, 56, 59, 114, 119, 151-152, 163-164, 166, 177, 254
   Innovation and competitiveness  152

# INDEX

Innovation policies 19-21, 28-29

**Internationalisation** 26, 64, 114, 139, 154, 161, 167, 255

## J

Jansen, Jonathan 5, 63, 66, 78

Japan 20-21, 23, 133-135

## K

Kenya 67, 149-150, 152, 159-160, 162

Knowledge 1, 3, 6, 9, 19, 21, 26, 30-33, 37, 43-44, 56-57, 59, 64, 66-70, 73, 75-77, 83, 97-98, 100-101, 103-105, 107-109, 114, 116, 120, 123, 131-132, 136-137, 139-141, 143, 156-158, 164, 175-176, 179, 181-185, 190-191, 194, 220-221, 231, 236, 246, 255, 261

    Knowledge and skills 68, 75, 164, 181, 184, 194

    Knowledge creation 66, 104-105, 107, 109-110

    Knowledge economy 6, 97-98, 102, 106, 152, 189, 191

    Knowledge production 11, 30, 56, 59, 66-68, 139, 175, 184

Kuhn, Thomas 8

## L

Latin America 27, 133, 191

Local ix, 1-2, 4-5, 7, 9, 12, 18, 21, 24, 29, 33, 38, 63-64, 66, 68, 70, 116, 136, 163, 177, 180, 254, 260

    Local and global 3, 11, 227, 263

    Local supervision contexts 5

Lockdown 12, 38, 253, 256-257, 263

## M

Mobility 2-3, 7-8, 10, 12, 18, 20, 23, 26, 31, 34-35, 38, 60, 91, 113-118, 121, 123, 131-134, 136-145, 154, 156, 161, 166-167, 254, 262, 270

    Academic mobility 8, 10, 90, 113-116, 120-122, 131, 133, 135-139, 143, 253-255, 270

    Dotoral mobility 10, 131, 136, 142

    Outward mobility 18

    Social mobility 11, 98, 100, 103, 115

    Student mobility 10, 18

**Multidisciplinary** 21, 22, 25, 87-88

## N

Neoliberal 6, 60, 101-102, 105-107, 110

New Zealand 68, 134, 218

North America 19, 27, 34, 45-50, 55, 57, 85-86, 133

## P

Paradigm 8, 25, 66, 77

Pedagogy 10, 56, 117-118, 121

## Q

Qualifications framework 68, 84, 160-162

Quality v, 4, 9, 20, 23, 25-29, 37, 43-44, 49, 56, 59, 65, 67, 69, 83-87, 90, 115, 137, 149-151, 153-155, 160-166, 168, 195, 241, 243, 255, 260, 262, 267

    Quality assurance 26, 69, 152-154, 157, 160-162, 164-166, 168, 180, 269

    Quality criteria 87

    Quality indicators 86, 256

## R

Rankings 6, 7, 29, 86-87, 102, 254

Researcher Development Framework (RDF) ix, 4-5, 63-64, 66-67, 71-78

Rhodes Must Fall 4, 63, 66

## S

Scandinavia 21, 50, 54, 89

Science, Technology, Engineering and Mathematics (STEM) 4, 22, 29, 153, 178, 181

South Africa 4-7, 9, 12, 17-18, 29, 44, 50, 54-55, 59, 63-69, 75-78, 89, 98-102, 133-134, 137, 149-150, 152-154, 159, 162-168, 175, 189-190, 209, 216, 235-236, 255-256, 267-268, 270-271

Student-supervisor relationship 45, 56-58, 232, 238, 246

Supervision ix, x, 1-5, 8-11-12, 18, 25-27, 43-45, 47, 56, 59, 65, 67-69, 73, 77, 107, 110, 113, 117-124, 142, 144, 153, 156, 159, 161, 163, 165, 180, 182-183, 215-221, 223-224, 232, 234, 237, 239, 253, 257, 259, 261, 263, 267-271

    Apprenticeship model 8, 10, 25, 123

    Cohort supervison 120

    Doctoral supervision 4, 44, 56, 118, 158, 176, 183, 226-227, 268

    Remote supervision 10, 117-118

    Team supervision 8, 10, 120-121, 123

## T

Trajectory 2, 10-12, 60, 153, 173, 175, 178, 209, 253, 258-259, 261, 263, 268

    Academic trajectory 10, 196

    Career trajectory 3, 8, 10, 259, 264

Transdisciplinary 1, 11

## U

Ubuntu 67, 77

United Kingdom (UK) 4, 10, 11, 20-21, 23, 27, 47-50, 52, 54, 69-72, 75, 85, 99, 131, 133-139, 143-144, 159, 175, 216, 218, 235-236, 255, 269, 271

United States of America (USA) 11, 17-18, 20-24, 27, 30-32, 37, 46, 52, 54-55, 69, 85, 89, 99, 131, 133-136, 140, 175, 181, 189-190, 198, 200-201, 213, 216, 218, 268-270

## W

Wicked global problems 175, 178

# CONTRIBUTING AUTHORS

**Eli Bitzer** is Professor Emeritus in higher education studies and a past director of the Centre for Higher and Adult Education at Stellenbosch University, South Africa. He has been a study leader to 92 master's and doctoral graduates and contributed over 90 articles to scholarly journals and chapters to academic books. He also chaired four international conferences on postgraduate supervision and published widely on the topic. Eli facilitates workshops on doctoral education and supervision and has a keen interest in promoting the quality of higher education in South Africa.
ORCID: https://orcid.org/0000-0003-4081-8053

**Jan Botha** is Professor in the DSI/NRF Centre of Excellence in Scientometrics and Science, Technology and Innovation Policy (SciSTIP) and the Centre for Research on Evaluation, Science and Technology (CREST) at Stellenbosch University. Formerly he was Senior Director of Institutional Research and Planning at Stellenbosch University. He participated in the development of a number of national policies, including the South African Doctoral Qualification Standard (2018). He is co-author and co-editor (with Nicole Muller) of *Institutional Research in South Africa. Intersecting Contexts and Practices* (SUNMEDIA, 2016). He is leader of the DAAD supported online DIES/CREST Course for Doctoral Supervisors at African Universities.
ORCID https://orcid.org/0000-0002-9765-0506

**Roxana Chiappa** is a Lecturer in the Centre for Higher Education Research, Teaching and Learning (CHERTL) at Rhodes University, South Africa. Roxana graduated with a PhD from the University of Washington- Seattle (2019), with a mixed-method study that analyzed the effects of the social class of origin on the careers of academics in Chile, which has recently received the award as the best dissertation of the College of Education at the University of Washington. Her research agenda is centered around the question of how and to what extent social and economic inequalities, manifested among social groups, institutions and countries, are (re) produced in the scientific and higher education systems. Roxana is an associate member of the Center for Innovation and Research in Graduate Education (University of Washington, Seattle), from where she coordinates a series of webinars about social justice and doctoral education. Roxana is also an adjunct researcher at the Center for the Study of Conflict and Social Cohesion (COES), linked to different Chilean universities.

**Sherran Clarence** is an Honorary Research Associate in the Centre for Higher Education, Research, Teaching and Learning (CHERTL) at Rhodes University. Prior to this she was coordinator of the Writing Centre at the University of the Western Cape, where her work encompassed staff and student academic development. Her book, *Turning access into success. Improving university education with Legitimation Code Theory* was published in 2021 (Routledge). Her current research uses feminist and social realist theory to explore experiences and practices in doctoral education,

and her practice focuses on working with doctoral and early career writers in thesis writing and writing for publication. She supervises students in higher education and gender studies and writes a regular blog on academic writing at the postgraduate level (https://phdinahundredsteps.com).
ORCID: https://orcid.org/0000-0003-2777-4420

**Liezel Frick** is an Associate Professor in the Department of Curriculum Studies, Director of the Centre for Higher and Adult Education in the Faculty of Education at Stellenbosch University (South Africa) and Research Fellow: DSI/NRF Centre of Excellence in STI Policy, Stellenbosch University. Her research interests are within the broader field of doctoral education, with a particular focus on aspects of doctoral creativity and originality, learning during the doctorate, and doctoral supervision. She currently holds a South African National Research Foundation C1 rating.
ORCID: https://orcid.org/0000-0002-4797-3323

**Cally Guerin** is an Adjunct Senior Lecturer at the University of Adelaide and a researcher developer at the Australian National University. She has taught, researched and published on doctoral education since 2008 with a focus on research writing and demystifying research cultures. Cally is a co-founder of the DoctoralWriting blog. Recent publications include 'Stories of moving on: HASS PhD graduates' motivations and career trajectories inside and beyond academia', *Arts and Humanities in Higher Education* (2020), 19(3), 304-324 DOI: https://doi.org/10.1177/1474022219834448; and Carter, S., Guerin, C. & Aitchison, C. (2020) *Doctoral Writing: Practices, Processes and Pleasures* (Springer).
ORCID: https://orcid.org/000-0003-0588-0804

**Karri A. Holley** is Professor of Higher Education at The University of Alabama. She earned a Ph.D. and M.Ed. from the University of Southern California, and a B.A. from The University of Alabama. Her research interests include organisational change, graduate and doctoral education, and qualitative inquiry. She serves as editor of Studies in Graduate and Postdoctoral Education. Prior to her faculty career, she worked in graduate admissions at Pepperdine University; was a research assistant at the Center for Higher Education Policy Analysis at the University of Southern California; and served as a US Peace Corps Volunteer in Ukraine.
ORCID: https://orcid.org/0000-0001-7168-7354

**Moyra Keane** is an Associate Professor in the Postgraduate School, University of Johannesburg, and independent consultant at various universities. She has worked in schools teaching science, in Non-Government Organisations as a researcher, and in Higher Education in Learning and Teaching Development. Her research areas have included decolonisation of science curricula; indigenous knowledge research methodology; supervision; research writing; ethics; and mindfulness. She also coaches PhD students. She has served as president of the International Organisation of Science and Technology Education; and on the board of AASIKS (African Association for the Study of Indigenous Knowledge Systems).
ORCID: https://orcid.org/0000-0002-8578-6895

**CONTRIBUTING AUTHORS**

**Margaret Kiley** has an adjunct position at the Australian National University. For many years, her research and teaching interests have been in the education of future researchers. She has worked in further and higher education in Australia, Indonesia, Malaysia and the UK, and facilitated workshops for doctoral supervisors and candidates in a number of countries. Her publications include (with Stan Taylor and Robin Humphrey) *A Handbook for Doctoral Supervisors* (Routledge 2018).
ORCID: https://orcid.org/0000-0002-9171-7423

**Mike Kuria** is an Associate Professor of literature and a graduate of the University of Leeds, UK from where he obtained his PhD in English. He has over twenty-five years' experience in higher education and specifically in quality assurance, teaching, research, and graduate supervision. In 2016, he joined the Inter-University Council for East Africa (IUCEA) as the Deputy Executive Secretary. Before Joining IUCEA, he was the Director, Center for Quality Assurance at Daystar University in Nairobi, Kenya. He coordinated an initiative to establish a regional quality assurance system in East Africa supported by IUCEA in conjunction with the German Academic Exchange Service (DAAD). His research interest spans across disciplines from quality assurance in higher education to representation of gender and language politics in African literature.

**Pia Lamberti** is a Senior Lecturer in the Commerce, Law and Management Faculty at the University of the Witwatersrand, where her sole focus is postgraduate writing. She is also an executive member of the Postgraduate Forum of Southern Africa. She has spent over thirty years in the education field, with twenty years in higher education development. In her capacity as Head of Research Capacity Development at the University of Johannesburg's Postgraduate School she had responsibility for postgraduate researcher development, and supervision development programmes for academic staff. Her research interests include researcher development, undergraduate to (post)graduate transitions, research/(post)graduate literacies, and argument and voice in academic writing.
ORCID: https://orcid.org/0000-0002-7896-7989

**Shosh Leshem** is a Professor in education, at Kibbutzim College of Education, Israel and Middlebury College, Vermont, USA. She is an Associate Researcher at Stellenbosch University, SA. Her research interests are: Doctoral Education, the Nature of Doctorateness, Supervision, Teacher Education, Second Language Acquisition, Mentoring. She co-authored (with Trafford) the book *Stepping Stones to Achieving your Doctorate*, Open University Press.

**Sioux McKenna** is the Director of Postgraduate Studies at Rhodes University where she also runs a PhD programme in social justice in higher education. Her research concern is with what is valued in higher education and how norms and values emerge as literacy practices. She has authored over fifty articles and book chapters, including co-authoring two books: *Going to University* (2018, African Minds) and *Calling for Change* (forthcoming). Sioux is the project manager for a number of international collaborations, including a national supervision development course, Strengthening

Postgraduate Supervision (www.postgradsupervision.com), and an online Creative Commons site, Enhancing Postgraduate Environments (www.postgradenvironments.com).
ORCID: https://orcid.org/0000-0002-1202-5999

**Anna Morozov** is a recent PhD graduate of the Adelaide University and a practicing immigration professional. Her research and publications are focused on challenges, benefits and consequences of academic mobility. She is passionate about providing an awareness of the diversity and potential that international university staff bring to Australian teaching and supervision practices.
ORCID: https://orcid.org/0000-0002-3837-7124

**Johann Mouton** is a professor and Director of the DSI-NRF Centre of Excellence for Scientometrics and STI Policy and professor at CREST. He is on the editorial board of five international journals including *Science and Public Policy, Science, Technology and Society* and *Minerva*. He has authored or co-authored 10 monographs including, *The practice of social research* (2002, with E Babbie), *How to succeed in your Masters and doctoral studies* (2001) and *Doctoral education in South Africa* (with Nico Cloete, 2015). He has also edited or co-edited 9 books, published 90 articles in peer reviewed journals and chapters in books, written more than 100 contract and technical reports and given more than 200 papers at national and international conferences and seminars. He has presented more than 60 workshops on research methodology, post-graduate supervision and bibliometrics and supervised more than 90 doctoral and master's students. He is currently working on predatory publishing, funding of science in Africa, the mobility of South African doctoral graduates and the state of knowledge production at SA universities.
ORCID: https://orcid.org/0000-0002-0339-7440

**Maresi Nerad**, founding director of the Center for Innovation and Research in Graduate Education (CIRGE) and Professor for Higher Education, University of Washington, Seattle, USA. A native of Germany, she received her doctorate from the University of California, Berkeley; directed research on doctoral education at UCBerkeley, as Dean in Residence at the US Council of Graduate Schools, as Associate Dean of the UW central Graduate School, publishing books and articles in this field. She served on national and international review committees and advisory boards in the US, South Africa, Germany; was visiting professor in Australia, South Africa, Germany, Japan, and India.
ORCID: https://orcid.org/0000-0002-8025-833X

**Murat Özgören** is a professor at Near East University, Faculty of Medicine, Department of Biophysics, director of Technology Transfer Office and board member of the Center of Excellence. He is a former Steering Committee member of the European University Association Council of Doctorate Education and has contributed to international and national higher education and innovation roadmaps. His research interests include applied brain biophysics, sleep and pathological processes. He is the national delegate on the European Strategic Forum on Research Infrastructures (ESFRI), as well as having served as the chair of Health and Food Strategy Working Group. He is the associate editor of *Sleep and Biological Rhythms Journal*. He is the vice president of the International Sleep Science and Technology Association (ISSTA). He is also a board member of the Asian Sleep Research Society.

ORCID: https://orcid.org/0000-0002-7984-2571

**Gillian Robinson** is Reader Emerita at Anglia Ruskin University where she was Director of Research Degrees and Coordinator of an International cohort-based PhD. programme for twelve years. She has supervised thirty-five PhD students to completion. Her research interests are in doctoral learning and issues of supervision, particularly in cross-cultural contexts and the supervision of creative practice-based PhD.

**Peter Rule** is an Associate Professor in the Centre for Higher and Adult Education at Stellenbosch University. He has thirty years' experience of working in adult and higher education in South Africa. He has published in the areas of adult education, dialogue and learning, reading education, disability and HIV/AIDS in education. His books include *Dialogue and Boundary Learning* (Sense Publishers, 2015) and (with Vaughn John) *Your guide to case study research* (Van Schaik, 2011). He has also worked in not-for-profit organisations involved in adult literacy, early childhood education and language education.
ORCID id: https://orcid.org/0000-0002-4746-8482

**Rebekah Smith McGloin** is Director of the Doctoral School at Nottingham Trent University. She has a track record in the configuration, set-up and delivery of regional, national and international doctoral training programmes. Rebekah has a national profile for policy work related to doctoral education. She chaired the UKCGE National Working Group on Diversity and Sustainability of Organisational Structures for Doctoral Provision and is co-author (with Carolyn Wynne) of Structural Changes in Doctoral Education in The UK (UKCGE, 2015). Rebekah is a member of the UKRI Bioscience Skills and Careers Strategy Panel and was an expert panel reviewer for the UK Concordat for Researchers (2019). Rebekah has published on doctoral education and the impact gap, new models of doctoral training and supervision.
ORCID id: https://orcid.org/0000-0001-9074-4596

**Marc Wilde** has been working with the German Academic Exchange Service (DAAD) since 2002 and is in charge for the programme "Dialogue on Innovative Higher Education Strategies (DIES)" which is jointly coordinated with the German Rectors' Conference. DIES provides a variety of measures aiming at strengthening institutional and individual capacities in the field of higher education management, including an online course for supervisors of doctoral candidates at African universities offered by Stellenbosch University. Marc Wilde holds a M.A. in Philosophy from University of Bonn and an MBA in Higher Education and Research Management from University of Applied Sciences Osnabrück, Germany.

**Gina Wisker** currently supervises doctoral students at the University of Bath in the International Centre for Higher Education Management. Previously she was Professor of Higher Education & Contemporary Literature at Anglia Ruskin University and then at the University of Brighton (now Emeritus), Head of the Centre for Learning & Teaching in both universities. She has published 26 books (some edited) and 140+ articles: *The Postgraduate Research Handbook* (2001; 2nd ed. 2007); *The Good Supervisor* (2005, 2012); *Getting Published* (2015); *The Undergraduate Research Handbook* (2nd ed, 2018). *Key Concepts in Postcolonial Literature* (2007); *Horror Fiction: An Introduction* (2005); *Margaret Atwood, an Introduction to Critical Views of Her Fiction* (2012); *Contemporary Women's Gothic Fiction* (2016). She was National Teaching Fellow, Principal fellow of the HEA, SFEDA, FRSA.
ORCID: https://orcid.org/0000-0001-8017-8244

www.ingramcontent.com/pod-product-compliance
Lightning Source LLC
Chambersburg PA
CBHW081203170426
43197CB00018B/2905